Dr Saheb John Borgall has given in his book an extraordinary account of the 'accidental' planting and growth of about 15,000 Christ Groups, a house church movement, all over India, through the ministry of India Every Home Crusade. He has ably portrayed the struggle between Western rationalistic and individualistic approach as against India's relational context in the ministry. This is a book every Christian leader and church planter should read who wishes to understand how churches in rural India, particularly in Karnataka state, are planted and multiplied taking into consideration the relational aspects, the past societal memories of bhakti and other movements and longings for social change.

Dr R Theodore Srinivasagam, General Secretary,
India Missions Association

Saheb Borgall tells a remarkable story. He began his Christian ministry as one of 1400 tract distributors delivering gospel tracts to every home in India in the 1960s, supported by a western mission agency.

Out of this national distribution ministry developed a 'people's movement' of families and local communities to become disciples of Jesus Christ. But the mission agency did not recognize what was happening. So independent 'Christ groups' formed in areas which had been resistant to the gospel of Jesus Christ for decades. Many have become strong congregations and churches.

Dr Borgall was himself part of this movement. He has now researched its origins, and interviewed its leaders and members. He offers an analysis of how a western ministry which concentrated on the mass distribution of one message to all its recipients became a movement of families responding to and sharing the love of Jesus with their communities. The age of mass movements to Christ, common in earlier periods of history, is not past and can now be understood in greater depth.

Canon Dr Chris Sugden,
Oxford Centre for Religion and Public Life

REGNUM STUDIES IN MISSION

The Emergence of Christ Groups in India

The Case of Karnataka State

Series Preface

Regnum Studies in Mission are born from the lived experience of Christians and Christian communities in mission, especially but not solely in the fast growing churches among the poor of the world. These churches have more to tell than stories of growth. They are making significant impacts on their cultures in the cause of Christ. They are producing 'cultural products' which express the reality of Christian faith, hope and love in their societies.

Regnum Studies in Mission are the fruit often of rigorous research to the highest international standards and always of authentic Christian engagement in the transformation of people and societies. And these are for the world. The formation of Christian theology, missiology and practice in the twenty-first century will depend to a great extent on the active participation of growing churches contributing biblical and culturally appropriate expressions of Christian practice to inform World Christianity.

Series Editors

Paul Woods   Oxford Centre for Mission Studies, Oxford, UK
Julie C. Ma   Oxford Centre for Mission Studies, Oxford, UK
Wonsuk Ma   Oxford Centre for Mission Studies, Oxford, UK

A full listing of titles in this series
appears at the end of this book

REGNUM STUDIES IN MISSION

The Emergence of Christ Groups in India
The Case of Karnataka State

Saheb John Borgall

British Library Cataloguing in Publication Data
A catalogue record for this book is available from the British Library

ISBN: 978-1-911372-08-0

Typeset by Words by Design
Cover design by Words by Design
Printed and bound in Great Britain
for Regnum Books International by TJI

Front cover photograph by the author

FSC
www.fsc.org

MIX
Paper from
responsible sources
FSC® C013056

This book is dedicated to my wife Rita
for her constant encouragement to pursue my research
when I faced uphill tasks to complete it,
and to my children Shirin and Paul
for their understanding and patience even when they needed me most.

I am also thankful to all my friends in the UK and elsewhere for their
timely support and prayers.

Contents

Acknowledgements

Foremost I would like to place this book at the feet of Jesus and express my deep gratitude and praises to the Triune God for His wonderful and divine help each step of my way.

First of all I want to acknowledge with a sense of deep gratitude and thanks to my two supervisors, Rev. Dr. Canon Chris Sugden and Rev. Dr. Canon Vinay Samuel, who were the main instruments in providing me with the input and academic direction. I am much indebted to Professor Derycke Belshaw for his guidance in the field survey and to Dr. Ben Knighton for his help in the academic process, Ms. Hilary Guest and Mr. Leonard Anderson for their help in proof-reading. I want to thank the OCMS community, especially Dr. Wonsuk and Dr. Julie Ma, for their encouragement and prayers. Also thanks to Carole, Blanche, Damon and Ralph for their great help.

I would also want to thank James Street Church family, especially Dr. John Hutchison, Professor in the Department of Materials at Oxford University and Mrs. Anna Hutchison who provided constant support and encouragement to me. I am thankful indeed to my two wonderful sisters in the Lord (late) Ms. Vivienne Stacey, a former member of Interserve and missionary to Pakistan and Ms. Eliazabeth Curry, a former missionary to India for their support and encouragement.

I am thankful indeed to the following Trusts and Charities who supported towards my studies – COMMIT, OCMS, Spring Harvest, Charles Wallce Trust, Daily Prayer Charitable Trust and Bishop Hannigton Trust.

Finally I would like to thank my wife, Rita, for her faithful and constant support to me. I am also thankful to my children, Shirin and Paul, my son-in-law Chris Sitther and grandson Nathaniel for all their support and bearing with my absences when they needed me most.

Foreword

The Emergence of Christ Groups in India: The Case Study of the Karnataka State is eye-opening research. It carefully and convincingly investigates the work of the Christ Groups in India, which have carried out extremely successful evangelism. The Karnataka region experienced a flood of missionaries from various denominations in the nineteenth and twentieth centuries, but the area remained mostly untouched spiritually by the overwhelming number of missionaries. Furthermore, the existing churches were steadily declining as forces of narrow ideas, political fights, and other challenges loom over them. In this midst of this dire situation, some churches made an effort to bring life and dynamism to the church through renewed zeal for evangelism and church-planting.

Christ Groups is one of the new initiatives. Its establishment and numerical growth has made a significant impact in rural areas among on churches and mission networks. Christ Groups played an important role in providing opportunity to rural churches to involve in practical ministry. It has indeed enabled the churches to employ an innovative way to rural evangelism and planting churches. The outcome has been extremely encouraging, thus, missiologically noteworthy. It also strengthens church and leaders in the region.

The research identifies the source of their enthusiastic evangelism in biblical principles found in the Great Commission. The disciples of Jesus Christ went out to the ends of the world following the command of their Master. The Christ Groups have also brought very much needed social reform. For example, it gives an equal opportunity to women and men and this is no small feat considering that earlier missions were unable to fulfil this. This came with heavy criticism, opposition, and even persecution from fellow churches and mission groups. However, the Christ Group not only persevered but also grew both in the region and outside of it. The training of grass-roots leaders for evangelism and ministry is another distinguished characteristic of this successful ministry.

The research showcases a successful evangelism that is locally initiated and motivated, thus, indigenous, while keenly relevant to the social context, thus, contextual. Undoubtedly, this is a model for other ministries to learn valuable lessons. The message of salvation is precious enough for bold proclamation, and Christ's church is called to be a witness of this good news in each given context. Ineffective methods of evangelism are the last things the church can afford, and for this, the Christ Groups have much to offer. Effective evangelism requires a close partnership between God's power and the faithful and wise obedience of his people. This research, therefore, is another important gift to the world church in reaching out to the lost with the living Word of God.

Julie Ma
Research Tutor, Oxford Centre for Mission Studies, Oxford UK

List of Abbreviations

AICC	All India Christian Council
BCC	Bible Correspondence Course
BGEA	Billy Graham Evangelistic Association
CGs	Christ Groups
CG Manual	Christ Group Manual
CGTC	Christ Groups Training Centre
CGTE	Christ Groups Training – Extension
ECFA	Evangelical Council for Financial Accountability
EHC	Every Home Crusade
EHC-I	Every Home Christ International
FEBA	Far East Broadcasting Associates
FT-5000	Final Thrust – 5000
IEHC	India Every Home Crusade
JAARS	Jungle Aviation and Radio Service
PAOG	Pentecostal Assemblies of God
PCs	Pioneer Crusaders
UNESCO	United Nations Educational, Scientific Cultural – Organization
YFC	Youth For Christ
YWAM	Youth With A Mission
WLC	World Literature Crusade

Chapter 1
Introduction

In the beginning of the 1990s, World Literature Crusade (WLC), an American Christian organization, in its publication called 'Everybody,' published an article stating that 15,000 Christ Groups (house-churches) were formed all over India by their sponsoring mission called India Every Home Crusade (IEHC).[1] This news was an indicator for many mission practitioners of phenomenal growth of church planting was taking place in India when communal harmony was at stake. It was also seen as a remarkable achievement in the area of 'church planting' by any one mission in the post-colonial and the post-independence period of India. 'Christ Groups' are like 'houses churches', or as Lee (an ex-President of WLC) calls them, 'baby churches', which are formed in the rural parts of India. Long before the publication of this news, that is, in the late 1970s, McGavran, after his visit to India, wrote an article commending the formation of Christ Groups by IEHC and the good support that the WLC had provided.[2]

Meanwhile, between the late 1970s and the middle of the 1980s, WLC underwent a period of crisis in leadership and finances. During that period, there were five successive Presidents so that WLC's ministry overseas underwent many different strategic changes and methods in its operation. One such move came from Dr. Dale Kietzman about the Christ Groups. Through his association with the World Magazine in 1986, a group of researchers was sent to do a sample survey of the Christ Groups. The teams were sent to a few selected States where the Christ Groups movement was claimed to be successful. One such team was sent to Karnataka State where the researcher accompanied them to guide and translate. The reports of researchers and subsequent visits of the Rev. Charles Wickman and Dr. Dale Kietzman, and their reports on Christ Groups suggested that they all tried to downplay the movement and, in the end (1987), Kietzman made a tactical move to end the support for the work of Christ Groups in India. He asserted that the WLC stands for the systematic distribution of the printed gospel booklet and will not divert its aim, therefore, saying 'no' to Christ Groups.

---

[1] *Everybody* 1994 A Report
[2] McGavran, Donald, 1976, *Everybody*, 10

On the other hand, the Indian leadership under the late B. A. G. Prasad tried to keep up the movement through many innovative ideas such as partnership with like-minded missions within India and sought financial assistance overseas from other missions. Even then, he was categorically forbidden by Kietzman to extend any sort of help for Christ Groups. Moreover, Kietzman wrote strong reminders to Prasad about his continuing interest in Christ Groups. After Kietzman's resignation in the late 1980s, Rev. Dick Eastman became the President of WLC and wisely avoided committing himself to mobilise funds for Christ Groups' work. The movement continued while Prasad lived and when the subsequent leadership in India folded due to the pressure from the WLC leaders, the Christ Groups movement coame to a halt.

In spite of WLC's and IEHC's disassociation and distancing from Christ Groups, the movement continues. How did these Christ Groups survive and what were the factors that helped them to grow and expand? How did the experience of their past religion or religious influence enable them to withstand the indifferent attitudes of their masters while they continued to live as Christ's witnesses and bearers of the Gospel and establish themselves? What was the perception of the members about Christ Groups? Who joined the Groups and why? How did the members manage to lead their Groups in the absence of evangelists who had led those Christ Groups but who were subsequently moved away by their mission to carry out the WLC's 'original aim'? On the one hand, why did WLC want to turn away from Christ Groups? What was their perception about Christ Groups? Did they acknowledge Christ Groups as their own?

On the other hand, why did the Indian leadership show interest in Christ Groups? Why and when did their interest fade away from Christ Groups? What made them to distance themselves from Christ Groups when they came under pressure from WLC leaders? Why did they choose to play a dual role with regard to Christ Groups? To have a better understanding of WLC and IEHC, it is important to consider the two different mission contexts and mind-sets in which they lived. WLC, on the one side, due to its linear context and under the influence of American 'Mass-Evangelistic' culture, showed entrepreneurial instincts and managerial efficiency. On the other, IEHC due to its relational context[3] tried to hold Christ Groups for a while but as pressure mounted from WLC leaders, their interest in Christ Groups seemed superfluous.

At the same time, in a wider spectrum, how did the established Churches perceive these Christ Groups? Were these Groups accepted as true churches or looked down on by the Churches? Have Christ Groups passed the test of time? Did these Christ Groups need any recognition from the Christian

---

[3] The relational context sometimes called the cyclical worldview, finds its roots in tribal cultures. It is intuitive, timeless oriented and fluid

churches, since their past religious experience and the influence of the pietistic movements of Bhakti and the Lingayats had given them the lead they needed to move forward. Today, Christ Groups, in spite of the turbulent times they have gone through, still continue even if not on the large scale of the 1990s. It will be interesting to see also how the Christ Groups saw themselves when they were disowned by their 'masters'. Did this affect their existence or development? If not, what were the factors that helped them to go on without realizing what was happening around them?

The research is primarily of a missiological discipline. 'Missiology' for Ivan Illich was more than a mission of the church. He sees it as a 'science' and 'history', which "studies the growth of the Church into new peoples, the birth of the Church beyond the linguistic barriers within which she feels at home".[4] Further, Natlino adds that missiology is an interdisciplinary subject that makes use of all the findings of the other branches of theology in order to discern better and reflect more about the proper mission of the Church.[5] Andrew Walls writing on David Bosch's great contribution to missiological studies calls him 'the most complete missiologist', and states that Bosch's understanding of missiology is the study of the range of disciplines and cognate studies used to assess the effectiveness of the mission.[6] Ben Eckman and A. F. Glasser define 'Missiology, or mission science, is the area of practical theology which investigates the mandate, message and work of the Christian missionary. Missiology is a multi-disciplinary and cross-cultural reflection on all aspects of the propagation of the Christian faith, embracing theology, history, geography, theories and methods of communication, comparative religion'. They further add, 'Missiology also dips into the behavioural sciences, namely anthropology, sociology, psychology, and linguistics. It is not a mere borrower from other fields, for these dimensions are related to each other in dynamic symbiosis'.[7] Jongeneel cites the development of missiology from 'a small discipline in the nineteenth century to a mature discipline in the twentieth century and thus concludes that 'missiology – is the totality of philosophical, scientific (=empirical), and theological studies of Christian mission'.[8] I do not claim any mastery over the different branches of the subjects mentioned here in this study except for looking mainly at their application towards the mission practice he is engaged on in this research.

---

[4] Illich, Ivan, 1974, 'Toward A Relevant Missiology', 6ff.
Bosch, David J. 2006 (1991) *Transforming Mission*, 620620
[5] Camilleri, Natalino, *Introduction to Missiology*
[6] Walls, Andrew F., 2002, 'Missologist of the Road', *The Cross-Cultural Process In Christian History*, 273
[7] ben@studentglobalimpact.com. Elwell, W. *Evangelical Dictionaryof Theology*
[8] Jongeneel, Jan, A.B., (1995) 2006 Conclusion and Perspective, *Missiological Encyclopedia, Part II*, 427

I made extensive trips to India and USA to collect data and archives and conducted interviews in the field with the members of Christ Groups and leaders of WLC and IEHC. Though the chapter on Christ Groups is placed in the middle of the book, the preceding chapters give a background to the study without which the study would have become incomplete and the analysis of the Christ Groups movement would have become more difficult. This research is the first academic study of Christ Groups in India. In 1989, a team (mostly of seminary students) from the US, was sent by the World Christian Magazine to India to do a brief survey, especially to assess their future. To gather the material, I first made contact with Mr. M. M. Maxton, then the executive director of IEHC, in 1998, to obtain permission to do a field survey in four Christ Groups in Karnataka. After obtaining permission, I then wrote to Mr. Albert Sudershan, the regional manager of IEHC Karnataka, to arrange for his visits to those fields. The manager wrote to his evangelists and asked them to cooperate in the field survey. For three weeks in February and March, I visited the four Christ Groups and collected data with open-ended questions from 200 people. Another two days were arranged with the field evangelists to validate the data collected from their respective fields. Then, one more week was spent to collect data from the leaders and staff of IEHC.

In 1999, I visited the USA to collect data from WLC and their past and present Presidents. WLC's office in Colorado Springs gave access to all Indian files in the offices of the President and vice President. Access was given to all the statistical data and journals. A board resolution on Christ Groups was made available from the Trust department of the WLC. Interviews were conducted with the President and vice-President of WLC and a telephonic interview was conducted with the former President of WLC. WLC office also allowed me to have the copies of some of the letters and statistical papers. I was given access to journals and magazines and to make copies. WLC office helped me find the reports on Christ Groups by Bayard Taylor and Charles Wickman.

I conducted a personal interview with Dr. Jack McAlister and Mrs. Hazel McAlister who took me to theirhome. Mr. McAlister provided some written material which otherwise was not available anywhere. He also made arrangements for me to speak to Mr. Yohann Lee, a former President of WLC, and asked him to provide the needed information. I conducted a personal interview with Dr. Dale Kietzman in his office at the World Mission Centre, Pasadena. Thus, I was able to gather first hand material from original sources which have been invaluable to the study.

It is important to study, (1) the socio-religious cultural contexts of the institution leaders, that is, of the United States and India, (2) their perception of Christ Groups in the light of their cultural contexts, and (3) the perception of the members towards Christ Groups in their own contexts.

I also examined many other contributory factors, both internal and external, that influenced the continuation of the Christ Groups movement.

The study on Christ Groups is not the same as Pickett[9] and McGavran's[10] study on Mass Movements and Church Growth. The study on Christ Groups ishows how the people took the message when it was delivered to them by their own countrymen. They were willing to own to it and appropriate it without divorcing themselves from their culture. This process would not have been possible if the same message was delivered by missionaries, who would have forced their culture on the natives. Thus, the intent of this study is to examine the context of Christ Groups, that is, their formation, development, and continuation. The contexts of the WLC and IEHC are also studied for a better understanding of the Christ Groups.

Field research has investigated the nature and extent of both social and religious contexts and related factors. At the institutional level, that is, of WLC and IEHC, what are their perceptions, involvement and exclusion of Christ Groups? Did this affect the Christ Groups or not? At the members' level, what are the factors that influenced them to join the Christ Groups? What are the contributing factors that generate their convictions so that they actively participate in the development of Christ Groups? What factors influence the involvement and non-involvement of members in evangelism, social issues and personality development?

The objective of the survey is to research the perceptions of the members, evangelists and institution leaders in the formation and growth of the Christ Groups, especially, looking at the future of these Christ Groups. The Christ Groups selected for investigation are: Bagepalli, Hosadurga, Pavagada and Bijapur. India Every Home Crusade claimed to form these Christ Groups during a nationwide, systematic distribution of tracts. They were selected on a chronological and geographical basis. Chronologically, Bagepalli represents the earliest group of the movement, that is, in the late 1960s, Hosadurga in the late 1970s, Pavagada in the middle 1980s and Bijapur in the early 1990s. Geographically, the locations of these places in Karnataka State represent the four directions, that is, Bijapur in the North, Pavagada in the South- Central, Hosadurga in the West and Bagepalli in the East.

All the four Christ Groups are in the State of Karnataka where the study has taken place and they are under the supervision of the India Every Home Crusade, Bangalore, Karnataka branch. An IEHC branch opened in Bangalore in the year 1964 under the leadership of the late Mr. G. Guruprasad. IEHC claims that it has twice systematically completed the distribution of tracts to every accessible home in Karnataka.

---

[9] Pickett, J. W., 1933, *Christian Mass Movements in India*
[10] McGavran, Donald Anderson, 1988 (1970,1980), *Understanding Church Growth*

At present, IEHC is engaged in carrying out many other programmes, conducting prayer seminars, literacy and distribution work. So, IEHC's focus has moved from the formation of Christ Groups to other interests of the ministry, as mentioned above. IEHC continues its connection with WLC (now EHC-I, that is, Every Home for Christ-International), which is the main donor. IEHC, on a national level, has its main office in Hyderabad and its branches are spread out in many States of India. One such office functions in Bangalore, Karnataka. These regional offices are operated by the local leaders. The person who heads the main office is the National Director and those who are in-charge of branch offices are the Regional Directors or the Regional Managers. The national director, while representing the country, also serves on the international board of WLC to give advice or suggestions, especially in matters concerning overseas ministry.

The purpose of the study is to see how and why the relational context plays a major role in forming Christ Groups and their continuation. Are there any other factors related to this relational context? The following hypotheses were investigated in this study: First, why and how did the members of Christ Groups respond to the printed message of the Gospel in families that was meant to appeal to the individual? What are the factors that influenced or were involved in this process? Second, did the people coming to Christ change their names, dress and family pattern so that they could be called Christians by the Christian Church at large? What are the theological and doctrinal positions Christ Groups need to adopt for them to be called Christian Churches? How do the members of Christ Groups see themselves in the Christ Groups and work towards their development, along with their own spiritual and other needs?

The study covers the period from 1978-98. In the year 1978, the Hosadurga Christ Group was formed and, during this time, Lee also speaks about his vision of 'Baby Churches'. The year 1998 suggests WLC and IEHC had finally moved away from giving any emphasis to the Christ Groups movement. These were the years of the Christ Groups movement when IEHC placed much emphasis on this movement.

An earlier assumption in the research process was that apart from the relational aspect, tracts, follow-up work and seekers conferences played some role in the formation of Christ Groups. As the research developed, the main assumption was challenged as further evidence emerged. Therefore, I examined the role of the tract, follow up work, and seekers conference to determine the role they played in the formation of Christ groups. The evidence became clearer that an entirely different process was at work, a process that linked with but was distant from the WLC's tract distribution. This required a field research into the cultures and religious backgrounds of the Christ Groups.

The study sheds light on the perceived ambiguity and tactical moves of WLC's leadership in their relationship to Christ Groups. It also reveals the dual role of Indian leadership in relation to WLC and Christ Groups. Moreover, the research provides important information for understanding how the members of Christ Groups viewed themselves and took active participation in the Groups and society.

The research is one of the first social science applications to Christ Groups in India, especially in the case of Karnataka State. I conducted personal interviews with the members of four Christ Groups, the national leaders of IEHC and with the WLC leaders including the founder of WLC, Dr. McAlister. The research provides insights into Christian Missions to evaluate their means, methods, approaches, while engaging with the rural Indian populace. The research suggests that Christian missions need to take the relational context seriously, especially in reaching the rural populace. It also makes suggestions for the Indian leadership to play their role in an appropriate way rather than trying to play a dual role to please their masters, on the one hand, and themselves, on the other. Since I was once an insider, my experience with the mission and sources used in the research will make them accessible for future scholarship.

Chapter one begins with the introduction of the background and main focus of the research. The second chapter sketches the development of mass evangelism, especially under the influence of modernity. The third chapter contains the history of the World Literature Crusade, its ethos, means, methods and failures. Chapter four discusses the dilemma of the Indian leadership over mass evangelism and Christ Groups movement. Chapter five describes the beginnings, formation and development of Christ Groups, and also their comparison in the light of other such movements. Chapter six is divided into two sections: section 'A' is on the field survey which explains the methodology of the research describing how both quantitative and qualitative methods are used and looks at other contributory factors influencing the growth of the Christ Group movement; section 'B', as a part of the field study, is a case study on Hosadurga Christ Group, of how the Christ Groups are formed, established and continued and also how their past religious context played a role in this process. Chapter seven is divided into three sections, which present the research results. Chapter eight concludes by discussing the study results and its implications and future research recommendations.

Chapter 2
An Overview of Mass-Evangelism as an Expression of Modernity and Western Mission of the Nineteenth and Twentieth Centuries

Evangelism, Mass Evangelism and Its Development

Evangelism[1] is good news or gospel. The word 'gospel' is the equivalent of the Greek word, *'euangelion'* or 'evangel' in English.[2] In the New Testament, it denotes the good tidings of the Kingdom of God, and of salvation through Christ, by faith in His expiatory death, His burial, resurrection, and ascension. The act of the evangel is called 'evangelize', in Greek it is *'euangelizo'*[3], which means to bring, announce or proclaim. The process of this evangelization or proclamation is evangelism. John Stott makes a distinction between 'the meaning of evangelism' and 'the aim of evangelism'. He states that evangelism is to preach the gospel and the aim of evangelism is to win or bring people to Christ.[4]

Ralph Winter defines three concepts in evangelism: E-1, E-2, and E-3. E-1 evangelism is sharing the gospel with others of the same language and culture as oneself. E-2 evangelism is seeking to reach people of a similar language or culture, and E-3 evangelism is a cross-cultural work.[5] In short, evangelism is proclamation of the good news of Jesus Christ to every creature that has not experienced rebirth in Christ. According to John Stott, "they need to hear or hear better".[6]

The premise of evangelism is based upon the life and teaching of Jesus Christ. 'Good News' means to proclaim, because "Jesus himself as an Evangelist"[7], brought good tidings to people. "The Spirit of the Lord is

---

[1] Note: Evangelism is the proclamation of the good news to non-believers... But Mission includes evangelism as one of its responsibility Bosch:1991 (2005):10, 11
[2] Vine, W.E., 1944, *Expository Dictionary of New Testament Words*, Vol.II, E-Li, 167
[3] Ibid. 168
[4] Stott, John, 1975, *Christian Mission in the Modern World*, 39
[5] Winter, Ralph, 1975, *Let the Earth Hear His Voice*, ICOWE, 215-216
[6] Ibid. 38
[7] Statements from the WCC Executive Committee Meeting, 1968 (Geneva, February 1968), *The Ecumenical Review*, vol. xx, no. 2, April

upon me, because he has anointed me to preach good news..." (Lk 4:18). Jesus commanded His disciples to become the bearers of good news. "Go ye into all the world and preach the gospel to the whole creation" (Mk 16:15). The act of proclamation is an obedience of Jesus' disciples to His command. This is vital to their life and testimony. Proclamation is through various forms: personal-evangelism, child-evangelism, youth-evangelism, mass-evangelism and so on.

Mass-evangelism[8] is a form of evangelism designed to reach the masses. Bryan Green defines mass-evangelism as "an attempt to reach a number of people at one time by the preaching of the Gospel".[9]

The common notion behind this strategy is, 'Why one, when thousands are passing by? There are other factors, like the imminent return of Christ (that "this gospel of the kingdom will be preached in the whole world as a testimony to all nations, then the end will come", Mt. 24:14) which brought the idea of 'World Evangelization'. The population explosion brought a sense of urgency. Technological advancement brought more openness to preach the gospel in different cultures and countries.

John Wesley was a firm believer in reaching the masses. Dr. Skevington Wood makes these comments in, '*The Burning Heart*': 'Once John Wesley had been convinced of the value of field-preaching,[10] it became noticeable how field preaching immediately assumed priority and became central to his schedule. Throughout the long years of evangelizing, he kept commenting on the value of field-preaching and said, "For usefulness, there is none comparable to it", and "I knew of no other way of preaching the gospel to every creature". His goal was a mission to the masses'.[11] John MacGregor, the founder of Open-Air Mission suggests, 'Christian people must go out to the masses and reach them on their own ground with the message of salvation'.[12]

From the time of Jesus, various forms of mass-evangelism have reached the masses, for example: open-air preaching, evangelistic campaigns or crusades, and mass-media evangelism. Open-air preaching reaches people wherever they are. In John MacGregor's words, 'reach them on their own ground'.[13] This iswhere the crowds gather, especially in market places, parks, and on busy streets and beaches. Evangelistic campaigns or Crusades are usually in a neutral place[14] in a city. Mostly they are inter-denominational. These campaigns are held for longer periods, from one

---

[8] Print, radio and television are grouped under 'mass-media'. Print or literature can be used for personal or mass evangelism (distribution) www.pgmindia.org.

[9] Green, Bryan, 1951, *The Practice of Evangelism*, Missions and Mass-Evangelism, 121

[10] This refers to open-air preaching, this is done wherever the crowd assembles

[11] Baker, Edwin & Alan Greenbank, 1995, *A Handbook on Open-Air Evangelism*, 3

[12] Ibid. 2

[13] Ibid.

[14] This refers to public grounds where all can come and gather

week to eight weeks. Mass-media evangelism includes print (literature), radio, television and satellite. These are impersonal methods of evangelism, but are effective.

Abbe Michonneau, in *'Revolution in a City Parish,'* observes that to speak of mass evangelism is in the strictest sense inaccurate, for, although the term is convenient, there can be no such thing as mass evangelism'.[15] Likewise, the development of mass-evangelism can be divided into two parts: 1. Pre-modern mass-evangelism, 2. Modern and Post-modern mass-evangelism.

Pre-modern[16] mass-evangelism is evident from the time of Jesus to modern times. On many occasions, Jesus spoke to large crowds. He once used a fisherman's boat as His pulpit and the crowd on the sea-shore listened to His message 'He got into one of the boats, the one belonging to Simon, and asked him to put out a little from shore. Then he sat down and taught the people from the boat'. (Lk 5:3). The Apostles spoke not only in the synagogues, but preached in the streets, market places and auditoria or wherever people were found. 'So he reasoned in the synagogue with the Jews and the God-fearing Greeks, as well as in the market-place day by day with those who happened to be there' Acts 17:1. '(Paul) had discussions daily in the lecture hall of Tyrannus' Acts 19:9.

A second century account describes an event where a man went to hear a notable Christian from Palestine, who was staying in Alexandria and preaching the good news to the crowd.[17] In the thirteenth century, the begging and singing preachers went about with bare feet, a coarse serge frock, and a girdle of rope around their waist[18] and preached the gospel to the masses. The early missionaries to Bulgaria, Moravia and Bohemia carried great pictures with them, which formed the texts of their sermons,[19] and preached the good news to crowds..

Modern and post-modern (see footnote 24) mass-evangelism can be traced from the time of the Enlightenment until now. During this period, the revolutionary changes in ideas took place and they affected society throughout the centuries. Modernity's replacement of 'top down' God-centred living with 'bottom-up' human-centred living represents a titanic revolution in human history and experience. It is basically an economic and technological transformation.

---

[15] Ibid. op.cit., 121

[16] Note: Hans Kung (1984:25; 1987:157) classifies Christian history into six stages: from the first century of Christianity to Protestant Reformation period Bosch:1991:262,349

[17] Young, William G., 1999, *Handbook of Source Materials*, for students of Church History, 47

[18] James, Maynard G., 1945, *Evangelize*, 33,34

[19] Ibid.

The Christian elements in modernity are as follows: All humans are created in God's image and have great value and worth. Each individual is called to personal faith, and to exercise responsibility in a continuous walk of sanctification, in comparison to modernity's emphases on free, rational choice and humanistic self-actualization.

To note some similarities between Christian faith and modernity:

1.   God is the universal ruler who governs the natural world in an orderly way and judges all peoples with equity. Modernity holds that both nature and society are governed by uniform, impartial laws.

2.   The NT teaches that each Church member has a distinct, valuable role. Everyone has a voice and participation. Modernity holds the ideal of democracy.

3.   In the Biblical view, history has a linear, positive direction. God's purposes are gradually revealed through history. They transform people and nations and come to completion at the end. Modernity emphasises ethnological, that is, transformation of the world or human race.

4.   Scripture emphasises the global mission of God's people, which will bring together people from all nations, tongues, races, and tribes. Modernity emphasizes universal conquest by its influence and following.

The Christian mission under the influence of modernity developed a worldview that perceived other cultures as primitive and pagan. It saw itself as a tool of modernization.[20] From the late eighteenth to twentieth century, mass-evangelism became one of the main Western missionary enterprises. In the eighteenth century, John Wesley and George Whitefield effectively used mass-evangelism. Field preaching was central to their ministry. Methodism grew out of it. John Wesley and George Whitefield along with their mass evangelistic approach strongly emphasized discipleship. They took their converts to church and nurtured them in the Word of God.

From the eighteenth to twentieth centuries, the world saw a great advancement in technology and communications. These technological advancements and inventions created more openness among the masses. The use of modern media in decentralized forms opened up traditional closed societies, and even centralized totalitarian states. This openness meant Christians faced the greatest opportunity to reach masses more effectively. In this period, American evangelicals used modern culture to its maximum effect in reaching masses with the gospel.

American Mass-Evangelism

The United States as the world's 'first new nation' and American mass-evangelism as Protestantism's 'first new tradition' both have features of

---

[20] Accorda, Corrie, 1993, 'Tradition, Modernity and Christian Mission in Asia', *Transformation*, October, Vol. 10, no 4, 18,19

modern culture that are constitutive of their very character and identity (for example, pluralism in the case of America and a reliance on technique in the case of mass-evangelism). This close affinity is an advantage because America and American mass-evangelism have prospered at the cutting edge of modern culture.

Andrew Walls sees the Americans' ability in invention and perfecting them.[21] He calls it 'first-rate technology'[22]. Uchimura observes 'it is their national characteristic'.[23] Americans have a deep historically rooted belief in the benefits of technology, starting even before the invention of mass-media. Walt Whitman, an American poet, in the nineteenth century, in his poem, *'Passage to India'* wrote:

Worship new I sing
You captains, voyagers, explorers, yours,
You engineers, you architects, machinists, yours,
You not for trade or transportation only,
But in God's name, and for thy sake O soul[24]

Rufus Anderson, in 1837, speaking on *'The Time for the World's Conversion Come'* saw that world conquest was now possible because of the scale at which technological advancement and global market expansion during that period. He said, 'Never till now, did the social condition of mankind render it possible to organise the army's requisite for the world's spiritual conquest'.[25] The whole climate of American Christian thinking was conditioned by expansion.[26] Zeal for world evangelization went in hand in hand with the use of innovative methods of marketing. To win the greatest number of converts at the least expense became their constant endeavour.[27] The nineteenth century Christian movement along the frontier and the evangelization of new cities brought new concepts in American mass-evangelism. D. L. Moody in the nineteenth century and Billy Graham in the twentieth century used and developed these concepts in mass-evangelism.

D. L. Moody's passion for winning more souls, allied with an uncommon tact, led him to adopt a new technique in mass-evangelism. 'Moody daringly used theatres and public halls, large choirs, popular solos

---

[21] Walls, Andrew F., 1990, *The American Dimension in the Missionary Movement, Earthen Vessels*, 1, eds. Joel A. Carpenter and Shank, Wilbert R., 1
[22] Ibid. 3
[23] Uchimura, Kanzo, 1926, Can Americans Teach Japanese in Religion? 357-61, *Christian Intelligencer*, Japan, 1
[24] Blodget, Harold W., 1953, *The Best of Whitman*
[25] Anderson, Rufus, 1967, *To Advance the Gospel*, Selections from the Writings of Rufus Anderson, ed. R. Pierce Beaver, 59-70, 65-66
[26] Ibid. 9
[27] Ibid. 1

and choruses, and the Inquiry Room with its army of workers to deal individually with the seekers, as methods of reaching the masses'.[28] Moody, before he became an itinerant evangelist, was an energetic, successful businessman. He had developed his skills in organization, publicity, fund raising and motivation. Speaking about Moody's business skills, McLoughlin comments, 'Moody brought to urban mass evangelism the sales and managerial techniques that were transforming the American economy'.[29]

Gordon observes that Moody's preaching and Sankey's singing was spectacularly effective.[30] Findlay remarks that 'Moody and ...Sankey, ...updated evangelism's idiom through their sentimental stories and gospel ballads, calling the weary sinner who had lost his or her way in urban America to accept the tender Saviour's invitation to come home'.[31] But, Kent remarks, Moody's and Sankey's primary intention was to lead people to their personal salvation.[32] Though Moody's use of modern business skills in mass-evangelism brought displeasure from conservative English and Scots religionists, he considered that he had urgent business to do for the Lord and that was to save the lost souls somehow, including in the power of God.

Billy Graham is the twentieth century's most world-renowned mass-evangelist. He used every mass-communication media to preach the gospel. From conducting 'Crusades' to relay through 'Satellite' he wanted to reach the masses. His team uses a familiar phrase, 'High Touch through Hi-Tech' to describe their use of high technology in proclamation. Graham grew up in a culture that trusted in modern technology in saving souls. Graham, when he was a teenager, developed sales techniques. Aikman remarks that in 1936, when Graham was a teenager he developed business skills in selling commercial goods door to door. By the end of that summer, he had become the best selling salesman in North and South Carolina.[33]

Though Graham's presentations were not filled with emotional appeals and sensational stories, he wore flashy clothes and delivered his messages dramatically. Pollock observes, 'Billy...wore loud hand painted ties and bright suits, that all the world might know Christianity to be no dreary

---

[28] Ibid. 19

[29] McLoughlin, William G., 1959, *Modern Revivalism*, Charles Grandison Finney to Billy Graham, 444-454

[30] Maynard, James G., 1945 (quotes Gordon), *Evangelize*, 181

[31] Findlay, James F., 1969, *Dwight L Moody, American Evangelist*, 233-244

[32] Kent, John, 1978 (1945), Gordon in *Holding the Fort*, chapter 6, 'Sacred Songs and Sankey', 181, *Evangelize* by Maynard G. James, 1945 pp.136-138

[33] Aikman, David, 1998, *Great Souls: Six Who Changed the Century*, 15

faith'.[34] George Marsden says about the mass-evangelist's appearance and dress that he 'looked like a business man;...dressed like a business man'.[35]

Graham's crusades, radio broadcasts, television and satellite relays provided full package delivery to the audience. They had bright soloists, large choirs, ensembles, bands, music and spotlights and, of course, Graham's dramatic delivery with his loud and clear voice. They had counsellors to counsel enquirers. The word 'counsellor' was used in education but never previously in religion. Follow-up work for new converts involved local churches and Christian groups, but Graham provided the materials. Graham's crusades to attract large audiences adopted the strategies and techniques of modern marketing, including advertising and promotion. In most cases, preparation for Graham's crusades started two years before they were launched. Graham fully believed in the use of modern mass communications to bring the Christian message to millions of lives around the globe.

The use of modern culture in the contemporary world brought extraordinary openness. In the last century and a half, American Christians have used every means, media, and methodology to reach the un-reached in an enterprise in creative ingenuity unrivalled in history. The explosion of the gospel was possible through modern media. The mass-production of Christian literature, the invention of radio, television, and satellites became the main American missionary enterprise. Marshal McLuhan and Neil Postman argue that the medium of communication shapes the content of the messages.[36] The influence of modern marketing, including advertising and promotion, television, and pop-culture, has caused profound changes in public discourse. That is from word to image, action to spectacle, exposition to entertainment, truth to feeling, conviction to sentiment, and authoritative utterance to discussion and sharing.[37]

The entrepreneurial activity, efficient organization, and financial rewards, which were characteristic of American business, became characteristic of American Christianity. American culture not only accepted business methods but also consecrated them to God and employed them in Christian activity. Patton in his book 'The Business of Mission' wrote, 'We are living in a business age, we believe as never before in business results. It is working'.[38]

Mass-evangelism as differentiation is one of the most popular theories of societal modernization, differentiation owes much to Emile Durkheim

---

[34] Pollock, John, 1966, *Billy Graham*, 52
[35] Marsden, George M., 1980, *Fundamentalism and American Culture*, 32
[36] McLuhan, Marshall, 1964, *Understanding Media*; Neil Postman, 1985, *Amusing Ourselves to Death: Public Discourse in the Age of Show Business*
[37] Ibid.
[38] Patton, Cornelius H., 1924, *The Business of Mission*, Foreword

(1858-1917) who observed differentiation in the division of labour in modern capitalist industrial societies; labour tasks became increasingly specialised in order to maximise production. In primitive societies, the various corporate activities of social life are still undifferentiated: production, education and health-care take place within the context of family and tribe; religion and its rituals are all part and parcel of daily life. Durkheim further explains that modernizing differentiation produces a cleavage between these elements of society so that societal activity is increasingly concentrated in differentiated institutional structures and one's life is divided accordingly. Production shifts from subsistence to commercial orientation, from the family space to the industrial space; health-care is less and less the responsibility of family or religious people, and is increasingly concentrated in professional public hospitals; education likewise is concentrated in purpose-built schools and colleges.[39] Durkheim states how during the Renaissance the rediscovery of the literature of classical antiquity, *literae humaniores*, provided a new standard against which the achievements of civilization might be judged.[40]

This new thirst for knowledge is expressed in the Renaissance concept of *ad fontes*, or back to the sources. The slogan of *ad fontes* meant a direct return to the title deeds of Christianity to the patristic writers, and supremely the Bible. During the Reformers' time, the importance of education was stressed. For example, Luther asked parents to have their children educated and insisted that the 'priesthood of all believers' meant that believers should be better educated. M. A. Noll said that Protestantism, in fact, marked the start of the move to universal education in Europe because its leaders insisted that all individuals had a responsibility to understand the world in which they lived and the spiritual world held out to them by Christian teaching.[41] Protestantism tended to act as a rationalising force through its inclination to 'disenchant' the world: it understood religious truth as certain fact revealed to man, rather than uncertain and incomprehensible mystery. Thus, adherents were encouraged to pursue truth to read the Scriptures and to enquire for themselves.

Mass-evangelism is a North American phenomenon, which involves the practice of reaching thousands of people in a short time. Motivation for this movement echoes the dictum of modern capitalism 'biggest is best', where mass-evangelism is a sign of religious prosperity and market success.

Mass-evangelism needs more administration and hence encourages a more bureaucratic administrative structure within the institution. The

---

[39] Ibid.
[40] Ibid.
[41] Noll, Mark A., 2005, an article accessed from the web and www.science.jrank.org education in 'Europe from Protestant Reformation Nineteenth Century', accessed on 8 June 2009

functions between personnel are increasingly differentiated: separate personnel are responsible for the functions of ministry, mission and finance. Such institutions sought more professional personnel to perform specific tasks: technicians, musicians, youth-workers with communication between the various levels of the institution is normally through formal means.

To support professional personnel, professionalism becomes increasingly important in an organization. Mass-evangelistic organizations are no exception. Fairely notes: 'secular modernism shows up in therapeutic, managerial, and professionalist shaping of its congregations, bureaucracies, and seminaries, but in an arrested form'.[42] Mass-evangelistic organizations offices are equipped with the latest technology, the use of multimedia to promote its work for more funding or for evangelistic meetings, like Billy Graham's Evangelistic Crusades, all contribute towards an efficient and professional bureaucratic mind-set. As a mass-evangelistic organization becomes accustomed to formal rationality in the modern period, there is a tendency towards greater organizational centralization and control. The organization is largely a construct of modernity corresponding to the pluralising nature of modernizing differentiation.

Mass-evangelism as 'commodification' refers to the process by which goods and services are increasingly produced for the market and thus the process by which society increasingly becomes orientated around market values. Pre-modern societies are characterized by subsistence or near subsistence economies and informal arrangements for trade. By contrast, in modernised societies, goods are produced for a monetary market value, which removes the need for any ad hoc arrangement for trade, such as bartering. In order to allow the 'exchange values' of the most radically diverse 'use values', commodification necessitates a formalization of exchange procedures and a defined market space. Commodification creates the possibility of mass production of goods and services and this has led to rapid industrialization and urbanization.

The metaphysical significance of commodity lies in the fact that the commodification externalizes the products of human labour away from the labourer. Marshall illustrates below, where the role of commodification in the formalization of exchange relationship between producer and consumer and consumer is illustrated.[43]

---

[42] Marshall, P., 1997 (quotes E. Fairely, 108), in 'Modernity and Post Modernity', M.Phil. Thesis, Queens University, Belfast, Northern Ireland, 136

[43] Ibid.

Commodity is mass-produced to a standard; within capitalist economies production is aimed at maximizing profits.		
Market relationship between producer and consumer is formalized through pricing, and through fixed standards and market place.		
Within capitalist economies, consumer aims to maximize consumption at lowest cost.		
Producer ▶	Commodity ▶	Consumer

The distinction between commodification and capitalism is that the commodification refers to a process of modernization that makes capitalism possible; capitalism exists where a society produces and sells commodities in order to maximise self interest. In this respect,t commodification is morally neutral, whereas capitalism introduces the questionable motive of self-interest. Commodification transforms traditional subsistence societies into modern societies where production is increasingly concentrated in mass industry; where disposable income allows society to consume as well as produce; where culture and leisure are increasingly commodified; where an increasing number of commodity options create the possibility of taste.

Mass-evangelistic organizations are increasingly conceived of as operating in a commodified market, competing with themselves and secular pursuits, for the time, loyalty and money of a limited clientele. In such a religious market, mass-evangelistic organizations have adopted the techniques and structures of the market. Hammond notes that religious organisations very much behave in their markets with an eye to mass appeal, advertising, and sensitivity to competition, profit, innovation, and so forth.[44]

In the secular modern era, individuals are free to choose non-participation in religious activity; mass-evangelistic organizations, therefore, are forced to 'sell themselves' in order to make people hear, read or see their products. The success of mass-evangelism brought many such competitors into the market place on an 'equal footing'. Moore comments that 'religious commodification accelerated...' in the twentieth century'.[45] Commodification has come to shape religion in the modern period in some very significant ways. Berger suggests five areas in mass-evangelistic organization* as it was expressed in modern culture, where a 'good deal of religious activity' came to be dominated by the logic of market economies.[46]

---

[44] Hammond, P.E., *Religion in the Modern World*, 1986, Chapter 6 in J. D. Hunter and S. C. Ainlay (eds.), *Making Sense of Modern Times*, 149, op.cit. P Marshall, 'Modernity and Post Modernity.' M.Phil. thesis, 1997, 119

[45] Moore, R.L., 7, in P Marshall, 1997, 119

[46] Berger, P.L., 1969, *The Sacred Canopy*, 138 (119). *Italics here and elsewhere in this section are mine. Berger instead uses the word 'Church' to describe all other Christian institutions or denominations

Berger understands twentieth century ecumenism to be an attempt by the Protestant mainline denominations to gain greater control of 'cost/benefit ratios'. This was true for mass-evangelistic organizations, which in promoting their work for more funding placed 'cost/benefit' ratios before their donors. For example, World Literature Crusade, a literature mass-evangelistic organization, when describing its work briefly, used slogans like, 'It is easiest, and economical'. However, the thrust of such slogans was to motivate their donors and to make them feel that supporting the mission in any endeavour was not a burden and that they were aiming at world evangelization.

Then Berger suggests that 'religious groups or mass-evangelistic organisations have become unashamedly commercial offering anything to which it thinks the general public will be attracted'[47]. Berger's use of the word 'anything' with reference to the work of mass evangelistic organizations is suspected because of the core-convictions on the basis of which religious groups and mass-evangelistic organizations function, with which he disagrees. Berger adds that 'various religious groups or mass-evangelistic organisations have adopted the ecclesiastical equivalent of product differentiation in their marketing strategy, attempting to make their religious product different from its competitors, but only just enough, so as not to lose the attractive element which all competitors share'.[48] Berger makes these comments from his sociological reflections, but fails to understand on what historical background these mass evangelistic organizations work.

Berger further adds that the Church has increasingly sold itself to youth culture as a means of bringing more families into the suburban congregations of the Church.[49] This is to a certain extent true with mass-evangelistic organizations. Their literature, radio, television and satellite messages mostly appeal to 'the young'. For example, the 'India Every Home Crusade' of World Literature Crusade, received a large number of responses to its tract distribution from young people, whose ages are from 9 to 16. Berger suggests also that in the modern seminaries there is a growing concern to teach trendy practical subjects such as counselling and organization management. This may not be fully true of mass-evangelistic organizations, but the messages that they relay all use trendy subjects.[50]

In 1886, Rollo Ogden commented: 'Indeed, so far has the Church or mass-evangelistic organisations caught the spirit of the age, so far has it

---

[47] Ibid.
[48] Ibid.
[49] P.L. Berger and D. Nash, *Church Commitment in An American Suburb: An Analysis of the Decision to Join*, archives of the Sociology of Religion, 105 in P.Marshall, 1997, Modernization and Post Modernization, 120
[50] Hammond, Phillip E., 1983, 'In Search of a Protestant Twentieth Century: American Religion and Power since 1900', 151 (121), *Review of Religious Research* 24, March

become a business enterprise, that the chief test of ministerial success is now the ability to "build up" a church or mass-evangelistic organisation'. In Christian ministries, executive and managerial success is now more in demand rather than the Christian commitment and dedication, which were once considered the highest requirement in God's servant.[51]

Though Berger's view appears over-cynical, the modern sociological expressions of mass evangelistic organizations have been impacted by commodification, and this has often been in very subtle ways. In a society that expects the salesman at its door, the mass-evangelistic organization has tended to sell itself as a commodity, which the consumer can either buy into or do without. This may be true in the case of World Literature Crusade, which took gospel tracts to every home. Though it was called 'Every Home Crusade', it tried to bring a religious fervour to its work, but the underlying principle was the same as a salesman.

Furthermore, capitalism has become sanctified in the thinking of many North Americans through a widespread belief in the Gospel of Prosperity. The Gospel of Prosperity is, in the words of Bromley and Shupe, 'the notion that Americans are a chosen people and that their individual and collective prosperity are the bounty of that covenantal relationship'.[52] The roots of this understanding lie in the cultural climate of early America where the new optimistic Armenian 'doctrine of free will created the possibility of improving not just individuals but also entire societies'.[53]

The ecclesiastical expression of the Gospel of Prosperity is the mass-evangelistic organization in which masses of people are reached in a short time and large numbers of converts are seen as a sign of spiritual prosperity. Leith Anderson believes mass-evangelistic organisations 'are market-sensitive and attempt to take current trends and needs into consideration, using such up to date methodology as tele-marketing, advertising and high-tech communications'.[54] When it comes to evangelism, the effectiveness of evangelical strategy has often been judged on the quantity of 'results'. Seel writes, 'Theological truth became increasingly judged by its results in the marketplace. Numbers came to trump truth. Ministers were evaluated by their ability to "get results", specifically the saving of souls in measurable amounts'.[55] In some instances, the techniques of marketing have been adopted wholesale in

---

[51] Lears, Jackson T. J., 1981, in Rollo Ogden, *No Place of Grace*, 24

[52] Bromley, D. G., and A. Shupe, 1990, 'Rebottling the elixir: The gospel of prosperity in American religio-economic corporations', in T. Robbins & D. Anthony (eds.), *In Gods We Trust: New Patterns of Religious Pluralism in America*, 249

[53] Ibid. 234

[54] Anderson, L., *Dying for Change*, 145-146, in P. Marshall, 122

[55] Sampson, P., 1994 (quotes J. Seels), in Modernity and Evangelicals: American Evangelicalism as a Global Case Study, Chapter 13 in P. Sampson, V. Samuel, C. Sugden (eds), *Faith and Modernity*, 293

evangelism. Seel quotes the marketing consultant, George Barna, who believes that the task of the church or mass-evangelistic organisation is 'the transaction in service of felt-needs'.[56]

Barna sums up the doctrine of mass-evangelistic organizations in the four Ps of marketing strategy: the product is the relationships (with Jesus and other people); the price is commitment; the place is with other believers; and the promotion is by word of mouth.[57] Summing up, there are certainly areas in which the mass-evangelistic organization, in modern culture, has accommodated the language, technique and behaviour of the market place.

A mass-evangelistic organization's involvement with a commodified culture will now be examined under three sub-headings: Mass-evangelistic organization and Performance culture; Mass-evangelistic organization and Christian literature; Mass-evangelistic organization and mass media culture.

Mass-Evangelistic Organizations and Performance Culture

Moore suggests that the 'antebellum revivals and revival camp meetings were arguably the first mass-evangelistic meetings in the United States.[58] At the camp meeting, the revival preacher was the main attraction and his words were calculated to impact on the masses, to convert the audience. Many preachers attained great fame on the revival circuit. For example, George Whitefield, a modern time mass-evangelist, the father of American revivalism, is regarded by Stout as a 'self-promoter with sure business instincts' who 'wanted to be a star.'[59]

To suggest that the revival meetings of the nineteenth century were oriented towards their total impact does not mean to say that the driving interest of this was not to lead people to Christ. About Whitefield, John Wesley said at his funeral, 'History records none "who called so many myriads of sinners to repentance".[60] The methods of Whitefield and Wesley provide, however, an indication of how mass-evangelists and organizations

---

[56] Barna, G., 1991, 'Marketing the Church' Seminar, Atlanta, Georgia, 29 January (quotes J. Seel), *Faith and Modernity*, Phillip Sampson, Vinay Samuel, Chris Sugden (eds), 299

[57] Barna, G., 1990, 'The Church of the '90s: Meeting the Needs of a Changing Culture', 47ff. (quotes J. Seel), in *Faith and Modernity*, Philip Sampson, Vinay Samuel, Chris Sugden (eds.), 299

[58] R L Moore., 1997, 44, in Marshall, 127

[59] Stout, H S., 1991, *The Divine Dramatist George Whitefield and the Rise of Modern Evangelicalism*, xxi & xxii, in P. Marshall (1997), 'Modernity and Post Modernity.' M.Phil. Thesis, 127

[60] *New Dictionary of Theology*, 1988, eds. Ferguson & Sinclair, 721

were able to draw upon the techniques of a wider performance culture to promote its cause.

Mass-Evangelistic Organizations and Christian Literature

Throughout the history of the Western Church, religion has been closely associated with a reading culture. In pre-Reformation Europe, orthodoxy was largely maintained through barriers erected by the Church, which restricted the path to literacy. However, the Reformation brought change. The Reformers believed that to encourage the study of the Bible, literacy was essential. Rather than leading to questioning, literacy could reinforce orthodoxy.

The early nineteenth century introduction of stereotype (more correctly linotype) printing and the steam-powered printing press to North America meant that printed material was manufactured in revolutionary proportions. At the same time, the huge capital investment that was necessary to make this possible required an expansion of the market through advertising, distribution and the printing of more diverse reading material with greater appeal. The trend intensified markedly during the second half of the nineteenth century because of the rise of mass production. The technology of production advanced so rapidly that the time came to manufacture profitably, products of only a few varieties in such great quantities and consequently at such low cost that the masses of society could afford them.[61] In the United States, 'the number of manufacturing establishments jumped from 40,000 in 1859 to over 200,000 in 1900 and accounted for an increase in the index of manufacturing production from 7.5 in 1863 to 67.6 in 1900'[62]. This indicates the enormous increase in mass production.

The first three decades of the nineteenth century saw the rapid growth in the publication of illustrated books and prints of all kinds. New mass publications emerged ranging from textbooks and children's stories to illustrated newspapers and magazines.[63]

Despite the persistent popularity of religious devotional material, printers were increasingly inclined to publish other more 'corrupting' material such as plays, poetry, tales, romances, joke books and almanacs. The Christian religious groups faced a new challenge. Moore suggests that Christian religious groups hesitated to use this new opening to provide contemporary Christian literature that people wanted to read.[64]

---

[61] George A. Steiner, 1979, Government's Role in Economic Life 1953, 82. (91) *Capitalism and Progress*
[62] Ibid.
[63] Johnson, Paul, 1991, *The Birth of the Modern*, 586
[64] Ibid. 17

It is at this historical juncture that Moore believes many North American religious leaders began to believe that fire was fought with fire. The Church in the States entered the market place of a reading culture with one eye on caution and the other on opportunity. Christian literature was produced by various Christian organizations for mass distribution.[65] This paved the way for such organizations to be involved in mass-evangelistic strategies through Christian literature. For example, SPCK, the Bible Society, SGM and the American Tract Society were all involved in such enterprises. In 1827, the Tract Society printed over three million items for distribution; by the end of the 1820s, the Bible Society was producing three hundred thousand editions annually;[66] between 1800 and 1830 it was estimated that the number of subscribers to religious journals rose from five thousand to four hundred thousand.[67]

As the nineteenth century progressed, Christian publishers realised that the nation's tolerance for religious instruction depended on utilizing many of the cultural innovations that were available outside the Church. Such companies, says Moore, were 'cultural entrepreneurs of the first rank'.[68] This growing awareness of the need to diversify Christian publications was expressed by the American Tract Society in an advertisement for a new list of 'steady sellers' for children. 'While, on the one hand, the committee wish to issue publications rich in the glorious truths of salvation, and to do what they can to counteract the prevailing thirst in the rising generation for the mere entertainment of high wrought fiction... they are aware on the other hand, that the young demand something more entertaining than mere didactic discussion'.[69] This suggests that Christian literature mass-evangelistic organizations produced literature that was contextually appropriate.

Mass-Evangelistic Organizations and Mass Media Culture

After the Second World War, as people's disposable income began again to rise, there was a new appetite for a Christian culture in North America. The growth of mass media culture presented a new challenge for the Church.

During the fifties, Hollywood converted much of the Bible into spectacular big screen epics such as De Mille's remake of *The Ten Commandments*. Many saw the potential of mass media. The primary object was the furthering of the Gospel: this was certainly so in the case of

---

[65] Ibid.
[66] Ibid. 18
[67] Hatch, O. Nathan, 1989, *The Democratization of American Christianity*, 141
[68] Ibid. 19.
[69] Thomson, Luckman, 1991, *Printing and Publishing Activities of the American Tract Society from 1825 to 1850*, Papers of the American Bibliographical Society of America, 96, in P. Marshall (1997), 126

Billy Graham's crusades. However, others saw the business opportunities, for example, Norman Vincent Peale, who linked religion to successful living. Mass media was 'the most effective means of communication'.[70]

Mass production and mass-media created more openness in the society. Product differentiation and commodification enhanced the performance and brought an effective 'cost-benefit' ratio in total manufacturing and modern market techniques created to bring possible measurable results. Among American mass-evangelistic organizations, World Literature Crusade, a Christian mass-evangelistic organization possibly used these modern market culture techniques to their maximum effect. This is the focus of the next chapter.

---

[70] Armstrong, B., *The Electric Church*, 108, in P. Marshall (1997), 129

Chapter 3
A History of World Literature Crusade

Background, History, Beginnings and Development of WLC

This chapter studies World Literature Crusade's history. WLC is now known as Every Home Christ International (EHC-I). WLC with its faith in mass production of the printed page driven and its western mass-evangelistic and individualistic[1] approach strove to evangelize the world. Mass evangelism was an invention of America and an expression of modernity, where mass-production and mass-distribution was an efficient way to reap the maximum results. Like other American organizations, WLC was interested in big plans, great numbers and economically viable programmes. To reap maximum benefit in the shortest time and simplest way was its motto. Going systematically door to door would achieve 'World Evangelization' in this generation.

A Brief Historical Review

The decade of the 1940s experienced the worst effects of the Second World War. The world leaders and people were looking for lasting peace, reconciliation and restoration worldwide. The decade also saw the rise of communism in many parts of the world. Christianity faced many challenges. During this crucial period, independent faith missions and conservative denominational agencies of North America[2] played an important role in defending Christian faith and encouraged the churches and Christians to take part in world evangelism.[3] Their enthusiasm and dynamism was evident when Christian mission and witness were decreasing worldwide.The reasons for the decline may be theological debilitation in the sending churches, the de-colonisation process that accelerated during 1945-55, the rise of national churches in the Two-Thirds

---

[1] One of the Enlightenment precepts was that everyone was an autonomus individual (Bosch:1991:273)
[2] Escobar, Samuel, 1991, 'A Movement Divided', *Transformation*, October, 7
[3] 'World Evangelism' assumes that the current generation is evangelized. This assumption is now questioned. Hesselgrave (2007:121-14)

World,[4] and restrictions imposed in some countries upon missionary enterprise.[5] Such a situation demanded a new type of missionary activity.

The independent faith missions' enterprise was mainly associated with militant conservatism in its theology. It is due to the influence of the Manichean ideology of the Cold War, whereby the Christian world was opposed to the Communist evil world.[6] Much Christian literature of that era wrote against Communism and its spread.[7] The review of WLC's literature shows such anti-Communist fervour.[8] WLC saw that the spread of Communism was possible because of the printed page. WLC felt that the new readership in the world should read the printed gospel before such could read the propoganda of Communism. This was one the factors for its interest in the printed page. The other factor was 'World Evangelism' in this generation, a motto for many Conservative Evangelicals of pre-millennial convictions who wanted to advance the Second Coming of Christ through evangelizing everyone in the world. To suggest such urgency, WLC used a phrase, 'on fast-footing'. In brief, pre-millennial means 'its reference to Christ's coming before the establishment of the millennial kingdom, after the destruction of all things and the end of human history'.[9] Another important aspect of pre-millennialism was the 'individual conversion', when people must make a decision here and now, which is evident in all the Gospel booklets of WLC.

World evangelism seemed possible from the technological advancement and the invention of mass media in the nineteenth century. America and American mass-evangelism grew in this modern culture. Moody brought modern market techniques into mass-evangelism, which paved the way for mass-evangelistic organizations to use more innovative modern methods. The mass evangelistic organisations of 1930s and 1940s like the Billy Graham Evangelistic Association and World Literature Crusade chose to play into the modern market culture in their venture to evangelize the world.

Beginnings: Jack McAlister and his Vision of Literature Evangelism

Dr. John A. (well known as Jack) McAlister, the founder of World Literature Crusade, when he was young, developed a vision of world evangelization through the printed page. Jack McAlister, a Canadian, was the son of the Rev. Walter E. McAlister and Ruth McAlister. McAlister's parents were concerned about his health because when he was very young

---

[4] Ibid.
[5] McGavran, Donald, 1976, *Everybody*
[6] Ibid.
[7] Lee, Yohann, 1984, *Everybody.*
[8] Lee, Yohann, 1980, *How I Survived a Communist Struggle*
[9] Macchia, F.D., 1999, *The Struggle for Global Witness: Shifting Paradigms in Pentecostal Theology, in The Globalisation of Pentecostalism,* 8-29

his right foot was affected by polio.[10] Rev. Walter E. McAlister served as pastor and the General Superintendent of his denomination. Then, he served as the Executive Vice-President of WLC, where he established the Stewardship Department.[11]

McAlister was voracious reader.[12] Obviously, the impact and influence of reading books himself convinced McAlister of the power of the printed page in the lives of its readers.[13] From a young age, McAlister had developed a disinterest towards having more worldly things. He challenged people to have only a few possessions.[14] McAlister claimed in later years that he never owned property or had a savings account.[15] Wes Wilson, the present vice-President of EHC-I (WLC), disagrees with this claim[16] as McAlister owned a big and beautiful house in a rich suburb of Los Angeles.

McAlister had leadership qualities. From a young age, he used to gather other boys to do some church jobs.[17] From the age of nine, McAlister earned all the money for his own clothes. He sold boxes and gathered old newspapers, collected cardboard boxes and used baskets from store garbage and gathered pieces of scrap iron. He took up a job of selling newspapers.[18] This suggests that McAlister was a born salesman who was able to sell even the 'pieces' of scrap iron or paper. McAlister on one occasion in reaction to a remark from Dr. Oswald J. Smith said he knew how to raise money for the printed page.[19] Dr. Smith had once told McAlister that it would be rather difficult to raise money for the tracts, when people are not even ready to support the other better methods of the ministry, like supporting missionaries and church planting.

Before McAlister became a minister, he worked at the La France Fire Engine Company in Toronto as a stenographer.[20] There he learnt about the importance of hard work.[21] In his early twenties, McAlister became an ordained minister of the Pentecostal Assemblies of Canada (PAOC), in Prince Albert, Saskatchewan, a small town of 16,000 inhabitants.[22]

---

[10] McAlister, W.E. Ruth, 1977, *Everybody*, My First Born, Vol. 3, No. 4, 8, 9
[11] Lee, Yohann, 1976, *Christ Group Manual*, 1.1
[12] Ibid.
[13] Ibid.
[14] Ibid.
[15] McAlister, Jack, 1976, *Everybody*, Vol. 2, No. 9, 20
[16] Wilson, Wes, 1999, personal interview. Wes served as a vice-President in WLC, Colorado Springs, USA
[17] Ibid.
[18] Ibid.
[19] McAlister, Jack, 1974, *Operation Last Home*, A One Evening World Missionary Tour no 21, 34
[20] Ibid.
[21] Ibid.
[22] Ibid. 1

Most of the above writing on McAlister is from Johnny Lee. According to McAlister writes, he (Lee) is an 'oriental' man, his 'English is peculiar', he is 'hard working' and his parents are 'godly' and so on.[23] In all their writings, McAlister and Lee seem to be patting each other on the back. Whether they wanted to present themselves as a new breed of 'Duo's' in American evangelical missions is not certain: like, Moody and Sankey, Billy Graham and Cliff Barrows, who attracted large crowds, gained wide publicity and raised enormous amounts of money for their missions and themselves.

McAlister and Lee were successful in raising money for their mission, while promoting each other's profile in the eyes of the American public. Lee wrote on McAlister when he was still the President of WLC. When McAlister left office, Lee and others did not speak the same about him. Lee wrote that McAlister had a 'dear and oppressive rule' and further said, 'there is a lot of fresh air in the office'.[24] McAlister's rule seemed like a dictator who had divided the staff and taken away their freedom.

McAlister's introduction to literature ministry

McAlister came to know about the effectiveness of the 'Tracts' through his maternal grandfather, Manley, who was a school teacher.[25] Mr. Manley used to stand on the street in the city and give them to people who passed by. McAlister helped his grandfather to fold the tracts.[26] McAlister was influenced by his grandfather's stories about how the lives of the people were changed by reading literature. McAlister developed a complete trust in the power of the printed gospel to bring others to Christ and coined the famous slogan, 'When God wanted to reveal the Living Word He chose the Written Word'. [27]

McAlister said that he was never called to the literature ministry, however, the burden of reaching every creature on the face of the earth made him go into literature ministry.[28] 'To reach every home on earth with the gospel of Jesus Christ' was his vision. He thought that the easiest, most effective and most economical way to do it was through printed literature. 'To reach the world population in a minimum time was another consideration for taking the literature ministry'.[29] American culture is typically innovative, always wanting to do something big, that no one has attempted and that is economically and commercially viable.

---

[23] McAlister, Jack, 1976, *Everybody*
[24] Lee, Yohann, 1980, A Letter, Studio City, California, USA
[25] Ibid.
[26] Ibid.
[27] Ibid.
[28] McAlister, Jack A., 1963, *The Song of the Soul Set Free*, 'Preface...Tried by Fire', 1
[29] Ibid. 1.1

The other influences on McAlister to take up the literature ministry

McAlister lists four illustrious men of his time, who influenced him most to take up the literature ministry:

Dr. Frank Laubach, a pioneer who developed courses for the illiterate to read and thereby come to Christ.[30] He encouraged McAlister to devote to himself to do the literature ministry. The principle behind this was that when you teach someone to read a vacuum is created and that vacuum should filled by the Good News of Christ.[31] WLC did not engage itself to teach literacy, but did the job of distributing gospel tracts to every home of the literate or illiterate. Later, in the 1970s, WLC, in partnership with Gospel Recordings, tried to place or play gospel recordings for the illiterate.

Dr. Robert G. Lee's soul-winning zeal impressed McAlister. For 25 years, Dr Lee preached the gospel message and led people to Christ.[32] From him, McAlister learnt how to appeal to the individual and lead them to Christ. Such an appeal is evident in all EHC tracts.

Dr. Oswald J. Smith's life of commitment and single-mindeness towards morning-prayer, which he exercised for 60 years, impressed McAlister.[33] Lee states that in the beginning of the ministry the advice of Dr. Smith played a crucial role[34] and McAlister's world vision grew under his influence.[35] This is quite evident in the life and ministry of McAlister.[36] For a period, McAlister titled one of WLC earliest magazine 'Read and Pray'. In India, IEHC entitled its magazine 'Prayer Bulletin'. McAlister challenged people to pray for at least 15 minutes a day.

Cameron Townsend was the founder of Wycliffe Bible Translators, Summer Institute of Linguistics and JAARS (Jungle Aviation and Radio Service). Townsend's concern for the least regarded tribes influenced McAlister's life to reach every creature of God on the face of the earth by some means, if not by literature alone.[37]

McAlister at some point unsuccessfully tried to introduce gospel recordings in different dialects. However, that method did not seem to interest WLC very much because it was at a much slower pace, which was not akin to the kind of ministry WLC wanted to carry out. On his television programmes, McAlister referred to great missionary characters like William Carey and John Wesley. As Leach pointed out, McAlister was good at getting closer to great men of his time and getting good

---

[30] Ibid. 14
[31] Ibid.
[32] Ibid.
[33] Ibid.
[34] Ibid. 1.5
[35] Lee, Yohann, 1983, 37 years of the Vision, *Everybody*, Vol. 1, No. 2, 3
[36] Editorial, 1960, *Read and Pray*
[37] Ibid. 15

commendation letters from them.[38] Taking the names of such great personalities to promote himself and his ministry McAlister tried to impress the American evangelical donors to raise more funds.

Other Considerations for Literature Evangelism

Rise of Literacy

In the year 1971, WLC believed that in spite of 700 million illiterates (according to UNESCO) there were 3700 million adult literates and it was estimated that 3 million new readers were introduced every week. WLC's policy stated that if there was some kind of illiteracy it wouldl use another means of communication like gospel recordings.[39] It depended on the national offices to provide such recordings, if they had funds. In India, WLC through the support of Australian EHC-I's office, provides funds to run literacy classes, which help illiterates to learn to read and write.[40]

In 1953, McAlister's trip to Japan, Korea, Hong Kong and India, was an eye-opening experience: the printed page had to be used if the evangelism of the whole world were to take place in the present generation.[41]

Literature and the spread of Communism

The grandson of Gandhi said, 'The missionaries taught us to read, but the Communists gave us the books'.[42] During his time, McAlister witnessed the growth of Communism through literature. His concern was that before communism could sweep the world and build a godless community, through mass-evangelism, especially through literature, people could be introduced to Christ.

Development of McAlister's Vision

McAlister was born in the era when mass media like print, radio, and television were gripping the minds and hearts of Americans. Evangelicals especially envisaged that world evangelism was possible with the invention of the 'trios'. Though McAlister was an ordained pastor, it seemed he had sold himself to the use of mass media, that is, to an impersonal method. The following five key stages that is, 'radio to tract club', 'supply of free literature or funds', 'literature for Europe', 'from tract club of the air to WLC' and 'from general distribution to systematic house-to-house distribution' show how the vision of McAlister developed.

---

[38] Leach, Eric, 1998, personal interview (an international director EHC-I, Australia), London, UK
[39] McAlister, Jack A., 1972, *Everybody*, 5
[40] Creighton, Fred, 1998, a faxed letter, Hamilton, New Zealand
[41] Ibid. 1.5
[42] McAlister, Jack A.,1963, *Daily Diamonds*, 68

From Radio to Tract Club

McAlister had a radio ministry in October 1944.[43] Between 1944 and 1946 McAlister initially used the radio ministry to establish contact and to gain the confidence of the people. In October 1946, McAlister launched his radio and literature ministry, 'The Tract Club of the Air', over the station of CKBI[44] in Prince Albert, Saskatchewan, Canada that became the birthplace of WLC[45] and a modest beginning.[46] McAlister's small church study was his first office.

It was a weekly programme of thirty minutes.[47] During this radio broadcast, McAlister gave Christians encouragement, instructions and gospel tracts to help them in their personal witnessing. He offered free printed gospel messages for his listeners to give out to others. In 1946, McAlister had a plan to launch a great 'Million Tract Campaign' over his radio programme.[48] McAlister dreamt big numbers from the beginning. His passion for mass media and the 'number game'[49]suggests that such a gimmick was used to attract more American donors to participate in his programmes.

Supply of Free Literature or Funds

The news of this ministry spread and missionaries began asking for translations of these tracts for overseas. In 1947, in response to foreign missionaries' requests, he began sending free literature or funds to buy literature, to missionaries in many countries around the world.[50] Then the ministry took on an international dimension.[51] Hundreds of Canadian Christians made up the charter members of the ministry. They began sending voluntary contributions to the ministry that enabled McAlister to send funds overseas to provide Christian literature under the name of WLC (not yet registered). In 1947, the first overseas mission of the Tract Club of the Air was launched in Europe and then, in November 1948, in Africa, in January 1949, China and South America, and in October 1949, Japan.[52]

---

[43] Ibid. 5
[44] Ibid. 1.1
[45] Lee, Yohann, 1976, *Everybody*, Vol 2, No 9, 7
[46] Ibid. 3
[47] Ibid. 12
[48] Ibid. 1, 3
[49] Coote, Robert, 1991, The Number Game in World Evangelization, 18, April, *Evangelical Mission Quarterly*
[50] A Report, 'Country-by-Country Summary of EHCs', 'Canada', 24, EHC-I, Colorado Springs, USA
[51] A Report, 1976, cited., in *Everybody*, 'They send missionaries by the millions', from 'Worldwide Challenge' magazine of Campus Crusade (1976), Vol. 4, No. 1, 4
[52] Ibid. 5

McAlister sent literature or funds to buy literature to the missionaries with whom he had established contact.

Literature for Europe

In 1949, McAlister made his first overseas trip to Europe. He had firs-thand information of the results of the most horrible war in history. He recorded his impressions for his listeners in Canada. He saw the need for literature in Italy and France. He promised the European leaders that he would send them funds to print gospel literature. On his return to Canada, he was able to send the needed funds to print a million messages for each of those countries.[53]

From Tract Club of the Air to WLC

In 1951, McAlister and his family moved to south to Los Angeles, California. The station KGER was the first radio station in the USA that aired WLC's programme out of McAlister's garage-converted office. In 1952, the name 'The tract club of the air' was changed to 'World Literature Crusade'. For radio and television, the change of name gave it an international look.

Tracts Distribution from General Use to Systematic Distribution

From 1946 to 1953, McAlister alone was leading WLC. During that time, he gained experience about the use of literature.[54] The tracts were then used for general purposes like in bus stations, on street corners, in parks and in shopping areas. There was not any strategic plan to distribute the tracts..

In 1953, McAlister visited the Orient. He visited Japan, Korea, Taiwan, the Philippines and India. He witnessed the different cultures of these countries.[55] During this period, the EHC plan was drawn and put into practice in Japan.[56] He launched the first EHC in Japan in 1953[57] with the cooperation of two missionaries of the Evangelical Alliance Mission, Ken McVety and Sam Archer. It was giving tracts to every home that the name 'Every Home Crusade' was born.[58]

Rev. Dick Eastman, the present President of EHC-I, writes that Charles Cowman of 'Every Creature Crusade', first started reaching 'Every Home' of Japan in 1913. It took five years to complete the task of reaching every

---

[53] Ibid. 1.1-1.2 Stout, H. S., *The Divine Dramatist George Whitefield and the Rise of Modern Evangelicalism*

[54] Ibid. 7

[55] Ibid. 1.2

[56] A Report, 1978, op.cit., *Everybody*, Jan, 4, from Worldwide Challenge magazine of Campus Crusade for Christ International

[57] Ibid. 7

[58] Ibid. 1.2

home by Cowman and his team.[59] On this 'The Oriental Missionary Standard' of 19 January 1918, brought the following writing:

> 'By the time this reaches our homeland readers, the great work of taking the Gospel to every home in Japan will have been completed. Shout the victory with us, and give Jesus all the praise! Sixty million Japanese have had the Gospel put into their individual homes. There waits but the touch of fervent prayer to set this land aflame with a mighty revival. Let us mingle with our shouts and prayers the faith-inspired cry, "On to Korea" '.[60]

Dick Eastman also writes that after the death of Charles Cowman, his wife, Lettie Cowman, tried to continue the vision, but her mission organization, the Oriental Missionary Society focussed more on training nationals for Christian mission than on systematic house-to-house distribution.[61] Betty Cowman's other organzsation, 'The Bible League' (formerly World Home Bible League), tried to continue the strategy of reaching every home. Though by now the above organizations had house-to-house distribution programmes, none of them claimed that their primary concern was to take the gospel in printed form to every home on earth.[62] McAlister does not agree that he was developing Charles Cowman's vision, but asserts that reaching every home on earth was originally his own vision.[63]

It is not certain whether the vision of reaching every home systematically was originally WLC's or whether it developed the vision which Charles Cowman had founded. Going to every home was originally a business strategy to sell goods. A 'Bottle Brush' company in USA sent its distributors to sell their goods house to house. [64] A similar impression is found in a quote of Charles Cowman, 'Why not in these days of colossal business schemes undertake the King's business as something that requires haste'[65]

In Patrick Johnstone's words, reaching systematically every home on the globe was unique to WLC. He remarks, 'I regard as the most globe-covering literature vision the world has ever seen is that of World Literature Crusade (EHC-I). The vision is very simple, but its out-workings have had extraordinary coverage and impact'.[66]

---

[59] Eastman, Dick, 1997, *Beyond Imagination: A simple plan to save the World*, 254
[60] Cowman, Charles, 1918, *Mission Warrior*, The Oriental Missionary Standard, 136, by Lettie Cowman op.cit., Eastman 1997:254
[61] Ibid.
[62] Ibid. 311
[63] McAlister, Jack A., 1999, personal interview, Los Angeles, USA
[64] McLoughlin, William G., 1959, *Modern Revivalism: Charles Grandison Finney to Billy Graham*
[65] Ibid. 253 (126)
[66] Johnstone, Patrick, 1998, *The Church is Bigger than You Think*, 232

Move from Canada to USA

In 1951, McAlister and his family moved south to Los Angeles (in a residential suburb), California, USA.[67] The station KGER was the first radio station in the USA to air WLC's programme. Out of his garage-converted office, he and one office worker started anew.[68] During this period, many Christian missions and agencies had their bases in Los Angeles, Pasadena and the surrounding area. McAlister foreseeing his vision of the worldwide ministry mades this tactical move to find more funds and enlarge the support-network. Later, WLC en-cashes on this support-network and opens, or finds links, in Europe, Australia and New Zealand. Then he moved in 1962 to other location. In 1970, WLC office moved again to another larger location. In 1975, yet again, WLC moved to another location in Studio City, Los Angeles.[69] WLC claimed that God's money is not for bricks and mortar. In 1962, WLC bought a property in USA through a gift, and the same happened again in 1975.[70] In 1990, EHCI moved from Los Angeles to Colorado Springs. This is the present location of EHC-I. This property is taken on a lease basis and attempts are underway to raise funds to build their own building.

WLC and its Aims and Objectives

WLC set-up of Board of Directors who were evangelicals committed to world evangelism. Apart from the President and vice-Presidents, it will usually have some leading evangelical 'business personalities', like, Andrew Duda, a businessman who is a long- standing chairman of WLC.

The WLC, better known as Every Home Crusade or EHC is a Christian, interdenominational, international ministry to provide the necessary tools of evangelism to every Christian who adheres to the EHC vision. EHC regards itself as a service organization, serving local Christians, local churches, missionaries in the field, and new believers. EHC caters to the very large interest of the missions. The word 'Crusade' has different meanings in Christian history. However, WLC used this word to explain its two-fold task: 1. To inform Christians of the power of the printed page in World Evangelism; 2. To provide soul-winning literature to missionaries overseas.[71] Today, WLC is not able to produce and provide tracts for systematic distribution. The name of WLC has been changed to Every Home Christ International (EHC-I).

---

[67] Ibid. 1.1
[68] Ibid.
[69] Ibid. 1.6
[70] McAlister, Jack A., 1976, *Everybody*, Vol 2. No 9, 20
[71] McAlister, Jack., 1978, *Everybody*, 'Attitudes toward other Christian organisations', Vol. 4, No. 6, 3

Original Vision Statement

McAlister stated, 'an Every Home Crusade is a systematic gospel literature distribution effort-welcoming the participation of all evangelical Christian workers whereby two soul- winning messages (in their own language) are placed in "Every Home" in a nation (one for children and one for adults)'.[72] 'With free follow-up Bible Correspondence Courses for all new converts, where the countries have 1,000,000,000 populations'.[73]

New Vision Statement

Every Home International (WLC/EHC) exists to serve, motivate and mobilize the Church to participate actively in the systematic personal presentation of a printed repeatable message of the Gospel of Jesus Christ to every home in the world, helping new believers to become responsible members of the Body of Christ.[74] During Kietzman's period, he tried to change several aspects of the ministry including the vision statement. Whether these changes were brought to meet the new demands in the wake of its financial crisis,[75] or suit his own style to run the show is not certain.

Hitherto WLC had placed its large interest and funding in India,[76] but Kietzman, when he became the President of WLC, wanted to curtail the activity and funding in India.[77] Kietzman in this new vision statement emphasized the involvement of the church that means WLC will play a catalyst role rather than an activist's role as mentioned in the original vision statement of WLC, where participation of the 'evangelical workers' (not church) is 'welcomed'. Previously, the ministry of WLC in India had taken a role of an activist, and Kietzman may have changed it to a catalyst role to suit his style.

Objectives

1.   To communicate to all Christians that EHC can obey Christ's Great Commission to reach everybody in the world with the gospel;
2.   To train, equip and support dedicated national staff and volunteers to deliver two gospel booklets to every home in the world and a special message to prisoners, hospital patients, the blind, students, soldiers and seamen;
3.   To provide effective follow-up Bible study for all new converts;
4.   To assist all new converts in developing Christian discipleship and guide them into local Christian fellowship;

---

[72] Ibid. 10
[73] Ibid. 70
[74] Kietzman, Dale, 1985, A letter to National Directors & Executive Directors, Nov 4, Studio City, California, USA
[75] Goodwin, Paul, 1985, A Report, Studio City, California, USA
[76] Goodwin, Paul, 1985, A Report, Studio City, California, USA
[77] Ibid.

5.   To mobilize worldwide prayer support for this task.[78]

All the above said objectives of WLC's are historical except for 'mobilizing prayer', that continues today, due to Dick Eastman, who is one of the leading personalities of our times in the area of prayer.

The Finances

WLC raised its money by appealing to its supporters through radio, periodicals, books and television. WLC's main supporters mainly came from Canada and USA. Later, EHC-I had support bases in Germany, England, Australia and New Zealand. WLC claims that no money is spent for non-essentials in the headquarters office or in the field. The publications were low budget projects.

WLC's claims to be a faith mission organization,[79] not a fund-raising organization. WLC claims primarily to be a ministry that always gives.[80] WLC once claimed that 60 per cent of its budget is spent on the care and feeding of new believers- initial and advanced Bible Correspondence Course (BCC), Bible portions, personal counselling letters, monthly publications containing devotional materials.[81] However, now WLC has moved to a catalyst's role rather than an activist's role.

WLC in its own way is a 'faith mission', though not in the way George Muller or others thought about a faith mission. WLC has to wait for funds to come from its supporters, but its claim as a 'not a fund-raising organization' is superficial. From the beginning, WLC was very much into fund-raising. A review of WLC literature shows its entrepreneurial instincts. In Lee's words, 'if this country (USA) provides "only" the funds' are emphatic.'[82] WLC's publications show that it regularly raised funds for its ministry overseas and, in the 1970s, it made strong appeals for funds to purchase a paper mill.

WLC's other claim, 'a ministry always gives' is close to its meaning. WLC often claimed that 85 percent of its income was sent overseas towards the needs of the ministry and only 15 percent kept for their office administration in the USA. The same proportion was asked of overseas offices in their spending. However, it is not clear whether this system was strictly followed in the WLC's USA or in their overseas offices. McAlister and Lee often claimed that compared with other ministries like the Billy Graham Crusade Evangelistic Association and Youth For Christ missions, about whom they (WLC) said had spent their (BGEA & YFC) money in

---

[78] McAlister, Jack A., 1976, *Everybody*, Vol. 2, No. 1, 2
[79] McAlister, Jack A., 1975, *The Story Behind the Television*, back cover
[80] Ibid. 3
[81] *Everybody*, 1972, 17
[82] Lee, Yohann, 1980, *Everybody*

reverse order, that is, 85 percent on themselves and 15 percent was sent to their overseas work.[83] Such claims and comparisons have neither been verified nor established.

WLC and its Overseas Mission

However, WLC before setting up its work overseas initially provided funds to missionaries for the needed literature in various countries where McAlister was able to establish contacts. There was no organizational set up overseas. The money was sent to a particular missionary or group of missionaries to produce the required number of tracts.[84]

WLC's first overseas mission was in Japan in 1953,[85] where the first time 'systematic house to house' distribution was planned and the name 'Every Home Crusade' was born for WLC's overseas offices. The choice of Japan took place due to McAlister's missionary friend Ken McVety who was a long associate and had received tracts and funding from him for his work in Japan. McAlister was also looking for an opportunity to start his work in the Orient, thus the choice of Japan seemed right. Lee was introduced to McAlister in1957.[86] In 1957, Lee began systematic house to house tracts distributions in Korea.[87] In 1958, Lee invited McAlister to Korea and both met in Seoul. This was where the beginning of the first full-scale EHC in the world began with an office, office staff, follow-up material, and prayer bulletins. 'Are You Happy?' and 'He wants to be your Friend,' tracts and 'The way to a happy life' Bible lessons were written there.

WLC experienced rapid growth from 1958-68 when EHC was organised and launched in 27 countries. 1969-79 was a decade of historic breakthrough as EHC outreach was expanded from 27 countries to 49. During the 1970s, EHC launched a programme of reaching every home where a million people lived. From 1980 to 1983, work was slowed down and a special consideration towards Communist and Moslem regions was given.[88] EHC's work spread to 210 countries of the world. It is not certain what sort of arrangements WLC had in these countries. Whether it just sent funds to print tracts and follow-up material or financially supported the nationals too is not known. WLC's newsletter 'Everybody' mostly printed news from India, South America, Africa, Korea and Indonesia. The news from other countries were seldom or rarely heard. WLC had some sort of

---

[83] Guruprasad, G., 1998, personal interview, Bangalore, India
[84] Ibid. 1.2-1.3
[85] Ibid. 7
[86] Ibid. 7
[87] Ibid. 1.3
[88] Ibid. 3

contact in those countries but without a full time EHC office like in India and Korea.

WLC's Polices for their Overseas Mission

Literature

EHC provides all its materials free of charge to any and every Christian who abides by EHC's evangelism method. This commitment was there until the McAlister and Lee's era ended. However, from Kietzman's period (1984) until now, WLC hardly produces any literature of its own or offers it to anyone.[89] Mostly, WLC overseas uses tracts produced by other mission agencies including the Bible Society of India. WLC once said it would never use 'text' without any comment or explanation[90] like the Bible Society.

Personnel

WLC does not reject the idea of sending foreign missionaries to the other countries but its goal is the total evangelization of a nation. This cannot be done by foreign missionaries; it must be carried out by national Christians.[91] In every country, nationals are encouraged to operate its ministry. WLC does not interfere in the administration of these national offices. EHC boards have their national leaders of different Christian agencies. Except on some occasions, WLC's representatives may attend these board meetings. WLC believed in the effectiveness of indigenous witness more than its direct role in it. WLC firmly believed in providing the needed support of finance and prayer to these overseas missions, than in taking a direct role.

WLC's workforce involved not only its staff but also distributors and volunteers from 415 denominations and organisations.[92] EHC reports that in the 1970s, 900 nationals were employed.[93] In 1978, WLC had 3,733 national staff worldwide in 27 nations.[94] Now WLC maintains a skeleton staff worldwide. This may be due to its financial situation and its current passive role in world evangelisation. The role of WLC in overseas mission has changed. Though the western missionaries are not operating directly on foreign soil, most of its national leaders overseas are directly under the control of westerners. Chapter 4 discusses how WLC moved from allowing a 'freehand' to their overseas missions to 'under their hand'.

---

[89] Sudershan, Albert, 2003, personal interview, Regional Manager, IEHC, Bangalore, India

[90] Lee, Yohann, 1977, *Everybody*, Why the Amazing Harvest?, 22, Vol. 3, No. 3

[91] Ibid. 5

[92] Ibid. 13

[93] *Everybody*, 1970

[94] Patterson, David, 1978, 'Here & There', *Everybody*, June, Vol. 4, No. 6, 2

Establishment[95]

WLC establishes itself in any given country on a permanent basis. It believes that the vision of reaching every home never ends. The ministry of reaching every home will continue until Christ's return. However, it also states that this could change because political change or wars, or any other reason could require it to close down entirely, temporarily or reduce the ministry.

Now (during 1984-1987), WLC has changed its policy regarding the establishment of EHC offices. It required that overseas offices seek prior permission from international leadership to setup of a council or board.[96] To appoint a National Director, those councils or boards should seek prior consultation and agreement with the international leadership.[97] Chapter 4 discusses how during Kietzman's period, he wanted to bring control over the Indian leadership and the board, since it was independent. Now WLC enters with the foreign EHC offices on a contract basis. This suggests WLC will not be totally responsible to provide any resources, whether partial or on an agreed basis.

WLC and its relation to other Churches

WLC ministry is not endorsed by any particular denomination. The staff members come from different denominational backgrounds and work together towards one goal of reaching every home systematically.[98] Though the original vision statement stated 'evangelical workers', in that sense WLC's ministry may be classified as the ministry of 'evangelicals' but not of the 'others'. WLC provides needed literature to churches including tracts, booklets, bible study lessons, monthly devotional magazines and New Testaments. By so doing, it stimulates churches to accept their responsibility to evangelize their fellow countrymen. The local churches benefit through WLC with the addition of new church members.[99] Now WLC hardly produces literature of its own, it is not in a position to provide any literature to churches.

WLC does not build churches in the sense of bricks and mortar. However, in WLC's overseas mission,s some churches have been built by EHC offices, especially in India.[100] WLC does not aim to establish any denominations. Its seekers and converts are channelled into local churches. Where there are no local churches in the area, Christ Groups are formed.

---

[95] 'Establishment' refers to WLC/EHC office establishments in the overseas

[96] Kietzman, Dale, 1986, A Report, International Policy Guidelines, Studio City, California, USA

[97] Ibid.

[98] McAlister, Jack A., 1976, *Everybody*, 'Come meet us... here's what we are', Vol 2, No 7, 5

[99] *Everybody*, 1977, Vol 3, No 1, 4

[100] A Report, 1980, A Statistical Report, IEHC, Bangalore, India

WLC does not compete with the churches or cause any conflict of interest. EHC is national with all the literature is in the local language and printed in their country.[101] However, in the Solomon Islands, Christ Groups have become a denomination of their own.[102]

EHC converts and the local churches

In 1977, the 106 churches that were formed were the direct result of EHC tract distribution and the follow-up work. In Peru, 39 new congregations were formed in one State through the direct result of EHC. These groups were introduced to the Baptist Church, the Assemblies of God, Brethren and the other evangelical denominations in Peru.[103]

The co-operation of all the churches

WLC desires co-operation but it is not always fully met. Some churches hesitate to co-operate with WLC, due to its inter-denominational and evangelical stand. The local churches can use EHC for their assistance in planning evangelistic work, training workers, and supervising the programme.[104]

WLC's Paper Missionary

EHC's main weapon to evangelzse the world is through the printed page, that is the gospel tract. Dr. Ralph Winter speaking on the printed word says, "there are two things in the entire history of missions that have been absolutely central. The one, most obviously, is the Bible itself. The other is the printed page. There is absolutely nothing else in terms of mission methodology that outranks the importance of the printed page. Meetings come and go. Personalities appear and are gone. But the printed page continues to speak."[105] Books (tracts) are powerful evangelists. Each book may be a missionary and may sometimes accomplish more than the living agent.[106] However, WLC called the printed page 'Paper Missionary'.

The Titles of Tracts

'Are you happy?' for adults and 'He wants to be your friend', for children, were written by Lee. These two tracts were widely used in all EHC offices internationally and were translated into the national languages. In India, other titles of tracts are used in distribution: 'From Darkness to Light', 'The

---

[101] Ibid.
[102] Eastman, Dick, 1999, Personal interview, Colorado Springs, USA
[103] Ibid.
[104] *Everybody*, 1976, Vol. 2 no. 3, 9
[105] Dick Eastman, 1992, A Report, Points for Praise, Summer, From the President's Pen, Colorado Springs, USA
[106] Colquhoun, Frank, 1948, *Give Ye Them To Read*, 14

Joy of Ramesh', 'Did you hear this?', 'From Death to Life', and so on. The tracts (except two), were written by the nationals to suit to their own context but they followed certain guidelines of WLC.

Are you happy?

It starts with the background of an ambitious young man and his obsessed thoughts about money and material possessions. It then describes, 'What is happiness, anyway?' Here it talks about real happiness and real problem of sin. Then the tract explains what sin is, the result of sin and the only answer to it. Then the tract invites the reader to take a decision and make a commitment.[107] The western individualistic approach is used in India, addressing individuals.

He wants to be your friend

The tract talks in the beginning about different kinds of friends and writer describes about his good friend and explains about him, especially about that friend's death. Then the writer writes why Jesus wants to be a friend and how Jesus can become a friend of the reader, and asks for commitment.[108] WLC believes that the gospel needs to be written keeping Jesus Christ as its central theme. WLC did not feel convinced in writing about Jesus Christ alone. It believed that by such writing the reader remains uninvolved, remote and unrelated to what isbeing said about Christ. WLC also did not believe in just compiling the Bible verses with no comment or explanation made.[109]

EHC's basic message contains six fundamental elements:

- Who is Jesus Christ?
- Why did He come into the world?
- What did He do when He was on this earth?
- How and why did He die?
- His resurrection
- Christ's invitation and the reader's response[110]

The approach and message of the tract was to appeal to the conscience of an individual. McAlister affirms WLC's ministry was targeted to reach the individual, 'the importance of the individual is the key to this... ministry both here and overseas. Always remember this when you see the WLC Emblem of Evangelism'. Furthermore, he adds, 'Overseas...people are being reached for Christ One at a Time. When we think and talk of a million every day, remember this vast number is madeup of single

---

[107] Lee, Yohann, 1975, *The Story Behind Television*, 3-7
[108] Ibid. 7-11
[109] Ibid. 22
[110] Ibid.

individuals. A distributor goes to one home and gives one gospel message to one precious soul'. [111]

WLC came to India with such a western perception of an individual. Though the tracts were distributed to every home, the message appealed to an individual. The above words suggest that WLC had no idea about India's relational context and culture. WLC's attitude suggests 'we have the message and you listen to it'. 'A Top-Down Order' and 'One message for all'. Though WLC claimed that those tracts were translated and printed in the local languages, the pattern of writing of the tracts and the content of the message in them and their aims were all filled with the western thought pattern. The letters were in local languages but the contents were foreign. In the 1960s and 1970s, the name of 'Jesus' was never heard or fully understood by the rural Indians. The researcher in the 1970s had a similar experience, while explaining to an old man who was not able to grasp even the name of Jesus. WLC produced these tracts to convince its supporters in particular denominations in America to show that they present the Christ of the Bible to the heathens or non-Christians.

The method of evangelism

There is a systematic distribution of EHC gospel tracts to every home in a nation. The firm belief in systematic distribution comes from EHC's understanding that this is the only sure way is to reach every home in a nation. Since 1957, the emphasis on systematic house to house gospel tract distribution features in all EHC's plans. EHC claims Acts 5:42 as its scriptural basis for reaching every home.[112] EHC claims that it is a nationwide outreach. It means that it does not isolate its ministry to a certain section of the nation but the entire nation will be covered in a specified time, which differs from nation to nation and region to region.

EHC has other intermediary plans to reach the people who for any reason are away from their home: prisoners, hospital patients, soldiers, seamen, lepers, orphans, and the blind. EHC also reaches university students and other groups of people who need separate and special treatment from the primary house-to-house distribution. Sometimes WLC used different methods to evangelise certain areas. The Amazon River Basin stretches four thousand miles across North-eastern Brazil, where four million primitive villagers live in inaccessible areas. These dense forest areas along the river were covered under 'Operation Trans-Amazonas', in January 1976. Three large motor boats were used to cover these areas.[113]

---

[111] McAlister, Jack A., 1966, *One Million Every Day*, Preface, A One Evening World Mission Tour, No 13, 5

[112] Ibid. 2

[113] Ibid.

WLC's methods suggest that their systematic house-to-house distribution and appealing to individuals is done in an impersonal way.

The National Directors are responsible for their countries and regions to distribute tracts systematically. Local maps are prepared, printed tracts are ordered, the assistance of local churches is sought and office staff and distributors are mobilized. All distributors speak the local language well and sign a pledge that they will distribute the literature only in house to house visitations. In remote areas where there are no local volunteer Christians, nationals are paid. They are called Pioneer Crusaders. [114]

McGavran agrees with the 'modus operandi' of WLC of its overseas mission. He adds that 'a team of five workers would arrive in a sub-sub district, visit a group of villages on one day, mark it off on the map, visit another the next day and then mark it off ...and when...completed, the team moved on to the next'.[115] He affirms that EHC team distributed gospel tracts systematically to every home.[116] In India, it is not certain whether every home systematically received the tract or not. Often IEHC said, 'We reached every "accessible" home'.[117] That meant 'in-accessible homes' which were left out for certain reasons are not covered or reached. Reasons like opposition, suspicion or neglect on the part of the pioneer crusaders can be the cause for not reaching the homes.

Coverage

WLC in 1972 did not consider one coverage enough for a nation. Rather it believed in subsequent coverages to receive more decisions for Christ.[118] WLC says that no one should miss being introduced to Christ. During the coverage, some homes were missed because of the lack of experience on the part of the distributors, or human mistakes. Some nations took a longer time to complete the nation-wide coverage. The persons to whom tracts were distributed may in the next ten years have matured or grown up. They need to be reached again. The experience which is gained in the process of the previous coverage may help all EHC personnel to use it in their next coverage. EHC says its goal is two or three coverages in every nation. The subsequent coverage may be because of the increased responses. Many churches requested EHC to assist them in planning their evangelistic outreach, training workers, providing literature and supervising the entire programme.[119] This emphasis was there while McAlister and Lee were there but once they left during Kietzman and Eastman's period it was a

---

[114] McAlister, Jack., 1972, *Everybody*, 6
[115] Ibid.
[116] Ibid.
[117] Oliver, J. J., 1994, a letter addressed to Dick Eastman, IEHC, Mhow, India
[118] Ibid. 17
[119] McAlister, Jack A., *Everybody*, 1976, March, 9, Vo.l 2, No. 3

different scenario. They asked 'Why more coverage?' and 'Why to feed twice?'

The Response to Tract Distribution

Responses received numbered 3.5 million during the period 1946-75, worldwide.[120] The figures were calculated from the reports WLC received from its worldwide offices. The decisions received were from the people who enrolled for the Bible Correspondence Course, but did not represent the people who actually made any commitment to Christ. The percentage of the total decisions received in comparison to the total distribution of tracts is 1 to 7 percent. In contrast, the total decisions received under the Final Thrust-5000 (this was one of the programmes introduced in India between 1992-96, under which personal and family evangelism was encouraged) was between 30 to 40 percent.[121]

The above comparison shows that, in India, when evangelists personally shared the gospel with the people, not just placing tracts, the response jumped from a mere 7 to 40 percent. In the Indian context, the spoken words of evangelists were more powerful in getting a higher response than just the power of the printed word, which was rather restricted to below a 7 percent response.

Response and Follow-up

WLC from its inception placed strong emphasis on the adequate follow-up ministry, as "Fruit that shall remain" was its main motto. WLC does follow-up work in two ways:

One is through sending four Bible lessons to the enquirers, who send their written responses to the office. The four Bible lessons are tailored to meet the needs of various readers. EHC's says that, in 1975, its BCC was translated into 68 major languages of the world. This course was designed especially for those who had no easy access to the established churches, or could listen to a missionary. This course would provide some help for people to study at home. The courses also catered for the converts who were new literates, and not had the opportunity for advanced education. Therefore, the course was developed to enable it to be easily understood. Even the very young can grasp its truths. From the beginning, WLC gavemore thought, while creating its literature to the cultural and religious backgrounds of the many people of these nations, so as to suit the literature to that local context. 'The gospel has to be explained in an oriental way to the Orientals; but using African concepts for the Africans and approaching

---

[120] Ibid. 2

[121] Prasad, B.A.G., 1994, an address in a directors' conference, Secunderabad, India

Latin's with their own mentality. This is the best and the most effective method'. [122]

WLC also claims that after this simple course of 4 lessons, it will go on helping converts to study the further 15 other Bible Correspondence courses. A brief Outline of the WLC Bible Correspondence Course:

1. Lesson One – The Three things you must know:[123]
   The Bible; God; Man
2. Lesson Two – The Three Things you must believe:
   Sin; Jesus Christ; Eternal Life
3. Lesson Three – The Three Things you must have:
   Faith; Hope; Love
4. Lesson Four – The Three Things you must do:
   Bible Study; Prayer life; Witnessing

The four lessons were originally prepared in Korea by Yohann Lee.[124] It is arguable whether they were culturally relevant in other countries. 'A reader easily understood the truths' is an assumption rather than reality, at least in India. This is due to the lack of understanding of Christian teaching and terminologies.

Secondly, by personal letters: Bible Correspondence Course (BCC) is not the end for a BCC graduate. They will carefully be followed up by personal letters and devotional reading materials on a regular basis. Many join EHC's prayer mobilization by becoming prayer partners. Some become EHC's Pioneer Crusaders.[125] Personal letters may suggest again the impersonal method was used. In Karnataka along with personal letters, personal visits were deemed to be effective.[126]

BCC Graduates

In 1972, WLC records show that there were 1,042,093 who had graduated, since the introduction of Bible Correspondence Course worldwide. People who send their enquiries to EHC offices after reading the tracts are enrolled for the BCC lessons. The graduates are ones who complete the first four Bible lessons. In 1999, graduates numbered 3,837,968.[127]

---

[122] Ibid. 24, 25

[123] Ibid. 12-13

[124] Lee, Yohann, 1976, *Everybody*, Vol. 2, No. 3, 1

[125] *Everybody*, 1976, March, Vol. 2, No. 3, 5

[126] Vasudev Rao, H.R., 1998, personal interview, Field Coordinator, IEHC, Bangalore, India

[127] Statistical Report, 1999, Worldwide Progress Report, 30-03-99, EHC-I, Colorado Springs, USA

The Seekers Conference

Seekers conferences are arranged for the new spiritual babes who indicated the commitment of their lives to Christ or have graduated from the BCC. For such people, those conferences and personal counselling meetings were conducted. Each conference lasts three days and two nights- in a village, under a tree, by a river bank or in a local church (wherever the seekers choose to congregate). About 60-80 are invited to meet other converts who have been led to the faith through EHC's ministry. The programme was simple. The basic Christian teaching is taught in these conferences. Prayer and fellowship times are always welcomed at each gathering; question and answer sessions are especially liked by the seekers. Bible study groups often end the evening with evangelistic meetings. Often dozens of new believers are baptised in water at the end of each conference.[128] It appears today that the same emphasis on the Seekers Conference is not there.

Paper Missionaries Called Pioneer Crusaders

Pioneer Crusaders are generally young men whose average age is 21 years. Many of them are WLC's own converts who become PCs. (During the first coverage in India, that is in 1966, almost all the distributors came from Christian backgrounds). Some left their well-paid jobs to be involved full-time in God's work. These are full-time distributors of EHC where no volunteers are available. Mostly they are single men. They are away from their homes ten months of the year. Each PC reaches an average of 175 homes everyday with two gospel tracts. They go on foot, ox-cart, boat and bicycles. They cook their own meals and sleep wherever space in available-indoors or out.[129]

In some countries, the status of Pioneer Crusaders has changed into Pioneer Evangelists. The Ppioneer Evangelists are between the ages of 18 to 50. Most of them are married and have children. The average distribution of tracts or reaching homes differs from region to region, and country to country. In the past, WLC was committed to a 'One Million a Day' tract distribution programme, which meant that in the areas where one million people lived, distribution of tracts was by 'fast footing'. Now such a commitment is not used. Instead, normal tract distribution is practised. For transportation, in some places, vans or jeeps are used.

WLC apart from effectively publicising their 'Paper Missionary' idea with their entrepreneurial interest to American donors, also repeatedly and impressively used the stories of Pioneer Crusaders to encourage funding. On the one hand, they created a very high profile of the 'impersonal persona' of a printed page and depicted it as an all changing powerful

---

[128] Lee, Yohann, 1980, 'World Progress Report', *Everybody*, 1980, June, Vol. 1, No. 3, 14
[129] Oliveira de, A. B., 1978, 'Here & There', *Everybody*, Vol. 4, No. 6, 2

modern missionary, who was filled with up to date ideas, discounted the efforts of the human beings, who carried and distributed them to every home. In this way, WLC was successful in appealing to modern Americans for funding. On the other hand, they used the stories of the 'living persona' of Pioneer Crusaders, whose hardships and struggles appealed to the hearts of American donors to raise more funding. The following 'Story of Pioneer Crusaders' will illustrate how effectively it was used to appeal for funds:

'The life of these Pioneer Crusaders is not easy, to say the least. They are all single men, because the life they are asked to live would be impossible for any married man. Their average age is 21. They must be physically strong as oftentimes they have to walk all day long to reach the next village. Where they walk is not a paved road, but no road at all. They must go across the hills and streams, over the mountains and jungle paths. They have to endure the heat, humidity, and numerous insects and they sometimes get lost. Often they sleep under a tree; their eating hours are very irregular. They constantly face opposition from the villagers and right now two of our workers are in hospital because they were badly beaten up by some Hindu fanatics. Scores of Pioneer Crusaders were locked up in jail for no reason some of them for days go without food. Their gospel literature is sometimes confiscated by hostile police; many of them have been held by force and have been ridiculed by gather mobs'.[130]

Though the stories are a bit exaggerated for example saying, 'scores of Pioneer Crusaders' instead of saying a 'few', most of the matter contains the truth. McAlister confirms that the income of WLC has risen from a few millions to 70 million dollars a year.[131] Partly, this money was raised using the stories of Pioneer Crusaders. Most of the stories of pioneer crusaders used to raise funds were of Indians.[132] McAlister during his time with me repeatedly spoke about Crusaders and the hard work they did, with what dedication they worked, and how it brought 'blessings' to WLC.[133] Here McAlister's word 'blessings' sounds like meaning how the 'money' was raised through selling their stories to the American audience. WLC then rightly called IEHC a 'jewel in the crown of WLC ministry'.[134]

However, sadly, those pioneers were paid in the 1960s $3 dollars a month and in the 1970s $5 dollars a month. McAlister was not sure how much was greed by him to be paid to the Crusaders, though he said that it should be much more than that.[135] Apart from this, many a time, Crusaders were looked down on by their own leaders or the office staff. As Creighton

---

[130] Lee, Yohann, 1975, *2 Giants*, 10,11
[131] McAlister, Jack A., 1999, personal interview, Los Angeles, USA
[132] Ibid.
[133] Ibid.
[134] McAlister, Hazel, 1999, personal interview, Los Angeles, USA
[135] Ibid.

says, for Indians becoming a pioneer evangelist means a 'demotion' to them but if they were taken to the office it means a 'promotion'.[136]

WLC periodicals

The first prayer bulletin was published on March 20, 1960.[137] 'Read/Pray' was published monthly sharing the opportunities in WLC. In 1975, this contained six pages of news.[138] The other periodicals published are, 'Everybody', and 'Straight from My Heart'. The main purpose of these periodicals was to seek support and prayer. Mostly articles were written to attract the prospective donor.

The Prayer Ministry

WLC from the beginning laid an emphasis on prayer. From the first EHC in 1953, a 24-hour prayer chain has ceaselessly reinforced the ministry. Prayer partners were encouraged to commit themselves to fifteen minutes every day, one minute every hour, or one hour a day. According to McAlister, until 1976, WLC had more than 14,000 One Hour Watchers. WLC claims that since 1953 to 1976 more than 44 million quarter-hours of prayer have been pledged.[139] Change the World School of Prayer for Boys and Girls began in August 1977, to help school boys and girls to learn how to pray for personal, local and world needs with the emphasis on World Evangelism.

Since McAlister's trip to Japan in 1953, during which it became obvious that World evangelism could be only through prayer, WLC began a continuous unbroken Prayer Chain. According Eastman, until 1977, there were 5000 one hour prayer watchers.[140] The numbers, McAlister suggests, referred to those who pray 15 minutes a day. However, the numbers which Eastman suggests are those who are in a chain prayer. The prayer ministry seems to continue under the present leadership of Rev. Eastman, though it is not certain now that it is a continuous, unbroken chain prayer.

Christ Groups

Another emphasis of WLC was on Christ Groups. Their aims were to form a worshipping community of people coming from other faiths who do not have any easy access to other organized churches, to nurture and mature the new believers. Though it looks an interesting turn in the ministry of WLC,

---

[136] Creighton, Fred, 1994, A Report on Indian Leadership to Dick Eastman, Hamilton, New Zealand
[137] *Everybody*, 1976 Editorial, *Everybody*, July, Vol. 2, No. 7
[138] Ibid. 31
[139] Ibid. 6
[140] Eastman, Dick, 1977, '33 centuries of prayer', *Everybody*, Vol. 3, No. 9, 18,19

it only remained in WLC thinking until McAlister and Yohann left. After their departure, the ministry of Christ Groups remained on the periphery.

In India, during the first coverage, the initial responses to the gospel not only came from individuals but families, friends and communities whoo responded positively. These people not only received the good news but became the bearers of the gospel to their own people. This was another important factor that forced the WLC leaders to rethink their strategy in the two-thirds world. The percentage of those making some form of commitment to Christ in comparison to the total tracts distributed in India was said to be about 1 percent, whereas the people making some form of commitment to Christ under the Christ Groups movement reached 30-40 percent.

The Christ Groups movement in India became successful because of India's relational context. The message in this relational context was addressed differently rather than to impose the western rationalistic and individualistic approach. Another important factor came in the form of criticism from the Indian churches, Christian agencies and missions. The ministry of Every Home Crusade was labelled as 'Hit and Run' ministry.[141] Their criticism was that EHC was not presenting the gospel responsibly, and not explaining the gospel content to the illiterate masses but was throwing tracts hurriedly inside homes just to reach their daily target, or to improve their statistical data.

The important criticism of these Indian Christians came during the 1960s and 1970s, asking what adequate measures EHC had taken to care for its new believers. Did EHC want to disown its new babes after giving birth to them? These questions were asked because most of EHC's responses came from rural and remote parts of the country, where there were no neighbouring churches to take spiritual care of these believers. During this period, EHC in India was in fact reporting numerous stories of Christian conversions. This unusual success story of EHC was in contrast to the Indian churches, who were struggling to win new converts.

It appears that the above said factors forced WLC and EHC in India to shift temporarily their emphasis from mass evangelism to Christ Groups. Now WLC is just sympathetic but not enthusiastic towards Christ Groups' work in India. WLC does not own the vision of Christ Groups. It asserts that its only vision is reaching every home. It is not certain whether WLC in future will to continue to do Christ Groups work in India. In India, WLC has engaged most of its Christ Groups workers to teach literacy to the illiterate,[142] rather than to form or nurture Christ Groups. The Christ Groups' work would have continued if McAlister or Lee continued in

---

[141] Shettian, D.P., 1998, personal interview, Bishop of KSD, Mangalore, Karnataka, India

[142] Sudershan, Albert, 1998, personal interview, Bangalore, India

WLC. With their better business instincts, they would have focussed Christ Groups to their advantage to develop rather than just to en-cash their western individualistic approach to reach every home in India's relational context. However, WLC prefers to do what it wants to do than to do what is needed to be done in a particular context.

Jack McAlister and his Use of Mass Media: The Radio Ministry

WLC came into being through Radio ministry. McAlister from the beginning of his career seemed to fall in love with mass media rather than his pastoral work. McAlister along with WLC's work established thirty minutes' programmes broadcasting mission information from around the world.[143] During this broadcast, WLC used to share exciting testimonies from all over the world. After McAlister's departure in the 1980s from WLC, the radio ministry ceased to function. Through 'Radio' in the 1940s he had built WLC ministry. During the decades of the 1930s and 1940s, radio marketing was prominent among the evangelicals in North America. Joel Carpenter comments that among evangelicals 'radio broadcasting became a strong trend...' and they '...saw radio's religious potential and developed their own radio programmes'[144]. The evangelicals in America found radio a new medium, and there emerged a new pattern. It was used to air revival messages in order to seek funds. McAlister was a product of his time and used this medium effectively to build WLC.

Television ministry

McAlister was born in an era when the use of mass media had become a sanctified mission method for most evangelicals. By the introduction of 'Television' as Lee said, WLC entered into 'trio-logy' of the ministry.[145] The television ministry of WLC started primarily to provide Christians worldwide with an opportunity to view WLC in action. Their goal was once in two years to reach all the cities in the US and Canada and Australia with a '5-hour special programme' presenting missionary opportunities worldwide.[146] Lee says that McAlister changed his radio programme to television in 1975 and called it, 'World Evangelism Special'. In its two different programmes, it visited all the major cities in America, Canada and Australia.

---

[143] Ibid. 1
[144] Carpenter, Joel A., 1997, *Revive Us Again: The Reawakening of American Fundamentalism*, 129
[145] Ibid. 1.7
[146] Ibid. Inside front page

Two goals of television and radio ministry

First it was to spread a vision regarding the strategic place of literature in world evangelism today and specifically, to spread the vision of EHC, and to promote the ministry.[147] Lee[148] and Patterson[149] agree that it was to promote the work. Secondly, to mobilize prayer for all aspects of world missions. Specifically, to mobilize a 24-hours-a-day Prayer Chain in USA, Canada and Overseas.[150] The review of WLC publications shows that the first and the second 'World Evangelism Specials' were both used to appeal for money. In 1977, on 'Change the World', it was used for prayer. In 1978, the 'World Evangelism Special' was used to promote prayer and funding.[151] Raising money in multiple ways satisfied the entrepreneurial instinct of some of the American evangelicals.

In the following quote, McAlister, while writing to Josias of Brazil, seeks his help to produce a 5 hours' television programme. He states that it will be televised in the US and Canada and mentions two things to him: 'the aim to increase funding from $200,000 to $1,000,000 every month'[152], and to show to all Christians 'the power of the printed page in countries all over the world'[153] McAlister asked Josias to get 'important testimonies'[154] and maybe stories of distributors and persecution and others to use in the programme.

The main aim of the TV show was to increase funding almost five times. To achieve the target was to find the 'most interesting stories' to present on TV. Communication professionals know how stories can be glamorized or manipulated for a particular audience. Lee speaking about the stories says, 'The stories are all true, factual and documented'[155] However, Goodwin disagrees with this claim and says, 'The stories...were so embellished and stretched to the point that they were untrue'.[156] Examples of the 'most interesting testimonies' happening only through the power of the printed page is seldom heard. As Prasad puts it, 'in India, people came to the Lord not because of a tract alone, but only through "Total Evangelism" were we able to do what we did'.[157]

---

[147] McAlister, Jack A., 1976, *Everybody*, 'Come meet us...here's what we are', July, 4
[148] Ibid. 1.6
[149] Patterson, David, 1978, *Everybody*, 'Here & There', February, Vol. 4, No. 2, 2
[150] Ibid. 4
[151] McAlister, Jack A., 1978, *Everybody*, 1978, Vol. 4, No. 2, 3
[152] McAlister, Jack, 1970, A Letter to Josias S Riberio of Sao Paulo, Brazil, September 4, WLC, USA
[153] Ibid.
[154] Ibid.
[155] Lee, Yohann, 1975, *The Story Behind The Television*, 14
[156] Ibid.
[157] Prasad, B.A.G., 1987 (1991), A letter to Dale Kietzman, Hyderabad, India..

McAlister and Lee, to suit their shows may have played around with those 'most interesting stories' to attract the new donors and find more money for the mission and themselves. These tactics were well known to the other leaders of WLC. However, they kept quiet because the funds grew from $4 million a year to $70 million dollars a year,[158] through the showing of those 'tampered' stories the WLC leaders claimed at the time.[159] Sadly, when WLC faced a financial crisis during and after Lee's period, the leaders of WLC levelled at him charges blaming him for manipulating those stories and they made some decisions to set right the past mistakes.[160] This development illustrates the truth that unless Christian mission works with true Christian ethics without excessive entrepreneurial attitudes, it cannot stand the test of time and shine like a light on a mountain top or as a lamp-stand. The television programme was also discontinued after McAlister's departure.

The resignation of Jack McAlister

On 6 February 1980 McAlister wrote his resignation letter[161] to the board of WLC. His resignation was accepted in March 1980. For 33 years he had led WLC as its President. About his resignation, McAlister wrote that he had thought about it in 1979 after spending much time in prayer for God's direction and guidance.[162] In his resignation letter, he stressed that all through his life he had worked and now wanted to spend more time in prayer and writing. Lee also suggests the same about McAlister's resignation.[163]

WLC became a Charter Member of (ECFA)

The Evangelical Council for Financial Accountability. ECFA is an association of evangelical, non-profit organizations requiring the highest standards of financial accountability and disclosure to government, donors and the Christian public. The purpose of the ECFA is to show to the giving public that their gifts are being handled and accounted for in a highly responsible manner. ECFA was brought together under the guidance of leaders from World Vision, Billy Graham Evangelistic Association, Moody

---

[158] McAlister, Jack A., 1999, personal interview, Los Angeles, USA..

[159] Ibid & Dale Kietzman, 1986, A Report..

[160] Goodwin, Paul, 1984, A Report, WLC, USA; Kietzman, Dale, 1985, A Report, WLC, USA..

[161] McAlister's resignation related to mishandling of finance. No evidence was brought. In a private conversation in 1999, Hazel indicated the same from her words, 'I am sorry for taking my husband from WLC'.

[162] McAlister, Jack A., 1980, a letter dated February 5th, 1980, Los Angeles, USA

[163] Lee, Yohann, 1980, Executive Directive-10, Jack McAlister Retires From WLC/EHC Presidency, February 15, WLC, Los Angeles, USA

Bible Institute, The Navigators, Campus Crusade for Christ and a 100 other evangelical groups.[164]

It is surprising to note that WLC became a member of ECFA once McAlister left WLC. During McAlister's period, WLC received the highest donations. As McAlister says, '$70 Million Dollars' a year![165] Why WLC did not become a member of ECFA during his time is not certain. Whether McAlister opposed the move because he had his own reasons, or whether there were any financial irregularities which occurred during his time is not clear. Through becoming a member of ECFA, it suggests that WLC wanted to assure their donors that their money was safe (whatever the rumours they heard about McAlister or WLC work) and that itwais duly accounted for in the eyes of the larger body of 'Evangelicals'.

Other Presidents of WLC: Yohann Lee

John Lee, or Johnny Lee, or better known as Lee, is a Korean, who supervised EHC's nation-wide tract distribution in 1957.[166] His maternal grandfather and mother were examples of commitment to serve the Lord. His grandfather was a missionary to China from Korea in early 1900 until his death in 1950, when under Communist rule, he was in prison.[167] Lee was impressed with his mother's prayer life and her ability to mobilize prayer partners in Korea.[168]

Lee's introduction to Jack McAlister in 1957 was through an old missionary friend who lived in Japan and who had visited Korea where Lee was his interpreter. It came after their first meeting in Kimpo Airport in the summer of 1957.[169] (Lee also suggested that the first time he met McAlister was in 1958).[170] For Lee, McAlister's vision of 'reach the last home on earth' gave him needed motivation to get involved in a world ministry like EHC.[171] In 1958, Lee resigned from his pastoral responsibility, left his weekly radio programme, and became the director for Korea's EHC.[172]

Lee became overseas director on 2 May 1961 and moved from Korea to WLC headquarters in the USA.[173] From 1961, Lee made many trips to different countries and tried to develop motivation among the Christians.[174] In the closing months of 1961, Lee visited Japan, Taiwan, Hong Kong, the

---

[164] Patterson, David, 1980, 'WLC-a charter member', *Everybody*, June, Vol. 1, no. 3, 13
[165] Ibid.
[166] Ibid.
[167] Ibid. 9
[168] Ibid.
[169] Ibid. 9,10
[170] Ibid. 1.3
[171] Ibid.
[172] Ibid. 1
[173] Ibid. 1.4-1.5
[174] *Everybody*, 1976, Sep, 10

Philippines, and Indonesia. Lee was appointed acting Chairman and President of WLC in March 1980. On 16 May 1980, Lee was elected as President of WLC by the board.[175] Lee resigned from his Presidency in 1984. The reasons behind Lee's resignation is not known but Paul Goodwin's letters indicate mishandling or mismanagement of the money in regard to the Paper Mill and using manipulated stories to raise money from donors. Lee was with WLC from 1957 for 27 years. For the last four years he held the responsibility of President.

Dr. Dale Kietzman

Following acceptance of Lee's resignation, Dr. Dale Kietzman, a former President of the Wycliffe Bible Translators, became the President of WLC in 1984 and continued in the office until 1986.

Rev. Paul Goodwin

As an interim President, Paul Goodwin continued for some time, until 1987. Goodwin was a senior staff member of WLC from the days of McAlister. He held many positions in the organization and for some time he was the vice-President of WLC. He still serves on the board of WLC.

Rev. Dick Eastman

He has been the present President of WLC since 1987. He too was a senior staff member in WLC from the days of McAlister. He led the 'Change the World' prayer ministry, known as the 'School of Prayer'.

The Paper Mill

WLC owned a paper mill, with the capacity to produce 1,000 tons of paper a month. This was to provide papers for other countries to produce the tracts.[176] (Lee also suggests that WLC/EHC friends contributed to construct a large, efficient World Printing Centre, located within minutes of the paper mill. Whether it was constructed or not, or what happened to the money raised was not clear).[177] Holy Paper Mill was purchased for 4.5 million US dollars in late 1978, at An-yang City, which is outside of Seoul. About money, Lee says, 'Christians through this country (USA) raised funds over a two-year period to purchase a paper mill in Korea'.[178]

The purpose of purchasing this mill was to produce Bibles, NTs, tracts, BCC, Bible study books, devotional materials and Christ Group publications. Unil the end of 197,9 this paper mill shipped 3,250 tons of

---

[175] Editorial, 1980, *Everybody*, Vol 1, No 3, June, 12

[176] McAlister, Jack A., 1978, *Everybody*, Jan, 3

[177] Lee, Yohann, 1981, *I Survived a Communist Slaughter*, 79

[178] Ibid. 79

paper and shipped to 21 EHC countries in Africa, Latin America, Southeast Asia, India and Europe. The mill was able to use recycled paper as its raw material and, in 1979, the mill was improved to produce 2,000 tons of paper every month. The principle in owning this mill was to cut down the cost of paper.[179]

The Analysis of Three Main Failures of WLCs

Failure of the entrepreneurial instinct

The 'Holy Paper Mill' was a failure among WLC projects. The huge investment, which was partly raised and partly borrowed from banks, did not bring the desired result as was thought. The paper shipment to India never materialized. The Indian Government did not permit EHC to import the paper.[180] The manufacture of paper for commercial use was a real step backwards. Management failure is the main factor in the closure of the Holy Paper Mill. WLC entered this field basing its experience once again on mass production, cost efficiency and maximum profit. WLC may have entered this unknown territory without realizing the market structure, the government policies, and the managerial skills required.

Goodwin in writing on the Holy Paper Mill says, 'because of bad management, or whatever', which gives lot of other meaning to these words. 'Whatever' may even mean to say that money might have been swindled or misused. He further adds, 'Paper Mill in Korea with millions of dollars of investment is gone'.[181] WLC like any other American mission wanted to establish hegemony over literature distribution on the for worldwide mission. Lee, knowing well the American thinking, that is, the entrepreneurial instinct, may have made the board of WLC give consent for such an investment, where the profit ratio was much higher than any other previous activities of WLC in tract distribution, radio, and television.

WLC from the beginning, especially, McAlister, often said, 'God's money is not for bricks and mortar'. However, for an investment in this kind, where profit ratio was high, may have made WLC's leaders forget their own words or agreed convictions. In the end, they blamed Lee alone without acknowledging their part. Goodwin, writing further admitted, 'We are not sure (clear) about the investments in the World Printing Centre.' He continueds, 'It is also quite possible that printing can now be done in your

---

[179] Note: The total price for the mill was for 4.1 million US dollars...*Everybody*, 1978, Feb, Vol. 4, No. 2, 3, WLC, Los Angeles, USA, God's Paper Mill, 1980, *Everybody*, Jan, Vol. 1, No. 1, 8

[180] Guruprasad, G., 1998, personal interview, Bangalore, India

[181] Goodwin, Paul N., 1985, A letter to U S Board of Directors WLC/EHC Executives Worldwide, dt February 14, Studio City, California, USA

country cheaper'. This policy was not new as it was there from the beginning, but the profit motives led the leaders astra. causing permanent damage to the ministry.[182] WLC contradicted its own stand on 'God's money', and invested a huge amount in this project. Donors may have become suspicious for WLC experienced a great decline in its income from its donors, which then brought great pressure upon their ministry worldwide.

The failure of the entrepreneurial instinct of WLC led them into indebtedness. It landed them with a serious problem. Paul Goodwin, writing to the US Board of Directors, informed them of the then current economic position of WLC. Further, speaking on securing a loan and the period it took from the bank he admitted, 'Discussion was given about the proposed consolidation loan we have been waiting on for about five and half months'.[183] He assurds the members, 'we will be able to take care of 1 million dollars of debt. Without being able to arrange for this loan to cover further indebtedness here in the States, there would shortly be no US Support Base. "The golden goose" would have been dead!'[184]

The resignations of McAlister in 1980 and Lee in 1984 affected WLC's income and led to a steep decline in donations. According to Goodwin, 'God was not punishing WLC/EHC for some specific person's sin or mismanagement problem' Though the statement is not explicit, this has an implied meaning pointing at Lee. During his time, and partly in McAlister's time, the indebtedness increased to 1 million dollars.[185]

It is surprising to ask why WLC was so much affected by this 1 million dollar indebtedness or 5 million losses on the Holy Paper Mill, or a few millions on the World Printing Centre. According to McAlister, WLC once used to receive about $70 million dollars a year, and now in 1999 received 4 million dollars a year.[186] It was almost 15 to 20 times less than what they received 20 years before. However, WLC on that income, and 1 or 2 million dollars from its support bases, was able to run its programmes. 70 million dollars a year may have been raised between 1975 (the first telecast) to 1980 (the last telecast in McAlister's period), or 1984 (extended telecast, Lee's period). In this period, WLC received a considerable amount of money. The donations that were raised in the mid-seventies and the late nineties show a huge difference between them, almost amounting to roughly twelve times. During the fruitful years, the money flowed into WLC, but where did it go? It is not a matter to be dealt with here but

---

[182] Ibid.

[183] Ibid.

[184] Goodwin, Paul N., 1985, 10 March, A Report of US Board of Directors WLC/EHC Executives, Studio City, California, USA

[185] Goodwin, Paul N., 1985, A letter to WLC/Executive Staff, April 29, Studio City, California, USA

[186] McAlister, Jack, 1999, personal interview, Los Angeles, USA

Christian missions must make every effort to maintain their accountability as Christians before God and His Church.

Failure of overseas mission, in the case of India

The effect of the failure of 'entrepreneurial approach' was to start affecting WLC's ministries overseas, especially, India. Once it was called the 'Jewel in the crown of WLC'[187] because an enormous amount of money was raised from Americans by 'selling' stories of India. Now India suffered severe punishment through no fault of her own, but by that of her American 'bosses, because they wanted to recoup their losses, which were incurred through their own 'mismanagement' and 'bad management'.[188] This was at the cost of effective ministry, which was going on in India through 'Christ Groups'.

Kietzman, a former President of WLC, suggested that WLC wanted to move out from nations where EHC has at least completed one nationwide coverage. He wrote, 'no one has a right to hear the Gospel twice, until everyone has heard it at least once.'[189] This statement was originally suggested by Dr. Oswald J. Smith, referring especially to the Western audience, where the gospel was preached over and over again. But Kietzman, to suit his strategy, interpreted the statement of Smith wrongly for his convenience to suggest that he (Kietzman) wanted to move out of India. Before him, other WLC leaders have said that India would have repeated distribution programmes. Glen Pitts, a vice-President of WLC once remarked that in India reaching every home would never end because of its vastness and growing population.[190] Kietzman, talking directly to the Indian leaders prepared a platform to launch his strategic retrenchment of WLC's ministry in India. For years, the Indian subcontinent had received a larger portion of the budget, and Kietzman intended to cut that down and 'stabilize' the finances of the US office and pay off the debts.

Kietzman added, 'In fact, as often as possible, we should seek to get our ministry done through others already established in places of national church leadership'.[191] He suggested moving from pioneer work to that of a catalyst. From active participation to that of an agent, or middle-man. He suggested that WLC would like to take on the role of a 'catalyst'. He asserted that WLC should 'place a much greater emphasis on research'[192] He intended to transform a 'Pioneer Mission' which had functioned for more than 40 years in the forefront of active mission to become a 'research

---

[187] McAlister, Hazel, 1999, personal interview, Los Angeles, USA
[188] Ibid.
[189] Ibid.
[190] Pitts, Glen, 1988, an address in an IEHC directors' meeting, Bangalore, India
[191] Ibid.
[192] Ibid.

mission' without having any research team available either in the headquarters or overseas. He also said, 'we must also be ready to stimulate co-operative efforts with other ministries. This included the development of relationships with denominations that will make available their memberships as volunteers and supporters of our work'.[193] This kind of co-operation and development of relationship would be suitable on other occasions like coming together during Crusades. However, the work is done overseas either by their links to the West or by indigenous missions who may not be willing to co-operate and share news and results with other missions that may hamper their own support. Dr. Phil Butler's 'Interdev' mission tried to build partnerships among Indian missions to achieve more effectiveness and conserve resources but had very little effect.[194]

He proposed a single unit operation over a continent. For example, 'The Central American project, which is encouraging distribution to every home in five countries in two years, is doing so without a national director or special EHC office in any of them'. Kietzman was full of ideas but without any appreciation of practical aspects. He proposed the same 'one unit' idea for the whole of India, though the 'unit' did not constitute one language, or one cultural background. This was a naïve assumption about India, where very diverse cultures exist even among the same castes of people of different regions. For example, high-caste people who live in coastal areas will eat fish as their main food but those who live in the plains do not touch fish at all because that is seen as a non-vegetarian food. India is regionally, ethnically, linguistically, and culturally a very diverse country.

Kietzman's suggestions and ideas lacked practical application. He would have rather suggested the closure of WLC's operation overseas for not being able to carry out its vision. He was unwilling to take a risk to carry out the vision but rather willing to abandon the WLC vision for which it had stood for decades. He also suggested the appointment of international leadership in each country. That is moving from national and regional leadership and bringing back the age-old pattern of appointing their 'own' people (mostly Whites) to lead overseas missions. This became necessary for Kietzman when he found that some national directors were objecting to or resisting his moves in their nations or continents. For example, Kietzman's letters to Prasad showed that how much he (Kietzman) was not interested to receive his (Prasad's) correspondence, often remarking to him that his 'letters are usually long'. For most of Kietzman's suggestions, Prasad had different perspectives and tried to explain to him about the prevailing culture, political or legal situation in the country, which Kietzman did not like. Kietzman thought such attitudes, in the long run, would become obstacles to the development of the ministry. Kietzman

---

[193] Ibid.
[194] Bowman, Jim, 2000, Personal interview during his visit to Bangalore, India

wanted men who thought like him, for example, Charles Wickman, who better understood and accepted his management principles. However, Kietzman, who would not listen to Prasad, often tried to express his suggestions, which were filled with sentiment or emotions.

Did WLC's 'workable plan'[195] work in India? Kietzman said 'no'![196] Interestingly, one of the senior directors of IEHC, Oliver, remarked that WLC has 'stopped' announcing 'The Last Home by the turn of the Century'.[197]

Failure of world evangelisation through mass media

I have discussed how some American evangelicals through technical achievements wanted to 'win the world'. WLC, which was born in that era, felt strongly to move away from the 'missionary in person' method. Lee felt, 'world evangelism is totally hopeless if we depend upon "mouth contact" alone!'[198] For him, 'mass media' seemed 'the answer'. He regarded Literature, Radio and Television as the most potent and fastest weapons for world evangelisation. He asserted, 'our hope of getting the task completed lies in Literature'[199] He further emphasized, 'the printed page is the most far reaching, the most strategic, the most powerful and the most effective tool in today's evangelism'.[200] Lee rather emphatically said, 'we know now that it is absolutely impossible to send enough missionaries to complete the job of world evangelism...and God has entrusted to us everything to meet their need....The answer (is) Paper Missionary'.[201]

Nevertheless, Paul B Smith, from the beginning of WLC's ministry, rightly warned and commented on their over-hyped view about 'Literature' alone! He said, 'I do not believe that any single method can be responsible for total world evangelisation'. He further added, 'the flesh and blood missionary will always be the most important...because he is God's method'. '... man always comes first and the method second' However, he quipped that we need to adopt the new methods as a new era dawns without neglecting God given methods which have been used for ages.[202] To realize their claim was mistaken, WLC took a very long period to be honest with themselves and about the nature of world missions. WLC in the end, rather painfully, had to admit the failure of their claim of 'world evangelization' through mass media.

---

[195] Ibid. 5
[196] Ibid.
[197] Ibid.
[198] Lee, Yohann, 1962, *Dawn of New Era*, 28, 29
[199] Ibid.
[200] Ibid.
[201] Ibid. 30
[202] Smith, B. Paul, 1962, Foreword, op.cit., Yohann, Lee, *Dawn of New Era*

On that subject, Kietzman made an honest confession about how mass-media had failed to fulfil the Great Commission, 'no one vision and no one organisation will ever fulfil our Lord's Great Commission to take the Gospel of Christ to the ends of the earth. Is television to take the Gospel of Christ to the ends of the earth? Television cannot do it alone. Radio cannot do it alone. Literature cannot do it alone. Evangelistic crusades cannot do it alone. No single denomination can do it alone'. He added about the failure of literature evangelism, 'less-evangelised nations need living human beings' recognising the importance of personal evangelism while distributing the printed page. He also recognises the importance of 'acts of Christian love and mercy',[203] which was for so long missing in WLC's ministry. WLC was critical at that time asking whether it would be better to provide food to the hungry or to share the Gospel that gives eternal hope.[204]

Lee's other claim, 'we know now that it is absolutely impossible to send enough missionaries to complete the job of world evangelism' was rather short-sighted. In the 1990s, the founder of Youth With A Mission, Loren Cunningham, claimed that he had personally gone to every sovereign nation on earth, all dependent countries, and more than 150 territories and islands, for the sake of the Gospel.[205] According to Gene Early, YWAM sent their missionaries to all nations on the globe.[206] This suggested it was possible to send enough missionaries to all the nations of the world to complete 'world evangelization' with or without the use of modern technology!

However, the question remains whether people are ready to hear the Gospel, when it is mostly misunderstood by the many religious fundamentalists groups in the world, when for them it is one more piece of 'western propaganda'. Political vendetta is not conducive in accepting the Lordship of Christ even in so-called 'Christian' countries. Philosophers have not yet come to any conclusion about their 'Messiah of the world'. The poor and needy have not yet been delivered from their poverty. Their self-identity, self-esteem and self-dignity are yet to be restored, and they have not yet come to know that they have been made in the 'image of God'. There are many 'hidden groups', who have yet to hear the Gospel.

What is important in carrying out world evangelization as Kietzman[207] reminds us, is that the 'body of Christ' should take and carry the Gospel. The human and 'high tech' touches are equally important in the determination to carry out the message. 'Word and Deed' cannot be

---

[203] Kietzman, Dale, 1987, Memorandum to Wickman, April 10, Re: Strategies of ministry, the same was sent to all the leaders, WLC, Studio City, California, USA
[204] Ibid. 30
[205] www.ywam.org accessed on 9 May 2009
[206] Early, Gene, 1999, personal interview, an ex-staff of YWAM, Oxford, UK
[207] Kietzman, Dale, 1987, a memo, April 10, Studio City, California, USA

separated when we see human misery and exploitation. Without standing on any higher ground the Gospel is to be shared on an equal footing with 'others'. We must help human beings to understand rather than misunderstand the message.

WLC's Contribution for World Mission

The false entrepreneurial instincts of WLC will not take away the contribution WLC made in the annals of world mission history. Entrepreneurialism is becoming the norm for many US or non-US evangelical Christian agencies, missions and churches. From the United States to South Korea, we witness today the growth of Mega-churches, which have thrived and grown under highly professional and market entrepreneurial instincts.[208] Such practice in Christian missions may increase and continue as much as market theories and skills increase and achieve more and more technical advancements.

However, WLC's contribution to world mission was remarkable when the decolonisation process had affected the inflow of western missions or had forced them to leave countries because the legislation of those countries prohibited the work of missionary agencies.[209] As Carpenter puts it, 'in the emerging Two-Thirds World, there was a reality that demanded a new type of missionary effort'. [210] WLC was able to find this new way of providing that missionary effort through their 'Paper Missionary'[211]. McGavran, in commendation of WLC's work in India, said, 'Jack McAlister's systematic plan works!'[212] As Johnstone rightly puts it, 'WLC's work in the worldwide mission is highly commendable'[213] because he thinks no other mission agency had ever taken on such a Herculean task before through literature ministry as WLC.

---

[208] Walker, Andrew, 1985, *Restoring the Kingdom*, 275
[209] Ibid.
[210] Carpenter, Joel A., and Wilbert R. Shenk, 1990, *Earthen Vessels*, American Evangelicals and Foreign Missions, 1880-1980, 7
[211] Ibid.
[212] Ibid.
[213] Ibid.

Chapter 4
India Every Home Crusade and Its Leadership

Background to the Study

This chapter proposes to do a brief study on the ministry of India Every Home Crusade (IEHC), with special focus on its leadership's attitude, behaviour and characteristics, in relation to the ministry, inter-personal relationships, finance and WLC officials and vice versa. On certain issues, how and why did they act in a particular way? How was their behaviour perceived by the WLC officials? Were Indian leaders successful in holding the two opposing currents of thought, which are western individualism or 'linear' thought on the one side and the Indian relational thought context on the other? How far did they try to justify their activities in two different or opposite contexts, while fulfilling 'The Great Commission'? On the one side, Indian leaders were trying to please WLC officials while carrying out the western individualistic mass approach, which was a sign of modernity. On the other, India's relational context demanded more of a personal and relational approach to have a better understanding of Christ and His good news.

The sources for the study in this chapter are the archives of WLC and IEHC to which I had unique access. For the first time, the relationships between the US leadership and Indian leadership can be explored through their correspondence. This chapter will argue that important differences between the American and Indian leadership will illuminate the different directions that IEHC went from the WLC model that led to the formation of Christ Groups. To have a better view of IEHC's work in India and the behaviour and the attitude of Indian leaders, I will briefly present India's past and present contexts.

India Today

In three or four decades, India will overtake China as the most populous nation on the globe with over 1.5 billion people.[1] Today, the world's largest democracy still survives in India and its population is over a billion. India

---

[1] Population Reference Bureau 1997: see http://nyac.aed.org.factsheets/India 1.htm

has hundreds of unreached people groups, including some of the largest, like the Chamars (48 million), Rajputs (42 million), Anasaris or Pinjaras (13 million) and Bhils (11 million).[2] There are reports of powerful manifestations of the Holy Spirit in all the mission fields of India today. Reports of bold evangelistic outreaches, multiplication of disciples and rapid church growth are taking place in various parts of the country, especially among the scheduled tribes and castes, and among other majority and minority caste groups. More than 450 indigenous Indian mission organizations are sending out over 45,000 missionaries (though some surveys suggest this number is 30,000), around 66 percent of them are working cross-culturally in India, and about 450 of them are overseas.[3]

Complexity

India is rightly called a sub-continent. It is more than a nation. India is comprised of 29 States, some of them are larger than European countries and 6 Union Territories and about 600,000 villages. 222 languages are spoken by more than 10,000 people each.[4] These include 18 official languages. More than 1000 dialects and 25 scripts are used. Varied cultural differences can be observed between north and south, between west and northeast, and between urban, village and tribal settings. Dr. K.S. Singh (2000) of the Anthropological Survey of India (1991) has identified 4,693 communities or people groups: 'Nowhere in the world have so many streams mixed, with such diversity'. The India Missions Association records 960 castes and tribes with populations of at least 10,000.[5]

According to Ebenezer Sunder Raj, former General Secretary of the India Missions Association, India is home to approximately 450 million Hindus. In addition, nearly 300 million people of lower castes have been classified as Hindus by the Census of India since 1931, but since they do not practice the Brahminical religion, they are not properly called Hindus.[6] In Indi,a we find the world's largest block of accessible Muslims, about 123 million, as well as 22.2 million Sikhs, 6.5 million Buddhists and 3.8 million Jains.[7]

Hinduism as a religion is embedded within the caste system. There are some caste groups, who are inside the caste-ladder and some other caste groups, who are outside the caste ladder. Traditionally caste divisions are related to occupational groupings and endogamous marriage arrangements

---

[2] India Missions Association, 1997, *Peoples of India*
[3] Johnstone, Patrick & Jason, Mandryk, 2001, *Operation World*, 311
[4] India Missions Association, 1997, *Languages of India*, Chennai... *World Christian Encyclopedia*, 2nd ed., 2001; Vol.1, 359
[5] Singh, K.S., 2000, Cited in a Research Workshop on February 3, 2000. The commonly cited number from Dr. Singh's 1991 study is 4,635 people groups
[6] Sunder Raj, Ebenezer, 2001, *National Debate on Conversion*
[7] *World Christian Encyclopedia*, 2001

(i.e. marriage within a *jati*, a similar social unit).[8] However, when combined with religious ideas of purity and social practices of hierarchy, it has become for many an instrument of discrimination and oppression. At a recent UN conference on racism in Durban, South Africa, Indian Dalit leaders argued unsuccessfully for the identification of caste discrimination as a form of racism in the Indian context. The "politically correct" term preferred in place of "caste" is "community."

At the top of the hierarchy, the Brahmins, the priestly caste, comprise only 4 percent of the population.[9] The next two highest castes, the Kshatriyas (warriors) and Vaishyas (traders), comprise 8.3 percent. These first three castes are called 'Forward Castes' by the Government, because they are considered to be relatively wealthy and developed. Even though the Forward Castes comprise less than 15 percent of the population, they hold the dominant influence in politics, education, and business. The lowest castes, called 'Backward Castes' and 'Other Backward Castes' (Sudras) are 45.3 percent of the population. Together these four groups, the only ones properly called Hindus, comprise only 57.6 percent of the Indian population.

Another 14.5 percent belong to the Scheduled Castes, also called Outcastes, Untouchables, or Dalits, renamed *Harijans* ('children of God') by Mahatma Gandhi. Another 7.6 percent are tribals, the 'Adivasis' or aborigines. Both the Scheduled Castes and the tribals were enslaved centuries ago by the four higher castes, but for political purposes often are referred to as Hindus. All other religious groups comprise about 20 percent of the population. The different castes are separated by social barriers with numerous prohibitions related to intermarriage, food, and ritual purity. Even though caste discrimination is forbidden by the Indian constitution, it strongly influences social behaviour and thinking for over 80 percent of the population, including many Christians.[10]

According to the official government census of 1991, Christians comprised 2.61 percent of the population. The provisional figures from the new 2001 census indicate that the percentage of Christians has dropped to 2.3 percent but these figures are open to question for a number of reasons. Operation World (6th edition, 2001) lists the percentage of adherents to Christianity as 2.4 percent, whereas the World Christian Encyclopaedia (2nd edition, 2001) cites 4.0 percent affiliated, with an additional 2.1 percent unaffiliated ('crypto-Christians'). Christians are concentrated primarily in the four southern states (Kerala, 19.3%; Tamil Nadu, 5.7%; Andhra Pradesh, 7.9%; and Karnataka, 2.1%) as well as the North-eastern states

---

[8] Fernandes Walter, 1981, *Caste Conversion Movements in India*, 2
[9] Ibid.
[10] Ibid. 2,4; Webster, C B, 1976, *The Christian Community and Change in Nineteenth Century North India*, 80

(especially Nagaland, 87.5%; Mizoram, 85%; Meghalaya, 64.6%; and Manipur, 34.1%). Most of the northern states recorded less than 1 percent Christians, and some less than 0.1 percent (Haryana and Himachal Pradesh).[11]

Indian Christians commonly speak in terms of three basic regions: the North (where Hindi is the dominant language, and where Aryan influence is strongest); the South (the seat of Dravidian culture, and where English is preferred over Hindi); and the Northeast (comprised largely of hill tribes who are racially and linguistically related more closely to China and South Asia, and who have been shaped far more by Christianity than by Hinduism or Islam). However, even within these regions, there are profound and important cultural, linguistic and religious differences.

The Church

Yet amidst all the pressures and changes, the church in India is growing more rapidly than ever before. D'Souza remarks that Indian churches and Christian leaders are surprised at the 'viciousness of the Hindutva forces' against Christians as a whole. These can be termed religiously and politically motivated attacks, as the Human Rights Watch (1999b) report 'Politics by Any Means' has described. The martyrdom of missionary Graham Staines, who worked in Orissa for over 30 years and his two sons in 1999, awakened the consciences of the Christian community at large to make them identify with other fellow suffering Christians.[12] The persecution has begun to bring together many Christian leaders, who have operated rather independently of one another in the past, to meet the challenge of the hostile Hindutva forces.[13]

Tradition traces the beginning of Christianity in India to the arrival of the apostle Thomas in 52 AD. There is little doubt that Syrian Christians had become established in Kerala by the fourth century. Roman Catholic work began in Goa in the sixteenth century, and Protestant missions began in the eighteenth century. Indian Christians recently celebrated the bicentennial of William Carey's arrival in 1793. Yet despite this long tradition, the percentage of Christians recorded in the 2001 census was still less than 3 percent. Of these Christians, 39 percent were Protestants, 27.6 percent were Independent, 29.2 percent were Catholics, and 3.8 percent were Orthodox.[14]

---

[11] Ibid.

[12] Ibid. 312, 313

[13] D'Souza, Joseph, 2000, 'The Indian Church and Missions face the Saffronization Challenge', *Global Missiology for the 21st Century*, 391. (Saffronization is the process of making India a Hindu nation, excluding Christians and Muslims from a core identity as Indians)

[14] Ibid. 31

Indian leaders commonly refer to two primary streams in the Protestant church: the mainline churches (including the Church of North India, the Church of South India, the United Evangelical Lutheran Churches, and the Methodist Church of India) and the evangelical/charismatic churches. We can define 'evangelicals' as those who hold to the full authority of the Scriptures, who believe in salvation by grace through faith in Jesus Christ alone, and who emphasize the need to share the gospel with those who have not yet heard or believed. We can define 'charismatics' as those who believe in the full operation of the New Testament ministries and gifts in the church today, though there are varying degrees of emphasis on speaking in tongues, or on a separate experience of baptism of the Holy Spirit.

These categories are of limited usefulness, however, because many of the mainline churches have significant numbers who are evangelical in theology, while in some regions traditionally 'evangelical' churches like the Baptists have been strongly influenced by non-evangelical theology. Lines between charismatics and non-charismatics are increasingly indistinct, especially in newer fields. There is also a growing fellowship and cooperation between charismatic Catholics and evangelical Protestants in places like Mumbai and West Bengal. In fact, Charismatics and Evangelical Protestants often find much more in common with one another than either find with the non-evangelical wings of their own groups.

Many of the mainline churches have been weakened by limited vision, political struggles, the drain of expensive institutions inherited from the missionaries, endless lawsuits involving church property, and theological pluralism. Although there is evidence of evangelical awakening in many parts of the mainline churches, the great bulk of evangelism, mission initiatives, and church-planting efforts are coming from the evangelicals and especially in urban areas from the Pentecostals and charismatic streams.

The Christians in India are distributed very unevenly by region and by caste. 70 percent live in the South, and 25 percent in the Northeast.[15] Only 5 percent of India's Christians live in the entire North of India, and half of them (2.5 percent) are from the non-Aryan Northeast.[16] Furthermore, more than half of the Christians have Scheduled Caste background, and another quarter are from tribal origin. The Syrian Christians of Kerala, the Goans of Goa and the Anglo-Indians together comprise 12 percent. Only about 25 percent of the Christians come from the Backward Castes, Other Backward Castes and Forward Castes, even though these groups make up 60 percent of the Indian population.[17]

---

[15] Ibid. 315

[16] Sunder Raj, Ebenezer, 2001, in D.R.David, India Leadership Study, [unpublished]

[17] Vasanthraj, S. Albert, 1999, *Unreached Mega Peoples of India*, 6

Whatever the official government statistics may say, it is evident that definite growth has been occurring in the last decade. Even though the census of 2001 shows only 2.3 percent Christians, most Indian Christian leaders estimate the percentage of Christians is actually closer to 4 percent, or perhaps even more, if you include all the secret believers.[18] These claims do not have any significant evidence as such but most of the churches agree that in many regions of the country, and in a number of people groups, the churches are growing at an unprecedented rate.[19]

Not only are churches multiplying, and but also the number of indigenous Indian mission agencies. A. Gnanadasan (1998) while working for the India Mission Association estimated that there were about 300 indigenous mission agencies in India. But since then new group numbers have continued to grow. Operation World in 2001 reported that there are 440 agencies, since then in 2003 the number of such agencies may have gone beyond 500. The uncertainty in numbers is due to some denominational mission agencies not being a part of the India Mission Association.[20]

The combination of local agitation as well as official harassment and media attacks have prompted Indian Christians to rethink their strategies of evangelism.[21] In many places, public meetings and street preaching have become nearly impossible, though in some areas well-publicized evangelism and healing services can still be conducted without interruption. However, in general there is a growing emphasis on friendship evangelism, home meetings, and practical service (e.g. health, literacy, AIDS prevention, environmental initiatives) that plainly benefit the entire community (non-Christians as well as Christians) and that win a hearing for the Christians.[22] Two common criticisms levelled against the Christians by their opponents are that (1) they are outsiders, not true patriots, mere agents of the West, kept alive by foreign money; and (2) all their "good works" are simply dishonest ploys to 'convert' (i.e. to rip away from their community and their culture) the ignorant.[23]

Change

India today is undergoing rapid changes in many areas. In the last decade and a half, the relaxation of restrictions on foreign investment, the privatization of a number of industries, the explosion of the Indian software

---

[18] Johnstone, Patrick, 1993, *Operation World*, 274

[19] *World Christian Encyclopedia*, 2001, 2nd edition, Vol.1, 838

[20] Jayaprakash, L.J., 1987, *Evaluation of Indigenous Missions in India*, 22-68

[21] Ibid. 403, 404

[22] David, D. R., 2002, India Leadership Study, 4, USA (unpublished)

[23] Ibid. 4

enterprise, and the introduction of satellite TV, have contributed to far-reaching changes in the Indian economy as well as culture.

Even though almost 41 percent of the people in the cities and 51 percent of the people in the rural areas live below the poverty line,[24] the middle class is growing rapidly[25] in purchasing power. In some cities, motorbikes and private automobiles are replacing bicycles and rickshaws. In urban areas computers, cell phones, internet cafes, and e-mail addresses on business cards are multiplying. Western soap operas, movie stars and rock bands receive wide exposure. Western values and morals are rapidly undermining many urban Indian social and family traditions.[26] Divorce rates are rising among city dwellers though still lower than the West.[27] Urbanized young people identify more with their peers in other Asian countries as well as Western countries than they do with their parents' generation. The influence of television reaches beyond the cities to the villages and rural areas. However, amidst these rapid changes, the gaps between the economic and technological 'haves' and 'have-nots' continue to grow.[28]

Apart from the growth of the middle class and the increase of urbanization and globalization, the other most obvious change in India today is the rise of religious fundamentalism. Abuse and persecution of Christians, as well as destruction of Christian properties, have increased dramatically in the last few years. Churches have been burned. Christians at prayer have been beaten up. Christian workers have been killed. All India Christian Council suggests that from 1999 there are more than 700-900 cases that have been registered with the police, and there may be few more hundreds which have not registered.[29] In the State of Karnataka alone, from 2001 to 2003, about 179 cases were registered with the police.[30]

Yet, even while the forces of religious fundamentalism are gaining strength, another great social movement is emerging. A wave of social discontent and political awareness has been growing within a large segment of Indian society.[31] The Other Backward Castes (Sudras) and the Dalits (Scheduled Castes, or Untouchables), who resent the concentration of power and privilege in the hands of the forward castes (Brahmins, Kshatriyas and Vaishyas), do not want to be identified as Hindus.[32] Some of their leaders have called on their followers to 'quit Hinduism' and convert

---

[24] Ibid. 361
[25] Ibid. 392, 393
[26] Ibid. 6
[27] Ibid. 394
[28] Ibid. 6
[29] D'Souza, Oliver, 2003, personal interview, Bangalore, India
[30] D'Souza, Oliver, 2003, *Atrocities Against Christians in the State of Karnataka*
[31] Ibid. 396
[32] Ibid. 33, 34

to Buddhism, Christianity, or any other option that offers them more dignity, respect, and social mobility. In another report, AICC reports that an event of mass conversion of Dalits to Buddhism, took place in the city of Delhi. There are conflicting reports on the number of conversions. The media reported 5,000 and above but some said 50,000 were converted to Buddhism.[33]

These changes are not to be deemed as sudden but as a gradual process that began during the colonial period and continued after the independence of India. The work of IEHC began in the post independence period of India when changes were slowly and steadily picking up. The period of the 1950s and 1960s were good for ministries like IEHC and Operation Mobilisation who were committed to aggressive evangelism, which today would be totally discouraged. This is in the light of the 'Hate Campaign' (media coined word) or targeting 'enemies of Hinduvata' launched by some of the fundamentalist groups against Christians and other minority groups.[34]

The Beginnings and Growth of IEHC

The work of IEHC started in India in May 1964 although George believes that it was much earlier. Officially, World Literature Crusade (WLC), under the banner of IEHC, started their work with the help of six Indian leaders[35] in 1964 and began their work to reach every home in the country. The selection of these leaders was by looking at their church backgrounds, especially those who believed evangelism and the positions they held in their churches, like pastors and elders. A good recommendation from the national leaders and also their educational qualifications were important.

Speaking of the post-independence Indian mission field, Dr. Donald A. McGavran reports that between 1792 and 1952 Christian missions trickled into every province and every district of India. These missions preached Christ night and day. By 1952, there were fourteen million Christian Indians and many self-supporting denominations – Protestants and Roman Catholics. Most of the evangelism of non-Christians was still by the missions. The churches did some 'near-neighbour' evangelism but 87 percent of the people of India cannot be reached by near–neighbour evangelism.[36]

Like some other American organizations, WLC was interested in big plans, great numbers and economically viable programmes. To reap maximum benefit in the shortest time and the simplest way was its motto. It

---

[33] Ibid.
[34] Ibid. 392
[35] Guruprasad, G., 1999, personal interview, Bangalore, India
[36] McGavran, Donald A., 1976, 'Testing Your Investment in India', *Everybody*, 10, Vol. 2, No. 2

thought that going systematicallyfrom door to door everywhere on the globe would achieve 'World Evangelisation' in this generation. After its successful house-to-house distribution in Japan and Korea, in the 1950s, WLC was keen to reach every home in India and China. This was because of the great number of their populations and 'heathen-ness'.

Threat of Communism

WLC's other consideration in launching its work in India was the threat of Communism, which was fast spreading after the collapse of China in 1949 to the Red Army under the leadership of Mao Tse-tung.[37] At that time, the western powers predicted that India would be the next target of the Communists. Lee commented, 'Mao's sinister hand continues to make India's Prime Minister Nehru miserable and mad.'[38] During that period, the Indian Government and its leaders after India's independence in 1947 from their colonial powers, leaned more or less towards Communist ideology rather than capitalism. Jawaharlal Nehru, the Prime Minister, realizing the unequal status of people, who were divided by caste and class, would not dare to take the country on the path of capitalism, which he thought would create a greater gulf between the rich and poor and the high and low. For Nehru, capitalism was the creation of colonial powers, which he saw as a force interested in wealth creation rather than offering an equal status to all people. Seeing the Indian context and the danger of capitalism, he was determined to lead the country more or less to Communism. During the tenure of Nehru and his daughter Mrs. Indira Gandhi, India developed closer ties with Russia rather than with the West. Reflecting on this time, Lee rightly remarked, 'with another Giant-India-hanging in the balance, the colour of Asia's map may change with no proper forewarning.'[39] This was also the period after the World War II when the new 'Cold War' gave the wake up call to evangelicals, especially in the United States, who were determined to take the gospel and 'evangelise the world' to stop the spread of communism.[40] W. H. Warren of the Christian Literature Society, describing such a situation in India, informs, warns and challenges evangelicals to match the commitment and dedication of the forces of Communism to impact the world, while spreading the gospel:

> In Madras we have had a striking example of the effectiveness of the printed page in the rapid growth of communism among industrial workers during the last two years. Around any mill or factory during the mid-day rest hour one can see groups of workmen, numbering anything from ten to a couple of hundred, seated round

---

[37] Lee, Yohann, 1980, *I Survived a Communist Slaughter*, 85, Fact One: Christian in our Country must understand Communism before they can help stop it
[38] Lee, Yohann, 1962, *Dawn of a New Era*, 6
[39] Ibid. 6
[40] Ibid. 86

one of their number who is reading aloud from some communistic book or magazine. A steady stream of books, magazines and handbills has produced a complete change in the outlook and mentality of the Indian industrial worker... Until we can get to grips with the masses as the communist workers have done we shall make no impression.[41]

Likewise, Yohann Lee remarked that the Communist Party made promises for the Indian people through their books and pamphlets, 'it would provide food, homes and money for the poor people. Because they suffered under the British Empire, the cause of misery of the Indian people was the colonial power, but now imperialism is dying; Communism is a new force for a new world'.[42]

Growth of Literacy

The other consideration was the rise in literacy in India. WLC thought India's emphasis after its independence would be on education. WLC expected a rise in literacy and these new readers would read any printed material whether Communist or Christian. This may be only partially true because India for the first three decades of its independence focussed more on agriculture and industry. India's emphasis on general education only really began in the 1990s when literacy rose from 30 to 50 percent. Nonetheless, the then 15 or 20 percent of literacy in the country seemed good enough for WLC to launch its literature ministry.

However, WLC used these challenging issues wisely, with urgency, to seek for funds to start and develop its work in India and launch its ministry into other such needy countries. Penetrating and decisive words were used when an appeal was made for funds: 'The gifts be given "now" while the opportunity is still before us!'[43] In the same book, Lee appeals, 'by united sacrificial gifts, "paper missionaries" will go into every home in India, your help is needed "NOW". You can help... but will you?'[44] Such appeals were evident in all WLC's literature.

WLC, for political reasons, was not able to launch its work in China. However, India, after independence from British rule was open to missionary work. The majority of the missionary groups in India left, once their colonial powers had left the country.[45] The new Indian Government was not in favour of any new missionary force coming into the country, which it thought had worked mostly in favour of the colonial Empire rather

---

[41] Warren, W H., 1948, op.cit. Colquhoun, Frank, *Give Ye Them To Read*, 13

[42] Ibid. 65

[43] Hinman, Nelson E., 1962, ed. Jack McAlister, *Japan's Golden Harvest, Part I*, Let's Finish the Work! 36

[44] Lee, Yohann, 1962, *Japan's Golden Harvest, Part II*, EHC Action in Asia, A Hungry, Angry, Giant Without Christ, 69

[45] Ibid. 10

than in the interest of the Gospel alone. Brian Stanley remarks, 'Christian mission played an essential part in the broadening of Britain's imperial objectives in India'.[46] At this point, WLC's introduction of 'Paper Missionary' seemed an answer to the problem. Paper missionaries were thought to be more effective than real missionaries. To print the paper missionaries was much cheaper than to raise money for the foreign missionaries. They could go where others cannot go. They could talk to a person when he is ready to read them and could not argue with him. All that seemed right and appropriate for WLC's work in India. However, WLC did not consider India's oral tradition and relational context. It failed to assess how India in the past preserved its history through such a tradition and lived in close relationship with its community.

In the words of Jack and Hazel McAlister, founders of WLC, the EHC ministry in India was once considered 'a Jewel in the crown of WLC work'. This is because WLC received enormous funding when its work was at a peak in India. WLC used wonderful conversion and pioneer crusader stories to appeal for the funding. The review of WLC's literature show such stories were widely used in all their books and newsletters. Dick Eastman, President, EHC-I, in his recently published book, '*Beyond Imagination*' has used such stories. Despite that, Dick Eastman does not express the same words about India as McAlister used about WLC's work in India. Dick Eastman emphatically asked 'why India should be reached for the third and fourth time, when there are other countries, which are not reached even once?'[47] WLC's future interest in India has definitely declined but the study of their past interest in India will help us to understand their strategy in India, how that was translated into the local situation and what impact it brought to the Indian relational context.

What is India Every Home Crusade (IEHC)?

It is a Christian organization, which was committed to the distribution of printed literature on a mass scale, containing the good news of Christ into every home in India. IEHC was a sponsored body of World Literature Crusade of USA. The 'Every Home Crusade' name was used to denote the house-to-house distribution programme of WLC. This name was first used in Japan 1953,[48] when WLC launched its nationwide house-to-house distribution programme.[49]

---

[46] Stanley, Brian, 1990, *The Bible and The Flag*, 98
[47] Eastman, Dick, 1999, personal interview, 12th March, Colorado Springs, USA
[48] Lee, Yohann, 1976, *Everybody*, 7
[49] Ibid. 12

Infrastructure of IEHC

IEHC started in India with the appointment of six national directors located in six strategic centres, in mid 1964, by Yohann Lee, Overseas Director of WLC. In the 1990s, there were 15 offices operating from 15 States, whereas now there are 12 offices in 12 States.

Administration and board

The Executive Director heads the organization on a national level. Under him he has 4 Zonal Directors who, represent North, South, East and West zones. Under them, there are Managers who oversee the work of their regions. A Regional Director for South Asia who represents India on international matters is in overall in-charge of the sub-continent. The IEHC board manages all the affairs of the organization. It guides and makes the policy on which the organization operates.

Nation-wide distribution programmes

In the 1960s, India's literacy rate was growing. There were 50 million new readers.[50] Oliver adds, 'The literacy rate was 23 percent'.[51] These new readers were hungry to read anything available to them.[52] WLC, from its inception, was driven with the intention of giving something good to the new readers before other forces of the world could reach them, e.g. Communism and the Jehovah Witnesses. WLC, through EHC in India, offered to new readers free literature, on a door-to-door basis and provided free postage to do the Bible Correspondence Course and then offered free books on the completion of the course.

IEHC was able to launch and complete two nation-wide tract distribution coverages under the banner of, Operation Last Home 1964-74 and Project Calvary 1975-84. Each nation-wide coverage took place once in 10 years. These two nation-wide house-to-house systematic coverages in India suggest that the Indian leaders were aware of the original vision of WLC and they adhered to it.

The 'First Coverage' or 'Operation Last Home'

This was conducted between 1964 and 1974. The actual full operation began in 1966. The population of India at that time was 560 to 600 millions. There were 15 major languages and hundreds of minor languages and dialects spoken and the literacy rate was 23 percent. Oliver observed, 'we reached every accessible home in the land. Millions responded but we

---

[50] Wolpert, Stanley A., 1993, *A New History of India*, 366

[51] Oliver, J. J., 1994, A letter of 22nd of November, to Dick Eastman, in response to Fred Creighton's 'Open Letter ', a former director and one of the founding members of IEHC, Mhow, India

[52] Willmer, Haddon, 2000, personal interview, Oxford, UK

did not have more to offer other than the Bible Correspondence Course and a copy of the New Testament. Because there were no churches nearby and no other organisation to take them over, many were lost. The Christ Group (CG) programme came very late in 1973'.[53]

The First coverage was by 'fast footing'. Robert Louis remarked, 'we just gave away tracts to every home'.[54] They handed the tracts out like postmen to every home and could not stop to share or explain things with people. Even then, it was remarkable to note that millions responded or sent their request to the IEHC office for more information. However, the response was merely 7 to 10 percent of the whole.

The 'Second Coverage' or 'Project Calvary'

This was started in 1975 and completed in 1984. IEHC had many hurdles to clear before completing it. The finance and manpower were not enough to carry out the work. To cover the Kashmir valley was the most difficult task before them, due to the conflict between India and Pakistan over the Kashmir issue. They had to get additional manpower from the Southern States of India and divert some additional funding to get the job done. Many staff from the southern states had difficulty in learning Hindi and Kashmiri languages, yet with much difficulty the coverage was completed in Kashmir. On the completion of the Kashmir coverage IEHC produced a book called 'Project Himalaya' to commemorate their effort in covering it. While doing so they came across many interesting stories of the Valley programme. In one instance they found a community of Muslims secretly following Jesus.

During the Second Coverage, the population of India grew from 600 to 700 millions. Literacy rose from 23 to 35 percent. Robert Louis aptly said of the Second Coverage, 'it was aimed to do carry out in-depth evangelism'.[55] Oliver speaking on the coverage remarks, 'again millions responded. We conducted Seekers' Conferences and formed Christ Groups. Over 4000 Christ Groups were formed. Some were handed over to local churches willing to take them in, but the leadership in WLC changed and the Christ Groups programme was discouraged. Many of our Christ Groups were left leaderless with no one to look after them'.[56]

The Second Coverage was better than the First Coverage because its emphasis was on 'in-depth evangelism'. That helped the general populace, and especially the village community to hear the gospel in a better way.

---

[53] Ibid.
[54] Louis, Robert, 1978, A Report on India Every Home Crusade Ministry in Karnataka, was presented at a conference organized by the Bible Society of India, Auxiliary, Bangalore, India
[55] Ibid.
[56] Ibid.

The Pioneer Crusaders gave more time to each house in this coverage. They not only handed the gospel tracts to people but also shared their testimonies and Scriptures with them. Unlike the First Coverage, the Second Coverage IEHC had produced additional spiritual books to be given to their contacts that helped to gather more fruit and make that fruit remain. This coverage was mostly geared towards more personal evangelism, so IEHC produced more fruit during the period. However, enough time was still not given for personal evangelism because the main emphasis of the ministry remained on systematic tract distribution. Moreover, over the years, the house numbers had increased and the population had grown. It was a 'time bound' project and had to be finished in 10 years. However, despite such constraints, whatever little effort was given for personal evangelism seemed enough to achieve more results in the field. Even then, the response stayed at 7-10 percent but the people who made a personal commitment to follow Jesus increased from 1 to 6-8 percent. Those who made a commitment through impersonal evangelism stayed at 1 percent.[57]

Third Coverage or The Final Thrust-5000

During Glen Pits' visit to India in 1988 he once remarked that India cannot be reached completely because of its vastness and ever growing population. So, the tract distribution in India should become an on going programme.[58] Prasad also affirms that 'India is to be seen as a country always ready for evangelism'.

The Third Coverage started soon after the Second Coverage. The emphasis of this coverage was similar to the Second, which is 'in-depth evangelism'. The Final Thrust-5000 or FT-5000 plan was set up in the 1990s. Prasad's visit to Amsterdam in 1985 to attend the 'Billy Graham' conference had sowed some seeds in his mind about of the 'Personal Evangelism'. He heard from more than 85 percent of the delegates who said that they were personally led to Christ because someone had shared the gospel with them. Whereas only a few of the delegates said that they were led to Christ because of literature ministry. Prasad was also attracted to some of the evangelical missions who were geared towards AD 2000 movements and had gained momentum and attracted donors to evangelize the world by the turn of the century. He then called the Third Coverage 'The Final Thrust-5000'. The '5000' may have signified having 5000 workers to complete the task in India and to establish 600,000 Christ Groups in as many villages of India. [59] The number changed from 600,000

---

[57] A Report on India, by India Every Home Crusade, 1990, A Report on India, 1, Bangalore, India

[58] Pitts, Glen, 1988, an address in an IEHC Directors Conference in Bangalore, India (Glen Pits was the Vice President of WLC, USA)

[59] George, C., 1978, A Report of Christ Groups, presented in the Asian Directors

to 300,000 as the years went by following the start of the project, when the aim of establishing 600,000 Christ Groups seemed a distant vision.[60] The other consideration for Prasad in launching such a big project was that during his leadership he had seen so many ups and downs in relation to WLC's policies and programmes, which swung from one extreme to the other. He also had seen how the interest of WLC was slowly drifting from their ministry in India. Through the introduction of this new project, he tried to attract WLC's attention again to the Indian 'market' and by giving them 'an American' type of 'product', filled with big numbers and ambitious plans to place before the American public in appealing for more funding. Prasad's correspondence and WLC's literature indicates that WLC showed some interest in the plan and looked to support it for a while. However, the untimely death of Prasad brought to a close the FT-5000 work.

The Final Thrust was a natural progression of the First and Second Coverages. The emphasis of this Coverage was to gather much fruit and make sure that fruit remained and grew. At the same time, the population had grown from 700 millions to 900 millions and was predicted to reach 1 billion by the turn of the century. According to Oliver, IEHC estimated that half the population of India would be under 15 years of age and that is 'a brand new population to be reached'.[61] Oliver speaking on the project said, 'the literacy rate is almost 50 percent and is growing rapidly with the Government Adult Literacy Programme. People are now more open and receptive than before. Twice we have failed to gather the fruit and establish the new babes in the faith. The FT-5000 plan is very effective, practical and fruit bearing'.[62] Oliver with passion further added, 'it must go on as earnestly as possible if we are to bring millions of souls into the Kingdom of God. I have been praying for 50 million souls in this decade'.[63]

Failures of the Programme, Leadership and other Concerns

The Final Thrust-5000 was sadly abandoned in 1995 by WLC and IEHC officials. WLC mostly referred this FT-5000 as 'Prasad's vision for India' because the tract distribution had gone to the periphery and personal evangelism had come to the front. During this project, Prasad asked the evangelists to spend half an hour in every house and explain the gospel to people and help them to understand it and give the tract at the end for their

---

Conference, 7-14 January in Bangkok, Thailand
[60] Prasad, B.A.G., 1993, *Prayer Bulletin*, 4, 300,000 Christ Groups by the end of 2000 AD
[61] Ibid.
[62] Ibid.
[63] Ibid.

further reading and information. During FT-5000, though the number of tracts distributed was not significant compared to the last two Coverages, the response to the personal evangelism rose from 1 to 5 to 30 to 40 percent. Christ Group formation increased from 4000 to 10,000 or 15,000. (This huge variation in the number occurs in the WLC's and IEHC's records, due to the incorrect maintenance of statistical data). This occurred while compiling the numbers received from the regional offices in India, who sent some incorrect numbers and later those numbers were corrected.

The FT-5000 vision did seem to catch the attention and imagination of a few Indian missions, like Friends Missionary Prayer Band, Indian Evangelical Team and other regional missions and a few churches. These came forward to enter partnership with IEHC and carry out the vision of FT-5000 in their mission fields, or the areas which were either assigned by IEHC or their partner agencies. Such partnership in the Indian mission was the first of its kind on the national level. However, other evangelical missions like Indian Evangelical Mission, Vishwavani and other missions and denominational churches, did not come forward to join the project. This may have been due to their mission ethos, or principles, or because they were inward looking. They did not want to cross their boundaries, or 'citadels', which they had built for themselves and their successors, or they found it unnecessary and difficult to share their resources with others, or felt they could not follow the vision of 'others' as their own.[64]

Leadership

After Prasad's death, FT-5000 would have continued if the other Indian directors had shared the FT vision. However some of the correspondence and comments show that some were sceptical of his plan. Fred Creighton, in his letter to Dick Eastman, mentioned that Pratapkumar, interim executive director of IEHC, said, 'FT-5000 is a failure in India'.[65] Another director, after Prasad's death when he was asked about the continuation of FT-5000 sarcastically said 'FT-5000 has gone with Prasad'.[66]. This shows what perceptions other directors generally had of FT-5000. As indicated in this chapter, the failure of FT-5000 can be attributed to lack of funding and human resources. However the method and its working in the context seemed more effective than the previous two distribution programmes.

To a certain extent, IEHC directors may have failed to understand or be convinced of FT-5000's vision for India. They may have thought it was an

---

[64] Rajendran, K., 2000, The Impact of Christianity in India, *Global Missiology for the 21st Century*, 322

[65] Creighton, Fred, 1994, A Letter to Dick Eastman on the 4th of November Creighton, Hamilton, New Zealand

[66] Samuel, C. Sam, 1995, in a private discussion (Sam C. Samuel is the Zonal Director of IEHC), Bangalore, India

ambitious plan or not achievable. They may have felt it too difficult to carry out the task due to lack of funding. They may have preferred to fall in line with the WLC officials to do whatever was asked of them rather than do the ministry in their own way. They may not have wanted to have a confrontation with WLC in order to continue to get financial support, for the sake of the survival of the ministry and their own. The behaviour, attitude and character of the Indian leadership were at times lacking proof of what they really wanted to do or to say. Time and again, they failed to express themselves. So, I now turn to a brief discussion on the Indian leadership in their relationship to the Ministry, Staff Concerns, Relational and Inter-Personal Relationship, Funding, and WLC and visa versa.

Ministry

When WLC came to India with its single vision to do systematic house to house distribution, what was the perception of Indian leaders? Did they accept the vision of WLC as their own, or did they use it as a means of evangelism to gain a wider understanding of mission in the Indian context? Did they take the vision of WLC per se or did they want to change it to something different?

The correspondence of Indian leaders and personal interviews shows that 'Systematic House to House' tract distribution or 'literature ministry' was one means of evangelism rather than 'The Method for Evangelism' as WLC claimed. Kietzman while writing to Prasad reminds him of the main aim of WLC, 'your current outlook (here Kietzman refers to FT 5000 project, which had moved away from tract distribution to personal and family evangelism) towards "literature evangelism" which is the principle goal of WLC' Prasad, in reply, disagreed with Kietzman's directives and suggested India needed a 'total evangelism'. That meant a distribution of tracts to every home would not help to complete the evangelism in India, because of its context, which needed a different approach for tract distribution is to be effective. Prasad further added, 'campaigns (open air or gospel meetings) and word of mouth methods' and combining them with tract distribution are equally important for effective work to reach every home, and that could help to complete the evangelisation of India.[67] Prasad commenting on 'literature evangelism' wrote, 'if the basis is only "literature evangelism" we will miss 64 percent of India's population' That included the rural people, illiterate or people who needed more explanation and more time to understand the message rather than needing a tract to read and understand themselves. Prasad's 64 percent was the proportion of illiterate as 36 percent literate was the national figure of that time. This 36 percent literate included those who only knew how to sign but were not

---

[67] Prasad, B.A.G. 1986, A Letter written to Dale Kietzman on 22nd December, Secuderabad, India

able to read and write. This means more than 64 percent or between 70 to 80 percent of the population could be missed 'if the basis was on literature evangelism' alone.

In the above quotation, Kietzman wrote, 'your current outlook towards literature evangelism' suggesings that Kietzman thought that due to the FT-5000 project IEHC had moved away from literature evangelism to personal evangelism. However, Kietzman failed to see from the beginning of WLC's ministry in India how the Indian leadership viewed tract distribution. Louis, director for Karnataka, wrote, 'the First Coverage which was nothing but just giving away the gospel tract,'[68] was not persuaded to use 'the tract method' alone. This is partly attributed to the comments made by evangelicals and some other Christians in India, who had commented that you just throw away the tract, or else work like a post-man only. Further, speaking on the Second Coverage he added, 'but this time it is very different, it is what is known as "Evangelism in Depth", that is to say "discipleship and church planting" '.[69] B. A. Prabhakar, the first national director, in 1970, while inviting all Christian workers and organisations in Bangalore for prayer and to supplement each other's work, mentioned, 'for example, the radio work (FEBA) can be followed up by literature or records (Gospel Records). YFC (Youth For Christ) work can be followed up with literature'.[70] This suggested Prabhakar had a wider vision of mission and showed willingness to prepare a stage for other missions to come together to work in support of each other to be effective. He seemed to be a person who preferred not to work in isolation or hold on to any one 'method' ideology, but believed in co-operative evangelism. Guruprasad, an ex-director for Karnataka put it quite bluntly that 'we never did all we were asked to do by WLC officials, but we did what was best for our context. We provided whatever the information they wanted from us but the ministry we carried out according to what was better suited for us'.[71]

This dilemma continues perhaps even today in the lives of the Indian leadership. Sometimes they have had the benefit in carrying out the ministry in the Indian context but sometimes they have lost that benefit for various reasons, as will be examined a little more in the following discussion of their relationship with WLC officials.

Staff concerns during retrenchments

IEHC between 1968 and 1986 had three staff retrenchments. Most of the field staff members were cut back. Fred Creighton (1994) writing to Dick

---

[68] Ibid. 1
[69] Ibid. 1
[70] Prabhakar, B. A., 1970, A Circular dated 21st Aug. to various evangelical missions in Bangalore, India
[71] Ibid.

Eastman explained to him some characteristics of Indians and mentioned, 'we need distributors... for productive work but in India this position (distributor) is seen as ...bottom of the ladder'.[72] This concern of Creighton's and WLC was, to a certain extent, hypocritical because when the worst retrenchments took place between 1984-86, Prasad's concerns and laments concerning the retrenched staff were unheard by Creighton and WLC.

In one account, Prasad wrote:

'Nearly an hundred of our staff from different offices goes by the end of this month. This is the saddest decision we have had to accept, for most of these men have been with us for above 8 or 10 years and some even more. It was painful because in India finding employment is just next to impossible totally unlike it is in the West. There are millions waiting for employment and these men and women after giving the prime of their life in one employment will not be even considered by any other employment now. We do not know what they will do with their families and we wished and prayed that this would be the last time that ...we will ever have to soil our consciences with a sense of guilt for what we had to do under these circumstances to nearly a hundred of our men with their wives and children'.[73]

(Prasad in another letter mentioned retrenching 520 out of 670 staff in less than two years).

On the same lines, Prasad wrote to Rev. Paul Goodwin[74] and to Martin Wilson.[75] This thought may have haunted Prasad through the years until the Lord called him Home. This speaks of an Indian attitude of relational thinking. Over the year,s the employer and employees had developed some sort of relation between themselves rather than that of a master and servant. This speaks of a sympathetic, but concerned attitude rather than the 'hire and fire' mentality that is very much based on western thinking. Often Indian leaders were forced to follow the American way of doing things but that rather troubled their minds and thoughts. At the end of the letter Prasad noted, 'on the whole our conference was solemn...in the midst of all sorrowfulness...this probably would be the turning point in the history of IEHC and also for our personal lives and ministries'.[76]

This shows how retrenchment of the staff not only affected the conscience of Indian leaders but also caused damage to their morale. The WLC officials' behaviour and attitude and the financial instability affected the minds of Indian leaders, who became more inward looking leaders

---

[72] Ibid.
[73] Ibid. 2
[74] Prasad, B.A.G., 1985, A Letter to Paul Goodwin on 11 May, 2, Secunderabad, India
[75] Prasad, B.A.G., 1986, A Letter to Martin Wilson on 20 June, 1, Secunderabad, India
[76] Ibid.

rather than becoming aggressive and adventurous leaders to challenge the WLC officials to find some alternatives, such as financial benefits, and employment in other mission agencies.

The sympathy and concern of the Indian leadership for the staff was hypocritical. Even though they moaned and groaned, they could have done much better than that to help their staff, at least as mentioned above. Chopra, speaking of the irresponsible behaviour of certain Indians towards their fellow human beings makes this strong statement, 'these Indians...are self centred...and...promotion of personal interests even at the cost of the community...have marked their character.'[77] Here Chopra reminds us that Indians live for and promote the interest of the community first and then the self. D'Souza commenting on the above criticism says, 'this could be applied to...Christians as well.'[78] It is important for some Indian mission leaders to be conscious of the context in which they live, work, and then meet its demands. Instead, they acted upon the words and directives of their western bosses, whose ideologies are mostly shaped by individualism and capitalism, which work towards the promotion of self

This also indicates that the Indian leaders were powerless to assist their colleagues through no fault of their own. They were faced with a new way of employing people, based on 'hiring and firing', which they were in no position to modify and were in no position to alleviate.[79] Though there are instances that some of the leaders, on their own initiative may have helped some of their retrenched staff, most of the retrenched staff suffered badly financially. Many of the staff had passed their prime age to get any other employment and some did not have good educational qualifications to find other jobs.

Whenever Christian missions from the West come and launch their work in countries like India, they have to think deeply about their strategies and the people they employ. Big plans, big statistics, and a large number of staff are not the sign of the success of their ministry. When such tactics fail, certainly the axe will fall upon the ministry and its workers. This may bring permanent damage to the conscience and minds of those staff and their families and it will leave a very bad image in the minds of the future generation, who would be unwilling to be involved in mission. Rajendran asserts that when missions fail to meet the welfare of their missionaries, 'the missions in India will diminish'.[80] It shows that the approach of modernity with its emphasis on numbers, speed, and efficiency can be

---

[77] Chopra, 2000, op.cit., D'Souza, Joseph, 394
[78] Ibid. 394
[79] Sugden, Chris, 2004, personal interview, Oxford, UK
[80] Ibid. 319

destructive of human relationships and well-being and be ultimately inefficient.[81]

Interpersonal problems and relational factors among the leaders

Unlike other western mission agencies, WLC from the beginning maintained a policy to appoint nationals to oversee the work in their own countries. In India, not only for the country, they also appointed leaders of the States to lead the ministry of their regions. WLC always emphasized 'from the natives, to the natives' for the effectiveness of the work. It is also a fact that employing nationals in their own context cuts salary costs by between 80 to 90 percent compared to what they would have had to pay to their own nationals.

However, WLC's policy immensely helped Indian leaders to develop their leadership qualities. Along with the main leaders, their deputies and manager also had opportunities to develop leadership qualities. Like Operation Mobilisation, which developed Indian leadership through their discipleship movement, IEHC also provided a lot of opportunities for the younger generation to develop their leadership qualities. Breeding leadership within the organization also bred interpersonal relationship problems among the leaders. Regionalism, ethnicity, favouritism to their own relatives and, as Charles Wickman says, 'a degree of nepotism'[82] crept in time and again and hampered the interpersonal relationships of the leaders and others in the ministry, and became a cause of concern to WLC.

Yohann Lee observed that Indian leaders were not working in the interest of the ministry but rather than were concerned more about themselves, their position and their jurisdiction. He writes, 'put the welfare of our ministry above your personal feelings'.[83] Lee's comments came when he saw the opposition of North Indian directors to his appointment of C. George as Christ Groups Director in 1977 and who then moved to Delhi. The opposition seemed to be that George being a South Indian, the North Indian directors did not like him moving to Delhi, because they felt he would interfere in their ministry. Lee (1977) writing on the same matter, requests other WLC colleagues to pray for Indian directors, whom he mentions, 'I have been deeply concerned and heavily burdened by certain situations there'.[84] In another letter out-rightly attacking those directors involved, Lee mentioned 'un-Christian behaviour' and, in the end, he

---

[81] Ibid.

[82] Ibid. 3

[83] Lee, Yohann, 1977, A Letter to All Every Home Crusade Directors on the 20th of September and another letter to all the Regional Directors on 21st of September, USA

[84] Lee, Yohann, 1977, writes a letter to C. George, J. J. Oliver, Robert Louis, BAG Prasad, M. M. Maxton, Peter Bose, James Ebenezer, D. C. Kaushal, E. D. Ashwal and S. C. Samuel, on 18th of October, 1,2, Los Angeles, USA

temporarily cancelled the appointment of George and stopped the implementation of the Christ Groups Ministry.

At a later time, in 1978, George was appointed as Christ Groups director to head the Christ Groups Ministry and did move to Delhi to oversee the work. During Kietzman's period between 1985-87. there was some leadership tension between Prasad and George. Kietzmam had appointed George to the International staff and had assigned him to look into some official matters in Sri Lanka that had irked Prasad. Kietzman in his letter to Prasad, writes, 'you want to make sure that your position of authority is respected'.[85] This was in response to Prasad's (1986) letter in which he had asked how George was asked to go to Sri Lanka without his knowledge. Such tensions among the leadership continue even now. It should be noted that relational factors are prominent in the Indian leadership ethos in all walks of life either to recommend some one in the same family, for better status, to promote their image, or to cover up their own flaws.

The Indian national leadership remained in the 'one family' tree. An Indian political party, the Indian Congress Party, even today is ruled by the Nehru clan. In a similar way, IEHC national leadership rested with B. A. Prabhakar, B. A. G. Prasad and B. A. Pratapkumar, who were all brothers. This happened in a mission run and sponsored by a western mission. Prasad, during his reign, while writing to Faustino Ruvivar about his brother Pratapkumar, reminds him to add his brother's photograph to the WLC's prayer map, when it seemed to be missing on one occasion. WLC once a year produced such prayer maps to update the official news. Further, in his letter, he dedicated three fourths of the page to describe his brother's credentials, sacrifice and commitments. He writes, 'Pratapkumar being a renowned linguist…for a whole year… he did not receive any salary from EHC'.[86] During this period, Pratapkumar worked for a Bible translation mission where he received salary.[87]

The Indian leadership gave more importance to relational issues at times like this even when the matter was not of any importance. The relational matters in ministry were key positive factors for developing the work but in crucial times like promotion or covering up some failing of family members, relational influences became a great weakness of the Indian leadership. Prasad, responding to Kietzman's letter regarding some of the criticism which was made against his brother B. A. Pratapkumar, writes in his support and exaggerates some of his credentials, 'he is a preacher in greatest demand in Andhra Pradesh drawing crowds by thousands. He has

---

[85] Ibid.

[86] Prasad, B.A.G., 1988, A Letter to Faustino Ruivivar on 8th March, Secunderabad, India

[87] Guruprasad, G., personal interview, Bangalore, India

opened the maximum number of Christ Groups, over a thousand, and also raised a maximum amount of local funds'[88]

It is true that the Indian context requires the relational approach to reach its people. But if this relational aspect becomes a tool to promote one's family members, a ministry like IEHC will become blind and will try to defend or protect its family member at any cost, and may be found wanting in accountability and transparency. There is no doubt that B. A. Pratapkumar was a good preacher in Andhra Pradesh, but 'the greatest preacher' is an exaggeration. In Andhra Pradesh, in the time of the 'Mass Movements', thousands of people had become Christians. As Billington remarks, 'Conversion to Christianity occurred in Andhra at a faster than in almost any other South Asian region.'[89]

The same interest was shown during the 'Christ Groups Phenomena,' whereby thousands of Christ Groups were established. 'The establishing of Christ Groups', was the work of the Holy Spirit and the evangelists. However, sadly Prasad gave the credit to his brother. The same can be said about 'fund raising'. Like Andhra Pradesh, Tamil Nadu, Orissa and Karnataka were raising more or less the same amount of finances. Fund raising in IEHC was attributed to the team effort rather than the work of one person.

IEHC produced lot of leaders for the kind of work it carried out. This also created lot of problems among the leaders. The 'Big Brother (Boss)' always wanted one hundred percent loyalty from his associates and they had to listen to him without any question. A vast correspondence between Prasad and Kietzman and George, shows the tension and the division created between Prasad and George. The correspondence in 1994 between Creighton and other directors, that took place during the selection of a new leadership in India, after the death of Prasad, when some of the directors made strong comments against Pratapkumar, showed that if any ministry produces many leaders it may do good to the organization, so that it can easily find a replacement for any loss of leadership in the organization. However, at the same time, it may cause concern, when it produces dissension, division and disharmony in the organization.

IEHC not only found such crises of interpersonal-relationships on a national level, butalso on a State level. It is better for international missions to look at the behaviour, characteristics and attitude of their overseas leadership in the context they live in, rather than looking at them as they want to look themselves in their own context. Creighton, while choosing the national director for India and relinquishing Pratapkumar from his appointment as an interim executive director, reminds Eastman, 'I should not get too involved. The more we get into this the more we may find more

---

[88] Prasad, B.A.G., 1986, A Letter to Dale Kietzman on 2nd May, Secunderabad, India

[89] Billington, Harper, Susan, 2000, *In the Shadow of Mahatma*, 184

complex things will arise'.[90] Creighton failed to understand some of the inherent cultural leadership qualities of the Indian leaders. Such a style initially appeared to him as if it was of the West but when he saw the complexity of Indian leadership behaviour, attitudes and style he then tried to withdraw from it.

Funding

WLC from the beginning struggled with its finances. IEHC found itself wanting enough funds to run the ministry. This affected the work and morale of IEHC staff and leaders. During Prabhakar's time, the year 1969 was crucial in regard to funding. After sending a few reminders to WLC, he sendt another circular to all the IEHC offices and prepared all the staff to be ready to face any eventuality. He wrote, 'inform our staff, pioneer crusaders and others… to be prepared to meet the situation even if the payments at the end of this month are delayed…until we review the financial position and seek the Lord's plans for His work in India'.[91]

Often, WLC and IEHC leaders went back and forth in their planning and attempted to evangelize India because of inadequate funds. This uncertain and fluctuating financial condition demoralized many Indian leaders and Christian workers about continuing in this ministry. They then went in search of 'greener fields' rather than starve in uncertain financial conditions.

During Prasad's time, between 1985-1987, it was an ordeal for him to face budget cuts on regular intervals. During this period, many offices were closed down, hundreds of workers were sent home and the ministry was severely hampered. This was the period when Prasad put in every effort to raise funds from within. Today, this attempt was a stepping-stone for IEHC at least to stand on its own feet.

Financial accountability

Creighton and WLC were rather suspicious about the financial accountability and honesty of the Indian leaders. He wrote, 'Hyderabad Centre needs looking into. Large sums are reportedly spent unwisely. The building is reportedly not in the name of IEHC,'[92] he wrote when referring to the Good News Centre building in Secunderabad. During Kietzman's period, his letters to Prasad pointed out some financial and personal accusations against his brother Pratapkumar.[93]

---

[90] Creighton, Fred,1994, A Letter to Dick Eastman on 20th December, 3, Hamilton, New Zealand
[91] Prabhakar, B. A., 1969, A Letter to all IEHC Directors on 20 October, Bangalore, India
[92] Creighton, Fred, 1994, A Letter to Dick Eastman on 4 November, Hamilton, New Zealand
[93] Kietzman, Dale, 1986, A Letter to B.A.G. Prasad on 18th April, Studio City,

Whether these accusations were true or false is not a matter to be dealt with here. Such charges, mostly of financial mismanagement were very often levelled against most IEHC leaders and their close associates. This was the most common allegation made against Indian leaders by the Westerners. Eric Leach aptly quotes the words of one his Indian friends, a veteran missionary, C. D. James, who now lives in Australia, that 'Indians can be 100 percent honest and vice-versa.'[94] It would be as well for international leaders to hold this opinion about any Indians.. Such charges will keep coming against Indian Christian leaders unless they take some measures to overcome their love for money.

Relationship of WLC with the Indian leaders and vice versa

From the inception of IEHC in 1964, Yohann Lee as the overseas director kept close links with the Indian leaders until his resignation in 1984.. During his period, except for a few misapprehensions, the relationship was good between WLC and IEHC leaders. Yohann Lee being an oriental from Korea had a better knowledge of Indian leaders and their inherent cultural characters and that helped the dialogue between them. They listened to Yohann's directions, vision and interest and, in turn, he listened to them.Johnny did not object to whatever the Indian leaders felt necessary in the mission fields to develop the work apart from the vision of WLC. Though there were instances of financial difficulties, when the plans and projects were readjusted and the endurance of the Indian leaders was tested against some financial difficulties, the relationship of WLC with the Indian leaders remained a good one.

During Kietzman's time and after Prasad's death in 1994, when Creighton took over his (Prasad's) position as a regional director for South Asia, the whole IEHC leadership tasted the different style of westerners' authoritarian rule. All the freedom they had enjoyed in Lee's period to develop the ministry had gone. They were made to listen to their bosses' directions and WLC's interest rather than suit their own context or people.

As earlier discussed in the chapter, Kietzman brought financial pressure on Prasad and directed him to close down the offices and reduce the staff, even then ignoring Prasad's request to spare them from such an action. At this juncture, Prasad wished that such an action would be the last one.[95] Prasad, who represented South Asia on the WLC's international board, had a fair knowledge of WLC's finances. Though Prasad thinks this 'would be the last time', he failed to understand Kietzman's underlying intentions.

California, USA

[94] Leach, Eric, 1998, personal interview, 12th November, London, UK

[95] Prasad, B.A.G., 1985, A Letter to Paul Goodwin and All IEHC Directors on 13th May, Secunderabad, India

Though Prasad had thought 'for the last time', in a year's time, Kietzman announced another budget cut and asked him to reduce staff again. If Prasad and other Indian directors had opposed Kietzman's first move and had stood strongly together in opposing the instruction, Kietzman would have changed his methods. Prasad expressed shock at another budget cut that puts his 'vehicle again into reverse'.: 'After your announcement in India that there will be no more budget cuts, I took it for granted and was planning for the development and implementation of various projects for India'. When he announced a 25 percent staff retrenchment, WLC leaders went on tightening the noose around the Indian leaders to make them listen to WLC directives rather than to run the ministry as they judged best.[96]

Kietzman's management tactics, 'putting pressure on the opponent' were working well. Kietzman after announcing two budget cuts announced the third budget cut within six months. Kietzman went on bringing greater pressure on the Indian leaders, whom he had rightly read would wilt under the pressure. Prasad when replying to Kietzman's letter, in which he discussed the further budget cut, wrote, 'it took a couple of days for me to settle down emotionally after going through your...letter'. Kietzman's letter suggested that India receives 'a large budget', which he wanted to cut down some more. This was unacceptable to Prasad, because the Indian budget was already cut down to the bone. It had made him remove nearly 520 out of 670 staff in less than two years.

Although pressurised, Prasad replied 'we are willing to fully cooperate with your ideas.' This shows he agreed to do whatever was suggested to him to do for the sake of his own survival and that of his associates. However, when Kietzman tightened the noose around the Indian leadership Prasad finds himself in a tough position and laments, 'but the way we are being driven is too hurtful'.[97] Though Kietzman tried to control Prasad, he was aware that Prasad was the surviving senior director, who had been with IEHC almost from its inception. He was also a well-respected leader among all the officials of WLC, except for Kietzman. On some occasions, Prasad would have been subservient, but on other occasions, Prasad showed some resistance to Kietzman's plans and that made Kietzman much more determined and he began to express more tactical moves to overcome Prasad.

Kietzman, in one of his letters, was irked by Prasad's reply, 'I do not appreciate having the long lecture', when Prasad had written to Kietzman about his reaction to George's proposed visit to Sri Lanka on some official business, which Prasad was not told about. On another occasion, Kietzman reacted strongly to Prasad's response to the issues about which he had

---

[96] Prasad, B.A.G., 1986, A Letter to Dale Kietzman on 1st May, Secunderabad, India
[97] Prasad, B.A.G., 1986, A Letter to Dale Kietzman on 22nd December, Secunderabad, India

asked Prasad for an explanation, and wrote, 'both the fact of allegations (personal and financial) as well as the time spent in trying to continue to justify them makes us wonder whether or not the ministry as now constituted in India is an effective one that we should continue to support. I am now speaking as a voice of the WLC Board in the United States'. Furthermore, 'it is natural that at times we might see the possibility of moving toward new opportunities rather than continuing to support organisations that, while effective in the past, may not be the vehicle for the future'.[98]

This judgement on the part of Kietzman, as a President, seemed uncalled for when the relationship between him and Prasad was becoming more and more strained. Was he hinting indirectly what would be the course of action in future regarding their ministry in India, and may be even ultimately the closure of their operation in India? The same words were also sounded through Eastman, 'why should India hear more times, when there are countries, which have not heard the good news even once'?[99] IEHC, which was once thought to be 'a jewel in the crown of WLC' had become a 'bone of contention' to WLC.

Prasad, with much perseverance, responded to the above letter and explained to Kietzman how ministry should operate in India. To Prasad 'every home' ministry could not be completed in India due its vastness and growing population. He suggested, 'our kind of (IEHC) programme in India should be on the list perpetually for evangelism'. Further, he pleaded with Kietzman not to take any such drastic decision against their operation in India as Kietzman threatened to take, 'consider the whole situation and refrain from taking any rash steps for the reasons mentioned ...but continue with their deep interest for a greater involvement in India'.[100] This is how WLC leadership made the Indian leaders listen to them rather than to run the ministry in the way which Indian leaders were interested in doing. WLC regarded their own interests as more important than the local or national or contextual interests.

Prasad was further troubled over Kietzman's final tightening of the noose around his neck, in which Kietzman had written, 'This also requires an examination of your current outlook towards literature evangelism, which is the principle goal of WLC, and therefore, the basis on which it wants to make financial grants to an overseas organisation'.[101] This meant a sudden death to IEHC work in India. By then India had moved away from

---

[98] Kietzman, Dale, 1986, A Letter to BAG Prasad on 18th April, Colorado Springs, USA

[99] Eastman, Dick, 1999, Personal interview with the researcher on the 14th of February, Colorado Springs, USA

[100] Prasad, B.A.G., 1986, A Letter to Dale Kietzman on 3rd May, Secunderabad, India

[101] Ibid.

literature evangelism to Christ Groups ministry, or 'total evangelism'. He certainly disagreed with the directives of Kietzman and said, 'if the basis is only literature evangelism, we will miss 64 percent of India's population in our programme for IEHC'.[102] From the beginning of the IEHC ministry, the Indian leadership did not stick to the directives of WLC. They preferred to follow the Indian context and tried to share the gospel effectively with their countrymen. In Prasad's words, IEHC apart from literature used other 'methods'[103].

Further, Prasad, while defending the budget tried to convince Kietzman that '75 percent of the budget should go for the Christ Groups ministry.'[104] This is what Kietzman wanted to warn Prasad against in his above statement that the grants will be given only for 'literature evangelism' and had stressed that was the main goal of WLC. As WLC disowned their staff who had worked with them for years, in a similar way WLC seemed to disown Christ Groups ministry.

Kietzman, Creighton and other WLC leaders often talked about the changes, insisting that the Indian leaders adapt to them and blamed them for their slowness. However, when an unexpected development took place, in the form of the Christ Groups, which was an entirely new outcome of 'literature evangelism', WLC's leaders failed to see the changed Indian mission context and capitalize on it for the extension of the Kingdom of God. WLC sought to follow their 'entrepreneurial instincts' for an easy, economic and efficient plan rather than investing in a project like Christ Groups which needed on-going support.

WLC did not want to take any risk whatsoever in investing in any on-going project. Prasad, on other hand, took a long time to realize Kietzman's real motive, Kietzman just wanted a centralized office for India,[105] and wanted to consider India as one unit. He intended IEHC to function like Scripture Gift Mission, with one office for India and to send the literature on request to the interested individuals, groups or churches for distribution. Kietzman threatened to cut the Indian budget like they did with Korea and Japan. Kietzman announced he would do this in '20 days' time (that is before January 1987).

WLC wanted IEHC to take a back-seat role rather than an activist role in India, to move from pioneer work to being a catalyst. At this point, Prasad rather than opting to close down the ministry in India, bowed down to the pressure, for his own survival or survival of his associates. He said, 'we

---

[102] Ibid.
[103] Ibid.
[104] Ibid.
[105] Ibid. 5

have no right to dispute it. After all, it is they who have the money (WLC board). We are prepared to go through another ordeal at this end'.[106]

Once Kietzman resigned in October 1987, it was a big sigh of relief for everyone in IEHC, especially, for Prasad. It was an ordeal and very distressing time for him. For a while, during Kietzman's period, everything looked finished for Prasad, but he survived and succeeded in completing his long cherished plan 'Final Thrust-5000'. This is what he had written to Kietzman about in his letters calling it 'a total evangelism' and 'co-operative evangelism'. This vision was alive until his passing in 1994. Beforel then, WLC was contemplating what step could be taken to stop Prasad from going any further because of the kind of position he had among some of WLC's officials. His death was a blessing in disguise for WLC to take control over IEHC work and not allow the Indian leaders to do what they wanted in their context.

Creighton in response to Eastman's letter wrote, 'I'm rocking the boat too much!'.[107] Creighton, writing about the current Indian leadership after Prasad's death, mentioned that the inflow of income may have to be cut down further, to curtail the other activities of the ministry and stick only to systematic tract distribution'. Furthermore, 'the need is to change the whole structure to "serve the requirement of the future" ',[108] which seems to suggest running the ministry as per WLC's directions or plan, but not like previously when Indian leaders had tried to develop the ministry in ways that seemed best to their context.

Until the death of Prasad, it was rather difficult for WLC leaders to break 'the ice'. He was an old timer who had worked under most WLC leaders of his time. He knew the pulses of WLC and its interests. During his time, IEHC emerged as a powerful evangelical mission, which was penetrating into the hard soil of India in rural evangelism. During Kietzman's period, he diplomatically and wisely handled the rather difficult situation, though he at times was humiliated and intimidated by Kietzman. However, he guided the ministry as much as possible by his personal convictions, and especially tried to become a champion working towards establishing and developing Christ Groups work in India.

The emphasis of WLC's leaders was working towards moulding the Indian leaders to think and become like them but not to do what seemed best to them for their nation. It seemed, after Prasad's death, the leaders of WLC tried to put a 'noose around the neck of Indian leaders,' so that they could not lead the ministry to their liking. After Prasad's death, WLC leaders truly got an open space to run the ministry to their way of thinking.

---

[106] Ibid. 4
[107] Creighton, Fred, 1994, A Letter to Dick Eastman on 21st October, Hamilton, New Zealand
[108] Ibid.

Creighton wrote, 'we have come to a crucial time for reassessment...this is an ideal time... to do it'.[109]

This shows the attitude of westerners towards their mission in the non-western world. As Bishop Azariah put it in the Edinburgh Conference of 1910, 'that it is a ruling colonial pattern more than a partnership model'.[110] Samuel in his recent paper 'Mission and Power' outlines the two kinds of powers exercised in the history of mission, especially in the case of India. He explained, 'Studies in power in social relationships identify two aspects of power. One is power over others and is about exercising influence. The other is power to enable others to achieve desired outcomes and is about power as capacity'.[111] He added, 'Power over others is directed at achieving the outcomes of those exercising power. Those exercising power predetermine outcomes, barriers are created or reinforced to mute the voice of those over whom power is exercised. It also means that those in power often suppress awareness of their unrealised interests or real interests determine the wants and needs of others. Such use of power is domination, control and rule from above'. Samuel further remarks 'that newer missions (including WLC) who have entered Indian mission fields in the last five decades have continued such attitudes, domination and top down order'.[112]

---

[109] Ibid. 3

[110] Azariah, V.S., 2009 (1910), in Samuel, V.K., Mission and Power, a seminar paper, OCMS, Oxford, UK

[111] Samuel, V.K., 2009, Mission and Power, a seminar paper, OCMS, Oxford, UK

[112] Ibid.

Chapter 5
A Study on Christ Groups
in Karnataka State

Sources and Background

The study on the Christ Groups is the first of this kind as previously no one has documented, investigated or analysed them. The sources for this study are original reports and accounts by those involved. The unique contribution of the study will add knowledge and open up many more issues for further research. As stated in Chapter 1, in 1998 the primary data were collected through open-ended questions. Again, the gathered material was verified with the field evangelists and documented in a structured format. Interviews were separately conducted with the evangelists, field-supervisors, converts and leaders of IEHC (past and present) and recorded on tapes. Files, letters, journals, statistical data and published books were collected from the IEHC office in Bangalore with the kind permission of Mr. Albert Sudershan, Regional Manager of IEHC, Karnataka.

In the second stage, a visit was made to the USA to gather material from the WLC office in Colorado Springs, Pasadena and Los Angeles. In WLC (now EHC-I) from the offices of President and Vice President, files on India, letters, journals, published books and statistical data were accessed. Interviews were conducted with the President, the Vice President and the former President and recorded on tapes. In Los Angeles, interviews were conducted with the founder and former President of WLC and his wife. A few books were collected from the founder's office. In Pasadena, an interview was conducted with another former President of WLC. A structured questionnaire was sent to another former President and his response was received.

Apart from the above material, my story is also evidence. I became a Christian in 1967 through the ministry of IEHC. In 1968, I started a Christ Group and led it until 1970 and then joined the ministry of IEHC. I worked in different capacities until I became the Regional Manager for IEHC, Karnataka and left the mission in 2000. The Christ Group that was started in 1968 struggled to continue once I had left. It survived and today it has been taken over by the Church of South India of the Northern Karnataka Diocese and has a church building and an ordained pastor.

Background

This chapter proposes to study the emergence of Christ Groups in Karnataka. Before that it will be helpful to know briefly the history of Christ Groups in India. Christ Groups formed accidentally[1], when nationwide India Every Home Crusade's (IEHC) house-to-house literature distribution took place from 1966. IEHC was started by World Literature Crusade in May 1964.[2] WLC is now known as Every Home Christ International,[3] an American organization geared to mass-evangelism through literature distribution, since 1946.[4] Dr. Jack McAlister, a Canadian, radio-gospel preacher, member of the Assemblies of God Church[5] founded WLC with the vision to evangelize the world by placing gospel literature systematically in every accessible home with the least cost.[6] This systematic house-to-house distribution earned WLC the name "Every Home Crusade".[7]

'World Evangelisation' at the turn of the twentieth century became an official slogan of American Evangelicals.[8] From the middle of the twentieth century, an average of about 400 'Great Commission' conferences per year were held by the evangelicals.[9] This passion was very evident in the 1940s and 1950s, when Communism was spreading in the world. During that period, Carl McIntire and Billy James Hargis stirred up anti-Communist fervour and later Billy Graham reinforced it.[10]

WLC too was apocalyptic along with other American evangelicals about Communism.[11] WLC wanted to thwart its expansion with literature distribution, which Communism was using to spread its idealism,[12] by placing a pair of eight pages' gospel tracts systematically into every home and in every accessible country before Communist literature could reach

---

[1] Lee, Yohann, 1999, Christ Groups Survey Questionnaire, 5.
[2] Oliver, J.J., 1994, A Letter, Mhow, MP, India
[3] A Report, 1985, Every Home Christ International
[4] McAlister, Jack A., 1970, *Everybody*
[5] Lee, Yohann, 1976, *Everybody*
[6] Ibid. 7
[7] Lee, Yohann, 1983, *Everybody*
[8] Walls, Andrew F., 1990, *Earthen Vessels*, 'The American Dimension in the History the Missionary Movement', eds. Joel Carpenter & Wilber R. Shenk
[9] Gary, Jay and Olgy Gary, 1989, The Countdown Has Begun, in *The Story of the Global Consultation on AD 2000*, 11
[10] Brouwer, Steve, Paul Gifford, and Susan D. Rose, 1996, *Exporting the American Gospel: Global Christian Fundamentalism*, 16
[11] Ibid. 16
[12] Eastman, Dick, 1971, *No Easy Road*, 11

new readers.[13] This was planned on a 'fast footing' basis creating a sense of urgency to mobilize its supporters.[14]

From the 19th century onwards, American evangelicals, at the turn of every century, created a sense of urgency in the missionary enterprise by using the pretext of any major world political or religious event to its own advantage to compete in the global market. American evangelicalism developed in this market culture within the aggressive American business and media culture,[15] in order to carry out its task of world-evangelization. 'World Evangelisation' seemed to be a possible achievement by means of technological advancement. During industrialization, the invention of mass production and mass communication gave American evangelicals another effective, easy and economic tool to reach the world.

WLC with its faith in the mass production of the printed page driven with a western mass-evangelistic and individualistic[16] approach set out to evangelize the world without understanding the context and culture of those countries. Mass evangelism was an expression of modernity, where mass-production, mass-distribution was achieved in an efficient way for greater success. WLC, under the influence of an American dominated culture with its globalizing methods wanted to reach 'every-home' with mass free distribution of tracts 'to win the billions of unsaved souls for Christ on the earth'.[17] The method of distribution and the contents of the message from the snowy mountains of Alaska to the remotest village in the Indian sub-continent was the same. Though WLC aimed to use nationals and translated the materials into the local languages, it kept its overriding culture of a universalized method and message.

WLC's plan was to distribute a pair of tracts systematically to every home and ask the interested reader to fill out the attached response card for further enquiry, which included a 'Bible Correspondence Course'. On its completion, a copy of the New Testament was sent to the successful reader. The impersonal method was thought to be totally adequate as the simplest way with the minimum cost. WLC, like other American evangelical organizations, had big plans to get greater numbers of converts.[18] Statistics and numbers were its main passions. The main emphasis of the message was on 'appealing to the individual conscience to have a personal relationship or born again experience with Jesus'.[19] The message was to change the individuals not the social structures. WLC's method of maximization did not work out the way it thought when it reached the

---

[13] Lee, Yohann, 1980, *How I Survived the Communist Onslaught*, 69,70
[14] Ibid. 11
[15] Ibid. 3
[16] A Booklet, 1970, *Individual*
[17] Ibid. 3, 14
[18] Ibid. 1
[19] Ibid. 3

Indian relational context, where people read those tracts not only for themselves, but also for their friends, families and others. People who wanted to know more about Jesus formed groups of their own and shared their experiences. This led to the formation of Christ Groups[20] in India. Whereas this is evident in the most of the States in India, the present study will focus on Karnataka State.

Karnataka State

Karnataka nestles between the Eastern and Western Ghats (mountainrange), of India, and slopes down into the Arabian Sea. It was formerly known as 'Mysore State' and home of the princely rulers.[21] The State is surrounded by Maharashtra in the north, Goa in the north-west, and the Arabian Sea in the west. It has a common border with Andhra Pradesh in the north-east, with Tamil Nadu in the east and Kerala in the south. The population is around 60,000,000. It is 191,773sq.kms (74,044 sq miles) in size. Karnataka State is the eighth largest, both in population and area. For administrative purposes, the State is divided into 27 districts (like English shires), and each district has several *taluks*, which contain towns and villages, and which come under its jurisdiction. The capital of Karnataka State is Bangalore, where the legislative assembly functions.

Karnataka, in an earlier era, was called 'Kuntala Desa'. It maintained communication with the early civilizations, like the Egyptians, Sumerians, Phoenicians and Romans. Karnataka was ruled by many dynasties. The East India Company took control of Mysore in 1799. The unification of Mysore State took place in 1956. On 1 November 1973, this State came to be known as Karnataka.[22] Before unification, Mysore was a princely state under which the royal families of such states had some privileges and benefits. However, in 1956, the Government of India passed an ordinance and took away all those privileges and all the princely states were brought under the rule of the Central Government and thus became part of and on par with the other states of India.

Karnataka and its religions

India is a land of religion and the birthplace of several of the world's religions. Karnataka is the proud inheritor of most of those religions. The religions of Buddhism, Jainism, Islam, and different sects of Hinduism have made their own impact on the people,especiallythe Bhakti (a mystical

---

[20] A group of believers gathered for praise and worship and for fellowship

[21] Duke, H.M., 1989, 'The Contribution of Karnataka Churches, a former Auxiliary Secretary of Bible Society of India', M.A. Thesis, Fuller Theological Seminary, Pasadena, USA

[22] Ibid.

or pietistic) movement in the ninth century and Virsaivism in the twelfth century. Today, Karnataka has twenty-two percent of the total population of Virasaivas or Lingayats.

The Bhakti movement played an important role in Karnataka. Bhakti emphasizes that mystical and devotional experience to attain absorption with Vishnu or Krishna. This was a direct reaction to Shankaracharaya's philosophy of Advaita Vedanta, whereby through knowledge one can overcome ignorance, dispele illusion (Maya), to attain absorption in Brahman and thus gain liberation.[23] Virasaivism or Lingayatism is a non-Vedic religion and was set against the Brahminical domination. In principle, it condemned temple worship, sacrifice, and pilgrimage as useless. The caste system is rejected, the sexes are declared equal, child marriage is forbidden, and remarriage of widows is allowed. Although in the course of time, the caste system reappeared.[24]

However, the popular Hinduism seen in Karnataka is traditional rather than intellectual, following ancestral, social and religious practices. . The religion of the common people in Karnataka is limited to holy places within the state boundaries or in the neighbouring state boundaries.[25]

Karnataka and Protestant Christianity

Protestant Christianity arrived at the shores of Karnataka in the eighteenth century, though Christians (Catholics) were present when Salvador visited Vijayanagar where he preached and became a martyr.[26] Hostein also confirms that Thomas Lopez mentioned 'Mangalore' as the home of certain Christians who sent a deputation to Vasco da Gama on his second voyage towards the end of 1502.[27] In the nineteenth and twentieth centuries, Karnataka experienced a great influx of Christian missionaries. Many missions belonging to various countries, and based on a different theological ethos, and with varied visions, arrived and worked in harmony with each other. These missions avoided any sort of confrontation and competition in mission work.[28] The Anglicans came in 1808 to Bangalore, the London Missionary Society came in 1810 to Bellary, Wesleyan Methodists came in 1821 to Bangalore, the Basel Mission came in 1834 to Mangalore, and the Methodist Episcopal Church came in 1874 to Bangalore.[29] Other minor missions like the Brethren Mission in 1874, the Pentecostals in 1914, the Evangelical Church of India of the Oriental

---

[23] Ibid.
[24] Nadimutt, S.C., 1941, *A Handbook of Virasaivism*
[25] *The Encyclopaedia of Religions*, 1987, Hinduism, Eliade, Mircea and Adam Charles (eds.)
[26] Firth, C.B., 1961, *An Introduction to Indian Church History*, 1961, 51
[27] Neill, Stephen, 1964, op.cit. Hostein (1946, 406), *A History of Christian Mission*
[28] Ibid. 252-254
[29] Ibid.

Missionary Society in 1944 and the Baptist Mission in 1954, are present in the cities and towns of Karnataka.

However, Karnataka was not a happy ground for a spiritual harvest. It never had a great deal of significant Christian influence. Wurth, a Basel missionary commented, 'there were many who without restraint would give vent to their anger and indignation, whenever they heard the name of Jesus'.[30] Mr Waidelich, another missionary commented, 'the inhabitants of Navalgund are ... hostile to the gospel.'[31] Not only foreign missionaries, but even now some Indian Christian agencies make the same comments about the Karnataka mission field. Missionaries carried out a lot of hard work in respect to the Kannada literature. Kittel produced the first ever English-Kannada Dictionary. They contributed to education, to medical work and to social work, but the impact of Christianity on the people was low. Rev. Duke suggested that if all these institutions and establishments had seriously taken upon themselves the task of evangelization, the history of the church in Karnataka would have been different.[32] However, even if these missionaries had evangelized there would not have been any dramatic impact of Christianity in Karnataka because the people were rather suspicious of the foreigners and their message. The majority of people thought Christianity would help the colonial rule rather than the Indian cause of independence.

Karnataka and Every Home Crusade

India Every Home Crusade (EHC) began work in Karnataka State,, in May 1964,[33] under the leadership of Mr G. Guruprasad, who by profession was a school teacher. Guruprasad wrote a gospel tract, entitled '*From Darkness to Light*', based upon a Vedic prayer, '*Asathoma Sath Gamaya*'. This was used in EHC's distribution programme. The tract was addressed mainly to the high-caste and educated people. Yohann Lee, a Korean, WLC's overseas director, wrote a tract entitled '*Are You Happy*?', addressed to the materialistic middle and rich class. At that time, about 400 million were living under the poverty line.[34] For a Hindu, materialistic blessings are from god. Poverty and non-possession of materials are a curse from god. These two tracts along with '*He wants to be your Friend*' or '*Joy of Ramesh*' and '*From Death unto Life*' children's tracts were distributed in the EHC's first and second coverages.

---

[30] *The Journals of Basel Missionaries of South Maratha*, 39
[31] Ibid. 41
[32] Ibid. 59
[33] Ibid.
[34] Ana, Santa, Julio de, 1977, *Good News To The Poor*

Tract Distribution Programmes and Aftermaths

First Coverage

EHC in Karnataka prepared the ground for distribution work by contacting churches and Christian leaders and informing them of what EHC wanted to do. IEHC launched the first Indian nationwide coverage called 'Operation Last Home' from 1966-75, although Karnataka EHC completed its first coverage by the end of 1969. Karnataka coverage used the manpower of 72 pioneer crusaders (distributors) and they took two and half years to reach 6.5 million homes.[35] Such a fast coverage brought many complaints from Christians about not covering or completing certain areas in the State. Though some houses were missed, considering the difficult terrain, heat, weather and opposition, distributors put their best efforts into the work.

Robert Louis (1974) writing on Crusaders' hard work mentioned, "Crusaders left their bases on Monday morning to do the distribution in their assigned areas but returned only on Saturday morning to wash their clothes and get ready again for Monday's work'. Looking at their work plans, he added, 'it puts us to shame to see how they carry out the work ahead of our planning".[36] The entire State was covered just using bicycles on the rugged roads.

The abstract statistic of the first coverage in Karnataka State:[37]

- Total number of homes   6,500,000
- Total Population   40,000,000 (during 1960s)
- Total number of tracts distributed   11,321,720
- Total number of enquirers   56,000
- Total number of BCC graduates   5,600
- (BCC: Bible Correspondence Course)

EHC because of the WLC connection was driven and consumed by the importance of numbers. The success of their programme was measured from that number basis.[38] 56000 enquirers out of 40 million people in the State show less than 1 percent response.

Second Coverage

A second coverage called 'Project Calvary' was held in India between 1978-88. Karnataka EHC's second coverage began earlier than in other

---

[35] Louis, Robert, 1974, A Report On Karnataka IEHC, Bangalore, India
[36] Louis, Robert, 1974, A Letter written to G. Guruprasad from Raichur, while visiting a mission field, Raichur, India
[37] Ibid.
[38] Walls, Andrew F., *Earthen Vessels,* in 'The American Dimension in the History of the Missionary Movement, eds. Joel Carpenter & Wilber R Shenk, 1990

parts of India because their first coverage was completed by the end of 1969. In this coverage, importance was given to personal evangelism with the tracts distribution and it was called 'in-depth evangelism'.[39] This was launched to avoid the complaints received during the first coverage that distributors overlooked some areas and were negligent in their work and also that IEHC had not given enough care to new believers in Christ.

The statistics for the second coverage as below:

• During this time about 8 million homes were visited
• 17 million tracts distributed
• 80,000 enrolled for the Bible Correspondence Course
• 23,000 had completed the Bible Correspondence Course

(Some said that they accepted Jesus as their Saviour and Lord).[40]

EHC valued numbers. To win the greatest number of souls with the least expense was its constant aim.[41] This was WLC's constant effort to show Americans that 'Paper Missionaries' are effective, economical and there is no need to send home missionaries abroad.[42] The number of enquirers and BCC graduates in the second coverage increased in comparison to the first coverage. This increase can be ascribed to the personal evangelism[43] method by the EHC workers as well as by the new believers. People responded more to the relational aspect rather than to a non-relational impersonal method.

Seekers' Conferences

Unlike 'Crusades', 'Revival Meetings' and 'Healing Meetings' of other missions, which were mostly held where a larger Christian population lived, IEHC's Seekers' Conferences were unique in providing space and opportunity for a rural population of other faiths to come and meet in a place near to their locality for a better hearing of the gospel.

IEHC, to meet the need of the context, moved from its impersonal to a personal follow-up strategy. For Prasad and the Indian leaders, the 'tract was not the means to an end itself, but it was only a point of contact to people'. Prasad called this 'total evangelism' or 'co-operative evangelism'.[44] Seekers' Conferences mostly attracted the student community, yet it helped to pave the way for a better impression and influence of Christianity and its message among the rural community. In

---

[39] Louis, Robert, 1976, a report on Karnataka, Bangalore, India
[40] Ibid.
[41] Ibid.
[42] Ibid.
[43] Ibid.
[44] Ibid.

the past, Christianity and its message was suspect due to its links with the colonial power.

'Seekers' Conferences' tried to erase the age-old suspicion of the people because the bearers of the message and messengers looked like themselves rather than outsiders bringing the message. This gained goodwill among people, which in later times, especially during the Final Thrust-5000, helped to produce more faith and trust and eventually became a launching pad for the formation of Christ Groups. From 1969-71, about ten Seekers' Conferences were conducted in Karnataka. Seekers from a *taluka*, or district, were brought together to a central location. Sometimes 50, 80 or 100 would come. At the end of three days of teaching, they were encouraged to follow Jesus Christ as their Lord and Saviour.[45] From 1971-95, about 80 Seekers' Conferences had taken place.[46] The small 'Bible Study Groups'[47] (the original name for Koinonia) that were formed out of the Seeker's Conferences were introduced to local churches if they were nearby. IEHC also gave the addresses of the new believers to Christian pastors and leaders. IEHC sent their own field workers to follow up those who did not live near any local churches.[48]

Koinonias[49] (or 'The Bible Study Groups') to Christ Groups

The first 'Koinonia' group began in Naragund in August 1968.[50] This Koinonia was from its inception linked to the Brethren Churches of Hubli and Dharwar, which were 36 miles away from Naragund. Before Christ Groups (officially) commenced in 1972[51], EHC in Karnataka accounted for 40 Koinonia groups.[52] Later, these were called Christ Groups.

The Vision of Christ Groups

Lee considered the years 1946 to 1956 to be the decade of pioneering and vision sharing, mostly in Canada and the US. From 1957 to 1966, there was a period of evangelizing and organizing. From 1967 to 1976, the actual experiences of EHC overseas were defined, refined and sharpened.[53] From

---

[45] Ibid.
[46] A Report, 1995, Statistical Details on Karnataka, Bangalore, India
[47] *Prarthisu*, 1969
[48] Ibid. 122
[49] Note: 'The Bible Study Groups', 'Koinonia' and 'Christ Groups' are synonyms names used for the newly formed believers groups
[50] Ibid.
[51] The first Christ Group was formed in 1968. In 1972, they were recognized as having been formed by WLC
[52] Vasudev Rao R., 1998, Personal interview, a field coordinator, IEHC, Bangalore, India
[53] Ibid.

1976, WLC entered into the trilogy that made up the Great Commission: Evangelizing, Organizing and Teaching. According to Lee, taking Mk 16:15 and Matt 28:19, WLC entered into this teaching ministry by forming and establishing Christ Groups.[54]

Though this looks like an interesting turn in the ministry of WLC, this interest remained in WLC only while McAlister and Lee continued to lead affairs. After their departure, the ministry of Christ Groups remained on the periphery.

What are Christ Groups?

Christ Groups are worshipping communities.[55] They consist of people coming from other faiths, who responded initially to the call of the Gospel through literature distribution and mainly through the personal witness of the new believers and the tract distributors.[56] Describing 'Christ Groups', Dr. Yohann Lee, gives a basic definition that 'a Christ Group is a small group of believers made up of our own Every Home Crusade converts overseas who meet regularly for worship, Bible study and prayer fellowship. Their purpose is to know Christ more and to do so in small groups; so we just simply call them Christ Groups'.[57]

Why Christ Groups?

Dr. Lee, explaining the idea of beginning Christ Groups, ' in 1972 when I made the annual survey trip around the world, I came back with the deep conviction that we had to do more to minister to approximately 2,500,000 new converts around the world'. Furthermore, '85 to 87 percent of them were living in areas where there were no churches or Christian bookstores. At that time the conviction gripped me that we had to do something about these people'.[58] WLC pretended to own the Christ Groups Movement although Christ Groups formation began in 1968.

Analysis of Christ Group Movement

Lee, while writing the Christ Groups Manual made this analysis of the Christ Group Movement:

> Christ: is all in all to a new convert, stemming from His saving power and through receiving a new power to live for Him.'[59]

---

[54] Lee, Yohann, 1976, *Christ Groups Manual*, 1.7
[55] Ashwal, E.D., 1989, *It Can Be Done!*, Christ Groups, 119
[56] Ibid.
[57] Lee, Yohann, 1976, 'Christ Groups', *Everybody*, 13, February, Vol.2, No.2
[58] Ibid.
[59] Ibid.

Group: No believer can fully mature alone. A group signifies smallness, and so provides the intimate and informal environment in which the exchanges of fellowship can be warm; personal and devoid of trappings.'[60]

Movement: according to Lee, this means a '...moving, changing, advancing, transmitting, and a vibrant rhythm-movement...Christ Group provides a station where (new) souls...board a train to go home. Also, it is a school where the beginners...start to learn'.[61]

Lee, in claiming Christ Groups as a movement, stated the following: 'From the historical perspective every major religious movement of significance has had at least thirty years of preparation.'[62] WLC was started in the year 1946 and with the 'Christ Groups Movement' in 1976, Lee thought that WLC had finished '30' years and entered into the beginning of a 'Religious Movement'. Lee called those '30' years WLC's years of preparation to become a movement or to enter into a history of its own. Leewanted to shift WLC from its 'years of preparation' to 'years of progress', but sadly after Lee's departure, WLC reverted into the 'years of preparation' rather than go on into the 'years of progress', which was not in line with their kind of thinking of the, 'easiest and economical'.

Christ Groups in Karnataka
Christ Groups started in the middle of 1968 in Karnataka.[63] Officially, their work began in1972. Before 1972, they were called 'Koinonias'.[64] There are now over 1000 Christ Groups in Karnataka.[65]

Stages in the development of Christ Groups
Christ Groups' work began in India in the late 1960s[66] and then gradually developed until 1992. From 1992, their development became very significant.[67] Their development in India can be seen in four stages. 1968-72 'The Early Stage of Christ Groups', 1972-76 'The Development of Christ Groups Concept and Work', 1977 to 1991 'The Advancement of Christ Groups Work', and 1992-96, 'A Significant Growth and Activity of the Christ Groups'.

---

[60] Ibid.

[61] Ibid.

[62] Peters, George, 1976, *Everybody*, Lausanne Congress on World Evangelisation, Sep, Vol 2, No 9, back cover

[63] Ibid.

[64] Ibid. 122

[65] Statistical Data, 1996, A Status Report of Karnataka IEHC, Bangalore, India

[66] Taylor, Bayard (Brian), 1989, op.cit., *It Can Be Done*, 129, E.D.Ashwal, *Christ Groups*

[67] Statistical Data, 1994, A Report on Karnataka IEHC, Bangalore, India

Formation of Christ Groups

According to Lee, 'on completion of a Bible Correspondence Course (BCC) ... If two or three agree to come together, EHC will send a Pioneer Crusader to form a group with them.'[68]

During my survey, I did not find that any Christ Group was started on completion of BCC lessons alone. The case study on Pushpamma and Hosadurga Christ Groups examines Christ Groups that started because of evangelists who personally shared the Gospel with the family. Another example was in the place where I came from which started in 1968. This was the first Christ Group of IEHC, Karnataka. This group was started due to personal sharing of the Gospel with others. I became Christian after a healing experience. This suggests Christ Groups were either started by the field evangelists or their contacts.[69] After completion of a BCC, IEHC office sent further books for reading and occasionally wrote some follow-up letters to interested contacts.

Lee attempted to impress upon WLC's supporters that 'impersonal' and 'personal' methods produced these Christ Groups. He suggested that both the methods could go together and that one complements the other. Of course, in the Indian context, no single method was effective. As Prasad says, 'India needs total evangelism'.[70]

In some places, the Christ Groups started on their own and the group members became the carriers of the good news to others and helped to form the group. These evangelists, while nurturing these groups, formed other groups on their own.[71] For example, Muniswamy of Pathpalya of Bagepalli taluka who was a Vedanthi (scholar of Hindu scriptures) became a Christian in 1969 after much reasoning and experience. He was then introduced to Anjanappa, an evangelist of IEHC in Bagepalli. Later on, Anjaneppa's work was extended from Bagepalli to Pathpalya, Chelur and its surroundings. At the same time, Muniswamy too shared the Gospel in the surrounding places of Pathpalya and established Christ Groups.[72]

Membership

Lee suggested that each CG should not have more than five and no less than three members in villages and towns where there are no evangelical churches at all. Each group was formed by the BCC graduates.[73] However, Christ Groups in Karnataka were mostly the personal work of the evangelists and their contacts. Their groups were formed due to personal

---

[68] Lee, Yohann, 1976, *Everybody*, 12, April, Vol.2, No.4
[69] Ibid.
[70] Ibid.
[71] Ibid.
[72] Muniswamy, 2003, personal interview, Bangalore, India
[73] Lee, Yohann, 1976, *Everybody*, Jan, Vol 2, no.1

evangelism not through the completion of BCC lessons. Most of the members of CGs were illiterate and village women folk, and would not have known what 'graduate' means. Lee's suggestion of BCC graduates may be true in other CGs, but iwasof minimal significance in Karnataka.

Lee's above description of a cell-like grouping was in reality unrealistic in the Indian context, where families were coming to know Christ. Most of these families had more than five members in each family. Most Christ Groups in Karnataka are large. Some groups have over 100 to 150 members.[74] Eastman writes that in Indonesia and Fij,i many Christ Groups have grown into big churches and some have 300 members.[75]

Baptism

When new believers should be baptised was left to the discretion of the Christ Groups Evangelists. Believers were baptised in groups. Only after someone showed willingness to obey the 'waters of baptism' were they recommended by the evangelist for baptism. The first baptism took place, when Mr. Vasudev Rao, a Brahmin (a high caste) came to Christ in April 1967.[76] This indicated that even while the First Coverage was still in its initial stages, Vasudev's baptism brought challenges to IEHC leaders concerning his future life as a Christian. Since Vasudev lived closed to Bangalore, where IEHC had its main office, he was introduced to a local church for his spiritual growth and was given a job in IEHC to do the follow-up work. This would have given him an independent life and economic stability to overcome any opposition from his family members. Though Vasudev now has died, he lived as a Christian until the end of his life, in 2001. Karnataka has recorded 700 baptisms by 1998.[77]

Traditional values

Lee in his manual stated that there was respect for traditional values by these new believers. Slowly they weree taught how to show Christian love to others. The Holy Spirit continued to teach them and prompt them.[78]

According to Lee, we must not change the often strange, local customs, traditions, and living habits of the people to whom we take the good news. The gospel is food for the soul, not the body. To be a Christian is to be a follower of Christ in whatever social, cultural or ethnic situation in which we live. We should gladly accept, even if we do not respect their culture.[79]

---

[74] Jairajan, P., 1998, personal interview, Pastor of Hosadurga Christ Groups Church, Hosadurga, India
[75] Eastman, Dick, 1997, *Beyond Imagination*, 95
[76] Ibid.
[77] Statistical Data, 1998, A Status Report on Karnataka IEHC, Bangalore, India
[78] Ibid. 12
[79] Lee, Yohann, 1978, 'Dog Soup', *Everybody*, Feb, Vol.4, No.2, 5

This means accepting the 'strange' culture of others for the sake of their new found faith, though we may not really approve of such a culture.

Lee, as an oriental man, better understood the Indian context and the strong traditional values among its people. The accommodation of traditions into the Christ Groups was rather suspect to so called evangelical and denominational churches because CGs did not function like them and did not adhere to their church principles. Some IEHC leaders found this accommodation rather difficult to agree upon.[80] Today, there are a large number of Christians in India who have not come out of their past European missionary mould. India is fast changing and it will take an entirely different stand on its religious tolerance and harmony. Amidst mounting opposition, Indians, on the whole, show more response to the gospel than ever before.However, Indian churches need to awaken now so that they may develop their own mission and theology which best suits the local context and culture, and is in the best interest of all Indian Christians and churches.

The Christ Groups Manual

Authored by Yohann Lee, it was translated in 49 languages in October 1975.[81] Lee claimed the initial thoughts about the manual began in 1972, and after four years, he completed it, in 1976. Lee does not specify into which languages it was translated. It was never translated into the Kannada language of Karnataka State. Christ Group formation began in the year 1968,[82] almost eight years before the CG manual was written. Lee's CG manual was a rather late response to what was already happening in Karnataka. By this time, CGs in Karnataka functioned mostly on New Testament principles and thus the CG manual did not find its way into Karnataka CGs. The manual sat on the bookshelves of the IEHC office. The year of publication (1976) suggests that Lee waited to see the first nationwide house- to-house distribution completed and then produced this manual for CGs.

Development and momentum of Christ Groups

Christ Groups were started as a follow-up of the BCC graduate scheme and by Christ Group Evangelists who went from village to village doing personal evangelism. The first method is the standard method used by IEHC in the first and to some extent during the second coverage. The second method arose out of the work of Christ Group evangelists. They

---

[80] George, C., 1978, in a letter written to all IEHC directors, George being a director for Christ Groups India airs his suspicion about theological stand of Christ Groups. This he writes after his visit to Christ Groups in Uttar Pradesh, India
[81] Ibid.
[82] Ibid.

used existing Christ Groups as staging bases for discipleship and evangelism in the surrounding villages.

Between 1972-1984, the Christ Groups work was in its initial stage. IEHC field teams were sent to areas to explore the possibilities of forming Christ Groups. The teams consisted of two or four members. Most of the team members were senior field-workers of EHC. The response to Christ Groups work in the first stage was mixed. It ranged between a moderate to a high response. A place called Bagepalli was the most successful mission field but the response was moderate in other fields.[83] Emphasis on Christ Groups began in January 1985, when a Christ Groups Leaders conference was held in Bangalore. 50 Christ Groups key leaders (except one, all the others came from other faiths) were invited to attend a week's conference. During that conference in 1985, the thrust was on the formation and reproduction of Christ Groups.[84] Through to October 1985, 97 new Christ Groups were formed, an increase of almost 700 percent over the previous year.[85]

CG Building

Lee wanted to move away from constructing any 'church' of formal buildings for Christ Groups. So, having that thought in mind, he called them a 'Group' rather than a 'Church'. Secondly, to maintain a small membership, he also used the term 'Group' and suggested if that number grew to more than five they should split into two groups.

Lee explained, 'a CG has no building or trappings so it does not need affluence to survive. It is small so it has to be personal and real or honest. It has no traditions dictated to it by some outside culture'.[86] Initially, the idea looked right but as groups grew and became a worshipping community, the need for a building was felt. Now Karnataka has built six churches: Bagepalli, Hirekerur, Pavagada, Hosadurga, Attibele and Madhugiri. A church building also gives stability and continuity to the group. For the people of other faiths, a place of worship is a sacred place. Just as Solomon, when he made his dedication prayer for the temple of God he asked that God will meet His people, He will listen to their prayers and supplications, accept their vows and wishes and that glory may always be manifest in that place. (II Chron 6). In a similar way, the new believers, who come from other faiths, have a feeling for holy places. For people, who came from the outcaste backgrounds touching or entering into holy places gave them a new possession and position.[87]

---

[83] Ibid. 75
[84] Ibid. p.123, 124
[85] Ibid. 75
[86] Lee, Yohann, 1976, *Everybody*, March, Vol.2, No.3, 17
[87] Jayakumar, Samuel, 1999, *Dalit Consciousness and Christian Conversion*, 15

Christ Groups as a denomination

Christ Groups cannot always remain a non-denominational group. Eastman stated that in Fiji and Indonesia Christ Groups have become denominations.[88] However, in Karnataka their position remained the same as non-denominational in some of their Christ Groups, and some other Christ Groups in Karnataka became a denomination of their own, like CG in Naragund,[89] which for sometime was a Brethren Assembly and now a Church of South India. In the same way, Christ Groups in other places have joined up with some other denominational groups. In Devanhalli and Siddalghatta areas, Marthoma Evangelicals[90] took over the groups and the Mulbagal area, where the Methodist Church[91] took over the CG groups.

Leadership training

The year 1985, starting with the training of 50 key Christ Groups leaders, looked bright for Christ Groups work. However, WLC during the year, due to a financial crisis, asked all the IEHC offices in India to reduce their staff to the minimal strength. Karnataka office retrenched 30-40 of its office and field staff, including Christ Groups' evangelists. This created a precarious situation in respect of the development of Christ Groups' work, which was in the eyes of IEHC's leaders their 'jewel in the crown'.

To stabilize and develop Christ Groups, IEHC leaders promoted the idea of training grass-roots level leaders. As Christ Groups started growing in size and numbers, the field evangelists found it difficult to visit all the Christ Groups of their mission bases in a stipulated period. This led the way to train key leaders of these groups so that they could take care of their groups on their own. The development of the groups' leaders was encouraged. They were trained either by coming to Bangalore for short courses or in the field itself by the evangelists. This kind of practical on-the-field training was ideal for the rural areas and more effective than classroom training.

Basic subjects like salvation, assurance, witnessing and Bible study subjects were taught. Vasuder Rao suggested, 'that part of the time was spent in building relationships to enhance mutual understanding and to remove past suspicions about Christianity from their minds, for example, whether they will be displaced from their home and loved ones, if they

---

[88] Ibid. 95

[89] Ibid.

[90] Thomas, P., 1998, personal interview, a former field director of Marthoma Evangelical Churches, Siddalghatta area, and a former field staff of IEHC Karnataka, Devanhalli, Bangalore, India

[91] Christopher, David, 2002, personal interview (an ordained pastor of Methodist Church, testifies to the fact that due to the handing over of Christ Groups in Mulbagal area, the Methodist Church began in that Area), Bangalore, India

continue in Christ'.[92] In the past, missionaries built 'mission compounds' and isolated new believers from their own people[93] as a place to nurture them in the Christian faith. They feared, if allowed to remain in their surroundings, that those new Christians would return to their old faith because missionaries were aware of the strong relational bonds of Indians.

Would they need to change their names and religion?[94] The western missionaries used these criteria for the people of other faiths when they embraced Christianity. There are still some Christian missions and churches in India that insist on these changes, when people embrace Christianity. It is another topic for research to see whether such changes will bring true changes in the lives of people. Indians are more interested in following Christ rather than to follow norms and conditions as in the case of Sadhu Sundar Singh and Narayan Vaman Rao Tilak, who wanted to know Christ in an Indian way of asceticism and devotion (Bhakti) rather than in a traditional Christian way. H.L. Richard, in his book *'Following Jesus in Hindu Context'* explores this aspect in regard to Tilak's new faith.[95]

The period of 1985-87 was volatile. The relationships between Kietzman and Prasad were becoming harder , and all the IEHC programmes and projects swung back and forth. Hundreds of staff members were retrenched, senior leaders asked to retire and many Christ Groups Training Centres closed down. Kietzman was determined to make Prasad listen to him rather than to run the ministry on his own, especially in the case of Christ Groups.[96] In desperation, IEHC in order to keep the momentum of Christ Groups going, moved from Christ Groups Training Centres (CGTC) to CGTE (Christ Groups Training, Extension). Puneeth Kumar speaking on the training through extension wrote that CGTE wanted to provide some solid spiritual food that they were unable to get from their evangelists, who only visited them once a month. The evangelists found it difficult to visit all these groups as the new groups sprung up. This led to ineffective discipleship among the members, whose spiritual growth suffered.[97]

This continued as Kietzman 'clipped the wings' of the Indian leaders. Kietzman's resignation in 1987 was a blessing in disguise when they breathed a sigh of relief at release from his intimidating and humiliating rule. Although Prasad, during the Final Thrust-5000 project, tried to bring back the training of key leaders, his untimely death, in 1994, ended that

---

[92] Ibid.
[93] Sunder Raj, Ebenezer, 2000, *National Debate on Conversion*, 15
[94] Ibid.
[95] Richard, H.L., 1998, *Following Jesus in Hindu Context: The Intriguing Implications of N.V. Tilak's Life and Thought*
[96] Ibid.
[97] Puneethkumar, 1985, A Letter Regional Director, IEHC, Karnataka, A letter written to Mr. B.A.G. Prasad on the 19th Sep, Bangalore, India

training. The future of Christ Groups relied on the ability of the members of the Groups. However, the impact of the training left a lasting impression of Christianity and its message. Recently, I was able to meet two such leaders, Mr. Venkatswamy[98] and Mr. Muniswamy[99] of Bagepalli, who continue to lead their Christ Groups in their surrounding villages.

Life cycle

The new Christ Groups and the new believers are often developed into daughter Christ Groups as the result of efforts by EHC Evangelists and their group members. Some Christ Groups failed to continue.[100] Although 1000 Christ Groups were formed in Karnataka,[101] over 100 have discontinued, or disintegrated, or the members moved away to other places, leaving about 900 Groups active. The dissolution of groups was primarily due to a lack of Christ Group evangelists to care for them, and also funding.

Now the emphasis of IEHC completely moved away from Christ Groups to literacy and teaching tailoring skills.[102] Interestingly, in Karnataka, the leaders who liked the idea of Christ Groups helped some Christ Groups to grow as churches. Some church buildings were built.[103] Initially, Christ Groups were not allowed to build such buildings as they would not be seen as the continuation of the established churches or the mainline churches, which have become more inward looking, spending money on the maintenance of the building rather than on missions. Although there was no theology of their own for the Christ Groups, they mainly functioned on the principles of the New Testament.[104] Without any denominational theology, these groups have survived and continued to achieve numerical growth. However, many churches which have a theology of their own have only experienced biological growth and failed to produce any numerical growth even after being established for many years.[105]

Persecution

On the whole, opposition to Christ Groups and Christ Group Evangelists had been not as serious as it was in the beginning in Karnataka. Persecution

---

[98] Venkatswamy, C., 2003, personal interview (pastor's a house-church in Oodavarpalli of Bagepalli *taluk* for last two decades), Bangalore, India
[99] Muniswamy, 2003, personal interview (pastor's a church in Chelur of Bagepalli *taluk* for the last two and half decades), Bangalore, India
[100] Ibid.
[101] Ibid.
[102] Sudershan, Albert, 1998, personal interview, Bangalore, India & Munivenkatraman, 1998, personal interview, Bagepalli, India
[103] Ibid.
[104] Ibid.
[105] Ibid.

in the form of social boycott was quite common in some places there.[106] The response of Christian churches towards persecuted Christians was sympathetic and helpful. However, the level of persecution has steeply increased. In 30 months from 2000 to mid 2003, in Karnataka alone, more than 170 cases of persecution have been registered with the police.[107] Christ Groups' work is notgrowing as in the past, and hence to compare the relationship between the development of CGs and persecution may not be appropriate.

Signs and wonders

A standard feature in the founding of most Christ Groups is the occurrence of healing. Sometimes they are dramatic, such as leprosy or tuberculosis, and sometimes they are less dramatic, such as relief from stomach pain.[108]

Opportunities

EHC does the greatest good and the greatest work where there are no existing Christian churches. Vast areas of Karnataka are virtually unreached..

The number and size of Christ Groups

Christ Groups from their inception in 1968 to 1996 have grown in number and size. On the national leve,l Christ Groups number vary between 10,000 [109] to 15,000.[110] This huge variation in numbers is due to improper maintenance of records or the difference in number may represent the Christ Groups of other nations, though it is not clear which numbers are correct.

The sizes of the groups vary from 10 to 300 people. According to Lee three, [111] but for Prasad ten,[112] is the smallest number to form a group, but the largest for Lee is 5 [113] and for Prasad is 300.[114] Some of the Christ Groups have grown into churches. As discussed earlier in the chapter, Lee's method was to divide a Christ Group if it grows to more than five.[115] This encouraged a large number of groups, which reflected WLC's interest in

---

[106] Ibid.

[107] D'Souza, Oliver, 2003, public address organised by the All India Christian Council, before prominent leaders of the social strata and pastors, including retired high court justice, Mr. Balakrishna

[108] Ibid.

[109] Statistical Data, 1998, A Status Report of Every Home Christ International

[110] Statistical Data, 1995, A Status Report of Every Home Christ International

[111] Ibid.

[112] Prasad, B.A.G., 1999, *Prayer Bulletin*, November, 17

[113] Ibid.

[114] Ibid. 17

[115] Ibid.

numbers.[116] Lee's method was not strictly followed in the Indian context, instead groups grew to large sizes. As Prasad, speaking on the number of people in Christ Groups wrote: 'Normally CGs consist of 10-20-30 or more believers. However, in some places there are Christ Groups with 100 to 300 members'.[117] This can be attributed to the relational context where people, families and community want to live and grow together. Christ Groups in the rural parts of India were effective, when, at that time, many Indian mainline churches were struggling to grow numerically.

Speaking about the period, McGavran commented that established churches were 'not finding new converts'[118] Rev. H.M. Duke, a former Auxiliary Secretary of the Bible Society of India, emphatically stated 'that this fruitlessness of the established churches can be attributed to their failure to carry out the main task of evangelism on which they were built. Instead they engaged totally in social action'[119] and were inward looking. This may be true with some of the Churches of South India and other churches as well but not in Karnataka.

The Impact of Christ Groups on other missions

The impact of this phenomenon was noted and emulated by other mission agencies: Revival Literature Fellowship, Navajeevan Ministries, Tribal Transformation-India, and Marthoma Evangelical Churches. In 1998, there were 1000 Christ Groups formed by IEHC and other mission agencies in Karnataka State.

The Emergence of Christ Groups and their effect in other countries

The emergence of Christ Groups, according to Lee said was an accident, or in the words of Prasad, something they (WLC and IEHC) stumbled upon.

The beginnings of the Christ Groups in the 1960s were limited to a few places but in later years, especially in the 1990s, their growth spread into several States of India and outside India. Christ Groups spread in India as a limited phenomenon.[120] Then the phenomenon also became evident in other countries like: Nepal, Indonesia, Africa, the South Pacific, and the former Soviet Union.[121] The spread of Christ Groups did not happen simultaneously in all these countries. Starting from the first Christ Group in 1968 in Karnataka,[122] the Christ Groups' concept spread over time and developed in other places. In India out of 600,000 villages, Christ Groups

---

[116] Ibid. 5
[117] Ibid. 17
[118] Ibid.
[119] Ibid. 65
[120] Ibid. 120
[121] Ibid. 232
[122] Ibid. 122

were found in less than 20,000 villages, that is about 3 percent of the total villages. It was significant, however, in comparison to the previous rural response, which for so long in the Indian mission field, before and after colonial rule, was not an area fully open to the gospel.[123]

In Karnataka State, before Christ Groups were formed, from the time the Gospel entered the shores of Karnataka in early 19th century about 200 villages had some Christian witness, out of its 30,000 villages.[124] With the formation of Christ Groups in Karnataka in the year 1995, it was estimated that it had over 1000 such groups in as many villages.[125] Christianity from its beginning in India was mostly found in the cities and was seen as an Urban and Western religion.

However, Christ Groups formation in the Indian states like Karnataka, Rajasthan, Orissa, Gujarat and Uttar Pradesh was significant in the post-colonial era, where in the past Christian activities were severely opposed. These states were once considered as barren lands for the gospel work by missionaries. A Basel missionary speaking on the Karnataka field commented, 'It is a hard ground, with a proud people and opposes the gospel'.[126] This situation was true even after the independence of India.[127]

In this latter period, Christ Groups' formation and their growth in numbers were significant considering the rural context and the previous fruitlessness of many established churches and mission enterprises. Christ Groups paved a new way into rural evangelism and church planting and became a significant phenomenon in the post-colonial era. Christ Groups also brought a fresh way of thinking to some missiologists and one suggested, 'The methods by which the Christ Groups are being formed could be emulated or perhaps easily improved".[128]

The study on the Christ Groups work in the rural parts of Karnataka has shown that the Christian message can make penetration into the rural populace, impact the society and establish that which was missing in the earlier mission approaches. The study has shown that when the Christian message is shared by their own countrymen or women, especially in an Indian way, it is more effective. Now I will explore some religious and societal factors to see how the past religious experiences enabled the Groups to continue in their new-found faith and to spread. The study has

---

[123] Ibid.
[124] Guruprasad, G., 1998, personal interview and a report on IEHC Karnataka, Bangalore, India
[125] Ibid.
[126] Wurth, 1920, *The Journals of Basel Missionaries of South Maratha*, 39
[127] Report, 1982, A Report On Karnataka, IEHC, Bangalore, India
[128] Ibid. 120

some similarities to the fulfilment theology advocated by J. N. Farquhar,[129] Ivan Satyavratha[130] and others, but I will try to locate some enabling and withstanding aspects of their past religious experiences in the new found faith.

Christ Groups and the Other Hindu Movements

Bhakti (Devotional) Movement

The Christ Groups concept reminded the villagers of the 'Bhakti' (Devotional) Movement' of the ninth century. Bhakti then became a widespread Hindu religious form. Bhakt Purandardas and Bhakat Kanakadas were notable from Karnataka State in the Bhakti movement. 'Bhakti Marg' (The Way of Devotion) to salvation was considered superior to other Brahaminical ways: 'Jnana Marga' (The Way of Knowledge) and 'Karma Marga'(The Way of Good and Ritual Works).

Rudolf Otto draws a close parallel between the Christian and Bhakti for those who lived in 'evil ways' then 'cast away all these things for the service of (God)'.[131] Bhakti produced revival sermons and songs, and the ideas of decision 'here and now', before it is 'too late'. Christ Groups brought back the memory of the Bhakti movement to the rural masses. This also suggests that whether Indians are literate or illiterate there is a deep desire in them to know of the 'Other' and spiritual matters. As D'Souza said, Indians are spiritual people.[132] If mission only emphaszses other needs, it is like a car driven without petrol. In principle, Bhakti opposed sacrifice and priesthood. Castes and sexes were treated equally to attain salvation through devotion. Devotees held their devotions in homes, fields or wherever it was possible. The place and time of pujas (traditional Hindu form of worship) became nonessentials in order to meet God in person or as a group through devotion.[133]

---

[129] Farquhar, J. N., 1913, *The Crown of Hinduism.* The key word in Farquhar's missionary theology was fulfillment. It is in thi ssense that Christ is the crown of Hinduism. Accessed on 15-06-09 www.diglib.bu.edu

[130] Sathyavratha, Ivan, 2001, God has not left Himself without Witness, Ph.D. thesis, University of Wales, UK

[131] Otto, Rudolf, Hogg, A.G., 1947, in A.G.Hogg, *The Christian Message To The Hindu,* 45 (66)

[132] D'Souza, Joseph, 2006, A Public Address on a T.V news channel, while expressing the feelings of the Christian community against the screening of the Da Vinci movie in India.

[133] *The Encyclopaedia of Religions,* 1987, Hinduism, Eliade, Mircea and Adam Charles (eds.)

Anubhav Mantap (Temple of Experience)

Christ Groups also bring to mind the twelfth century 'Anubhav Mantap' in Karnataka. 'Anubhava Mantap' is a discourse of disciples, which was encouraged in the early stages of Lingayatism. Lingayatism was founded by Basavanna in reaction to the Brahminical order and gave common people a closer look at God, which was absent in the Brahminical hierarchy.[134] 'Lingayatism' encouraged discipleship among its followers, who met in a specific place for worship and fellowship. Such a place was called an 'Anubhava Mantap (Temple of Experience), where devotees shared their experiences with other fellow devotees to enrich their devotion to God. In a similar way, the members of Christ Groups regularly met in a certain place to worship and to pray and shared their experiences with each other. These religious groups had a significant effect on Hinduism for a time, but, slowly all these were assimilated into Hinduism which maintained temple worship and kept caste and sex discrimination.

The Nudi Movement

'Nudi' means 'word' or 'the prophetic word', Kalagnana means the knowledge of the future and Kodaikal is a name of a Lingayat mutt (shrine). The origins of these movements are not certain. It is surprising to see that the movement survived until the arrival of missionaries in the 18th and 19th centuries. In the late nineteenth and the beginning of the twentieth century, a large number of followers of 'Nudi and Kalagnana Movements' (The Movement of Prophetical Word) of Lingayatism came to missionaries to become Christians.

According to N.C. Sargent, 'One hundred years ago the Kalagnana and Nudi movement gave to the Basel Mission in Dharwar district a small harvest of converts'.[135] Writing further on the Kodaikal movements he states 'the Kodekallu Vachana movement also gave to the LMS missionaries in the Bellary district from 1891-99 a small group of converts'. Kodekallu is a Lingayat mutt (shrine) of Raichur district. These followers had sought fulfilment in Christ which accorded with their Hindu teaching. One of the disciples of the movement, Kodaikal Basavanna, foretold, 'In the East, in a Carpenter's house, a Saviour of the World will be born'.[136] Sargent also confirmed that these movements saw the fulfilment of their prophecies in the coming of Christ. The Vachanas were verses containing certain prophecies that were fulfilled in the preaching of

---

[134] Ibid.

[135] Sargent, N.C., 1969, *The History of the Christian Church in Mysore State*, The Karnataka Christian Council, A Souvenir of its Silver Jubilee, 1944-1969, and the Pastors' Conference, 35, Bangalore, op.cit., Basel Mission Magazine, 1841, 284, This was earlier published in the Bulletin of Church History Association of India, May 1962

[136] Ramalinga, 1987, '*Nitivantan Bhikar Kole*' (Murder of an Innocent)

Christianity.[137] However, a large number of disciples of these movements were rejected as Christian converts. Missionaries, in an attempt to develop western and 'pure' Christianity, did not accept the way the followers of Nudi, Kalgnana and Kodaikal understood Christ and so did not accept them as Christians.[138]

Though these movements slowly faded, their teaching was widely prevalent among the villagers. TheChrist Groups concept brought back the memory of the Bhakti, Anubhava Mantap, Nudi, Kalagnana and Kodaikal movements to the rural folk. Christ Groups like the Bhakti movement followers met in no fixed place; worship services took place on any day or time of the week without any discrimination of sexes.[139] Prayer, worship and service were open to all the members. Members shared their experiences of the Lord with others[140] to encourage them to follow the way of the Lord and share their Christian experiences with their family members and others. The Christ Groups' main emphasis was on devotion to Christ rather than to Christianity and the Church.[141] Legality and rigidity of religion are absent in Christ Groups.[142] Christ Groups provided equal opportunity for all to worship Christ and Christ was seen in a more Indian way.

Christ Groups and Social Change: Social and Economic Equality

India, after its independence, introduced Five Year Plans to achieve national growth in agriculture and industry.[143] Social means like untouchability were banned.[144] Equal status was granted to women, including equal rights of inheritance with males.[145] Widow and inter-caste marriage was encouraged.[146]. Christ Groups, at this period, created a common platform for people, who were seeking some form of social change in society for the common good. Christ Groups may have provided unity in society when religious tensions were present, and when the country was looking for some form of unity among all castes.

---

[137] Ibid.
[138] Ibid.
[139] Ibid.
[140] Ibid.
[141] Ibid.
[142] Ibid.
[143] Wolpert. Stanley A., 1993, *A New History of India*
[144] Ibid.
[145] Ibid.
[146] Ibid.

Caste Equality

The Indian Constitution ensures equality of all caste groups. The Indian Government advocates secularism and affirms the protection of the rights of all caste groups. Most of the Christ Groups in Karnataka in some form overcame caste differences. During 'Christ Groups Festivals' all the caste groups sit together to eat their food, which is a very rare scene among all caste groups. 'Christ Groups Festivals' are held once a year, when the members of different Christ Groups of one particular *taluka* (region) are invited to come together for a day's meeting, when a meal is provided for the participants.[147]

Literacy

The Government has taken steps to increase literacy in Karnataka, but it takes a long time for the benefits to 'trickle down' to the most disadvantaged. Some IEHC field staff try to teach their new believers who are illiterates. Some workers try to help their new believers at least to memorize the verses from the Bible. Now IEHC has more literacy classes for all different kinds of people and groups without openly referring to Christian contacts.

Christ Groups and the Relational Context

The relational context demands a relational approach. People in India, especially villagers, respond more positively to it. On the relational context and the spread of Christianity, R. D. Paul wrote:

> It is remarkable that from the very beginning of the movement in favour of Christianity in this part of the Telugu country, the work of evangelization was carried on by the infant native Church itself, commencing with the one individual and then extending, by natural and inevitable growth, like that of a living tree. There was no organized plan. The people followed their own impulses... The quiet conversation when visiting friends and relations... produced fruit in fresh accessions to Christianity.[148]

Lesslie Newbigin writing on the relational context mentioned:

> I have seen the Gospel spreading from village to village without any kind of organization and finance, which we have been accustomed to think of when we think of a missionary approach to a new area... this kind of spontaneous communication of the Gospel from village to village by those who have believed, and upon whom, from the very moment of baptism, the full responsibility has

---

[147] Ibid.

[148] Paul R. D., 1967, *Triumphs of His Grace*, CLS, n 113, in *Asian Christian Thinking, Evangelism*, 107

been placed for the spiritual nurture and care of the new congregation. I have seen illiterate coolies taking the lead in this work....[149]

Christ Groups were formed in villages where its members lived among their own people. It gave them a common goal. It did not detach them from their own contexts and cultures. Rather it helped the members to share their experiences with their own friends and families. The word of mouth sharing is effective in the relational context where people can notice a real change in their lives rather than only the words they speak. Pushpamma's story suggests that through her most of her family members became members of a Christ Group. This suggests that people in a relational context want to hear the message through experiences of their own people. The message in this relational context needed to be presented differently from the western rationalistic and individualistic approach.

Christ-Groups and the Traditional Churches
(Differences and Similarities)

The equivalent word to 'Christ Group' in Kannada language is 'Christa Balaga'. The Kannada language is the official language of the Karnataka State. The word 'Christa' is 'Christ', and 'Balaga' means 'relatives' or 'clan' or 'family circle'. The word 'Christa Balaga' appeals to the people and gives them the feeling of the family.[150] The word 'church', which traditional churches use, gives a western connotation and something to do with 'foreignness'.

The formation of a Christ Group was spontaneous, but a traditional church was formed with the intention of becominganother church within a denomination. Christ Groups formed primarily to help the converts of EHC coming from other faiths rather than minister to the Christian community of existing churches. Christ Groups were formed where there were no churches but traditional churches were formed to cater for the needs of their congregation.[151]

Though worship and prayer in Christ Groups is led by the evangelist, other leaders, including women, equally take part in the leadership.[152] However, traditional churches are led by ordained persons and a hierarchical order is maintained in leading worship and prayer.[153] Christ

---

[149] Hargreaves, A.C.M., 1979, ed., *Report of the Conference of British Missionary Societies*, 107, by Lesslie Newbigin, 1958, 9
[150] Vasudev Rao, H.R., 1998, personal interview, a field coordinator of IEHC, Bangalore, India
[151] Ibid.
[152] Ibid.
[153] Murphy, Soans, 1998, personal interview, an ordained pastor of Church of South India, Bijapur

Groups are not fully dependent on the evangelist alone because of multiple leaders in the group whereas traditional churches are fully dependent on the clergy. Christ Groups promote a free style of worship and prayer but traditional churches follow the order of worship and prayer. Traditional churches are fully organized bodies but Christ Groups are loosely organized bodies. Their continuity fully depends on the faithfulness and commitment of their members. Christ Groups regularly practice baptism and communion, the same as traditional churches.[154] Traditional churches had their own western theology to govern them. Christ Groups' theology was developed in the context.[155] Western theology was imposed upon its congregation but the theology of Christ Groups was made in the context. Western theology demonised all the local cultures[156] but Christ Groups' theology respected all the local cultures without denying the Lordship of Christ. Western theology tried to see its converts in a western way.[157] Christ Groups theology allows its converts to maintain their identity. Western theology displaced and disassociated its converts from their context and community. Christ Group theology did not threaten their converts' community and sense of belonging.

Western missionaries kept their converts in mission compounds. They detached their converts from their context and place, provided some material help and made efforts to nurture them. The converts in mission compounds were excluded and grew in an alien culture. Rather than becoming a help to the furtherance of the gospel, they became a hindrance to it.[158] Christ Groups, on the other hand, nurture their converts in their own context and place and never detach them from their own settings. Christ Groups' main activity is to help the converts to grow in their faith in Christ with no material help attached to it.[159] Material help is received in the form of divine healing and blessings and deliverance from demon possession. The liturgy and traditional hymns are completely absent in Christ Groups. Popular vernacular spiritual songs are sung and, in the place of liturgy, the Christ Groups' members offer prayers and praises and share their testimonies or blessings received.[160] No restrictions deter Christ Groups' members to conduct their marriages, engagements or funerasl in a Christian way.[161]

---

[154] Ibid.
[155] Ibid.
[156] Ibid. 2
[157] Ibid. 15
[158] Ibid.
[159] Ibid.
[160] Jairaj, P., 1998, personal interview, pastor of Hosadurga Christ Groups, Hosadurga India
[161] Ibid.

Over and against western based traditional churches, Christ Groups which are born in the soil would pass the test of time in regard to their Indian-ness. Christ Groups in being Indian find it possible to maintain their distinct character as Christians, while accommodating some form of Indian culture and context. Christ Groups that have based their faith and commitment upon the teaching of the New Testament will have to prove from experience when faced with challenges and accusations from some evangelical bodies of accommodation and syncretism of other cultures. To establish and continue as a true Indian church, Christ Groups should produce their own theology, which both honours the good in their own culture and context while keeping 'Christ' as Lord and God over them.

Christ Groups and Church Growth, Mass, House Church Movements

This study briefly will look into the two main differences between these movements.

Theology

Both movements claim that their movements are based on New Testament theology. Christ Groups' emphasis is on the personal experience of Jesus Christ, a criterion by which to become a member of the group, though enquirers and interested people are allowed to attend the meeting.[162] Church Growth's emphasis will be on all those who come to the meeting, with or without any personal commitment to Jesus Christ, and who are welcome to become members of the church. The same can be said about the baptism and Holy Communion. They are not strictly observed or else are completely absent from the worship in the Church Growth Movement.[163] Christ Groups stress that the both are important ordinances to obey and observe as His disciples,[164] but Church Growth does not emphasize either.[165] This shows Church Growth has a broader view on the church, but Christ Groups follow some form of conservative evangelicalism.

Multi-geneous groups against homogeneous groups

Christ Groups encourage all caste backgrounds to come together for the meeting. The field survey shows that out of 200 Christ Groups, only four were homogeneous units, and all the other units were multi-geneous. Multi-geneous groups have shown better growth than the homogeneous groups. In the Indian context. multi-geneous groups seem to be a better option to unite the country without promoting any sectarianism and ethnicism. For a long

---

[162] Ibid.

[163] McGavran, Donald, Anderson, 1980, *Understanding Church Growth*, 8

[164] Ibid.

[165] Ibid.

time. the Indian population has suffered tensions between high and low, powerful and the oppressed. For 5000 years or so, the oppressed caste experienced human degradation by the dominant and influential high caste people.

McGavran developed his homogenous group method to plant churches while studying the Mass movement on how particular people groups and communities became Christians, and how churches were planted. The mass movement, as briefly mentioned below, has its own historical context on why and how people became Christians, but today the Indian context is entirely changed, where a large portion of people groups and communities of all castes are showing interest in Christianity or have become Christians. Is it appropriate for Christian missions and agencies to create divisions and build tensions among such worshipping communities of castes and sub-castes? Or will we try to build bridges while breaking the old barriers, which kept these communities apart, and create a brand new situation for these worshipping communities to sense and feel what Christian fellowship really means, where everyone is equally treated and will have open access to 'worship God in Spirit and truth' (Jn 4.24).

Christ Groups Movement and the Mass Movement

For a better understanding of these two movements, I will briefly attempt to draw out the major differences between them. About the 'Mass Movement' as Kabis asserted: 'the first instance not a spiritual one...' and furthermore, 'it is their distress...which led them chiefly to us'[166] Some wanted 'a well and land',[167] some for 'immediate causes'[168] some bargained as if they were 'redeemed for their debts'.[169] For Loffters, the Mass Movement was seen as means where, 'the outcastes...who were socially and culturally excluded from...Hindu society, could better their situation and cultural valuation by turning to Western Christianity'.[170] For Jayakumar, it was for their 'social mobility'[171] that the oppressed class embraced Christianity.

Some may say that these are 'rice and rupee Christians'[172] and that this was an 'evil inducement to help people to become Christians'.[173] However, G. Isaac, an Indian pastor, puts it that 'material help is a channel to deliver people from their sufferings and encourage them to embrace

---

[166] Houghton, Graham, 1983, op.cit, Kabis, Q110, 114, *The Impoverishment of Dependency*, 114
[167] Ibid. Q111
[168] Ibid. Q112
[169] Ibid. Q113
[170] Lofters, 1999, 684
[171] Ibid. 15
[172] Ibid. Q14, 186
[173] Ibid. Q118, 115

Christianity'.[174] Jayakumar stated that Christianity gave them self-worth and dignity in Christ.[175] Rajshekar, a Dalit leader, counted on the deliverance of the oppressed community from the shackles of Hindu bondage through conversion to other world religions, including Christianity, and remarked that as a result 'they breathed fresh air.'[176]

On the other hand, Christ Groups not only attracted the out-castes but other castes too.. As Hwa-Yung remarks, 'salvation of the person includes conversion, physical healing, blessing and peace'.[177] Moreover, there are Indians who always love and respect Christ and His teaching. This was true during the Mass Movement or Christ Groups movement. As McGavran asserted, 'in this era more men (women also) love Christ'[178] As someone remarked about Christ's teaching and life, 'many had the greatest respect, some respected his superior doctrines and 'some were ardent, seeing in the character of Christ, portrayed (sic), perhaps their highest ideal of human perfection'.[179]

As Kabis put it, 'Christianity means conversion and believing in Christ'.[180] Christ Groups created space without attaching any sort of gift of material or physical benefit. During the Mass Movement, people fully depended on missionaries for their material and spiritual help. Even today, in many churches that were founded by missionaries, congregations cannot even lead their own prayers unless someone teaches or does it on behalf of them. Whereas Christ Groups are not fully dependent upon evangelists because members know how to worship and pray without any one's assistance or following some worship order.

Christ Groups and the House Church Movements

The book of Acts and the Pauline epistles show us how the first century Christians met in houses for worship and prayer. Kreider remarked that, 'in Rome the first congregations were literally house churches. Meeting in the largest rooms of their members who were rarely wealthy'[181] From the first century until Christianity became a State religion in the fourth century, people met in houses, open places and catacombs for worship and prayer.[182]

---

[174] Ibid.
[175] Ibid.
[176] Rajshekar Shetty, V.T., 1983 (1977), *Apartheid in India*
[177] Yung, Hwa, 2000, op.cit., Samuel Jayakumar (1999, 97), op.cit., Neil (1972, 68), Forrester (1980, 83f), Kingdom Identity and Christian Mission, a lecture in OCMS, 31st August
[178] Ibid. 6
[179] Ibid. Q70, 133
[180] Ibid. Q121, 115
[181] Kreider, Alan, 1995, *Worship and Evangelism in Pre-Christendom*, 5
[182] For further reading see Transformation, Sep, 1986

From then onwards, Christians mostly met in huge Roman, Norman and Byzantine, decorated and ornamented churches and cathedrals.

In the twelfth century, the Waldensian group for a period met in houses. During the Reformation period, some splinter groups from Protestant churches like Wesleyan and Anabaptist churches met in houses, barns and open places. Though there is much written on the 'House Church Movement', was the Christ Groups phenomenon unique to India or to the work of Every Home Crusade?

My study shows that between 1960-1990, House Churches outside the established churches were developing in some parts of the world. The distinction here made about the house churches outside the churches, is to show that during the same period, house churches functioned within the established churches. The biggest church in the world introduced 'Home Cell Groups' to strengthen its members and attract new membership.[183] In Britain, the House Church movement began inside and outside the established churches.[184]

According to Walker, 'House Churches' are inappropriate labels, looking at their form, diversity and growth in England.[185] In the 1960s, South Chard and North Fellowships set the way for the house churches in Britain.[186] In the early 1970s, under the emergence of a 'Restoration Movement', house churches became a household name in Britain.[187] Restorationists go back to the Pentecost experience of the early church and assert that the 'House Church' origin is found in the book of Acts 2:42.[188] Neighbour argued, 'nor was there a separation between the secular and the sacred' suggesting that 'House Churches' had an equal place like Jewish synagogues.[189] In the USA, the 'Shepherding Movement' developed the house churches concept.[190] In China, the 'House Churches' concept spread.[191] Watchman Nee, under the influence of Brethren Missionaries in China, started house churches.[192]

Though Christ Groups and House Churches may have begun in the same era and may have some similarities, the nature of their formation has some distinct differences. House Churches formed in reaction to established

---

[183] Cho, Paul, Yongi, 1981, *Successful Home Cells Groups*, 51, 52
[184] Walker, Andrew, 1985, *Restoring the Kingdom*, 28
[185] Ibid. 26
[186] Ibid. 28
[187] Hewitt, Brian, 1995, *Doing a New Thing*, 200
[188] Ibid.
[189] Neighbour, Ralph W., 1990, *Where Do We Go From Here?* 112
[190] Ibid.
[191] Hunter, Alan and Kim-Kwong Chan, 1993, *Protestantism in Contemporary China*, 81-82
[192] Ibid. 52

churches and traditional Christianity.[193] They wanted to see an end to 'Clericalism, church order, standardized liturgies, denominational certainties and dogmatic doctrines'.[194] Their (House Churches) emphasis was on experience, relationships, freewheeling and no overt leadership.[195] However, absolute submission to spiritual authority was a similar or more overt leadership style in them. Even 'freewheeling' was not without its limitations. To some this seemed to be rigid, legalistic and heavy handed.[196] Christ Groups formed where there were no churches or easy access to churches. Christ Groups formed primarily to hand them over to the interested churches.[197] They did not see continuity in themselves. Rather, they sought to integrate with the interested churches for their continuity and stability.[198] It is not clear whether IEHC tried hard enough to hand over these groups to other churches[199] Christ Groups' emphasis was similar to the house churches' movement in, experience, relationships, freewheeling and team leadership. However, they had no absolute requirement of submission to spiritual authority. The authority was in the group, given to all. They were encouraged to show their obedience to Christ together.

House Church formation was intentional, purposeful and planned.[200] Christ Groups formation was accidental,[201] spontaneous and unplanned. The 'House Church' phenomenon took place amongst Christian communities,[202] whereas Christ Groups formed from people coming from other faiths. My field survey of Christ Groups shows that over 99 percent came from other faiths. Over the period, most of the House Churches have moved away from that stance. They have grown big to become fellowships or centres with the purpose of creating wealth, running worship, providing coffee and even a swimming pool for their disciples or adherents.[203] This indicates they may have a bright future.

Christ Groups may have to survive on their own if they are the true disciples of Jesus Christ. Their originator, WLC, has disowned them because unlike some of their (other American mission enterprises) countrymen they cannot raise funds out of them, but rather they (Christ Groups) need huge funding to run them. Their own IEHC leaders have rather submissively let Christ Groups go and find their own destiny for

---

[193] Ibid. 30
[194] Ibid. 58
[195] Ibid.
[196] Ibid. 111
[197] Wickman, Charles, 2000, Christ Groups an Option for Adoption, 1
[198] Ibid.
[199] Ibid.
[200] Ibid.
[201] Ibid. Questionnaire 13
[202] Ibid. 56
[203] Ibid. 266

survival. Already, some Christ Groups have disintegrated but it appears that scores of others by the grace of God, and in the power of the Holy Spirit and on their strong will to survive, are continuing for the glory of God. Christ Groups will have, if not a glittering, certainly a shining future.

Christ Groups and the Indian Leaders

Some matters related to this aspect have been already discussed in Chapter four. Here I will briefly discuss the perception of the Indian leadership towards the Christ Groups and their vision. Was their perception fulfilled and what are their future plans for Christ Groups? Prasad, without any hesitation, admitted that Christ Groups were not in their original plan but they stumbled into them.[204]

IEHC openly argued that CGs were not formed due to reading the printed page, but through the earnest efforts of field evangelists.[205] Prasad illustrating this dilemma narrates an example of a fisherman and says, 'his heart is more on the fish than the net'.[206] He further explains, 'we were caught up with the rush of reaching last home…forgot…the ultimate goal…which is the saving of souls and adding to the church'.[207] Robert Louis and J. J. Oliver expressed the same opinion about the tract distribution.[208] B. A. Prabhakar mentioned the 'Koinonia' principles to other Indian directors, which Jack McAllister had discussed with him.[209] This suggests that the reports about the formation of small groups in Karnataka and other places were given some food for thought to McAllister and the Indian leaders. Prasad was happy to take on board the work of Christ Groups and he was able to foresee that CGs would become fully-fledged independent churches and aimed to plant 200,000 Christ Groups.[210] George speaking on CGs wrote, 'now entering the promised land'.[211]

Though the funding was not great, the interest and enthusiasm of the Indian leaders about CGs did not diminish. To keep up the Christ Groups' momentum, for the first time in the history of IEHC, they partnered with World Vision to run their programmes.[212] From the very start of the ministry, IEHC was totally sceptical about engaging in social aspects of ministry because of its evangelical convictions that were of the time. The funding was meant to help the CG members develop their skills and learn

---

[204] Prasad, B.A.G., 1991, *Prayer Bulletin*, December, 24.
[205] Prasad, B.A.G., 1999, *Prayer Bulletin*, November, 17
[206] Ibid. 14
[207] Ibid.
[208] Ibid.
[209] Ibid.
[210] Ibid.
[211] George, C., 1985, *Christ Groups* 28.
[212] Ibid. 26

to earn more money. However,the support which came from World Vision was to meet the general need of the people rather than just CG members. It was a time limited project and it took care of one or two villages. The impact of using such help on CGs was minimal.

Indian leaders found it difficult when WLC discussed with them and instructed saying, '...let the Christ Groups choose their own destiny...' and gave them three years do that.[213] This directive unsettled the minds of Indian leaders over the future of CGs. Robert Louis strongly reacting to this directive on 'three years' says, '...we have to approach this statement very cautiously...(in given) time span...Christ Groups workers...should be certain that when they leave the place, the group...can survive and grow....' Jesus said, '...you travel about on sea and land and make one proselyte; and when he becomes one, you make him twice as much a son of hell' (Mt:23:15). 'We do not want this to happen to us and our ministry'.[214]

This directive came rather surprisingly from Lee. He expressed the real inner feelings of WLC leaders about Christ Groups. By this time, Lee had perceived his days were numbered too. He was preparing the minds of Indian leaders on the future destiny of the Christ Groups. Until Prasad's death in 1994, the future destiny of Christ Groups was in his hands. After his death, though the leaders, as discussed earlier in the chapter and in Chapter four, tried to continue with that vision for some time, until the leaders of WLC made the Indian leaders listen to them rather than wanting to run the ministry in their own way. Now the Indian leaders became spectators rather than the leaders of Christ Groups, in order to find some safe basis for their own continuity and connectivity with WLC.

---

[213] George, C., 1983, *Christ Groups*, 18

[214] Louis, Robert, 1976, a Report on Karnataka, December, IEHC, Bangalore, India (was the director for IEHC, Karnataka and the treasurer for IEHC-India, a senior member of IEHC)

Chapter 6
Field Survey Section A: Methodology of the Research

Introduction, Methodology, Hypotheses and Research Method

After a historical overview of Christ Groups I turn to the field survey and a detailed case study.This chapter is divided into two sections, Section 'A' is the 'Field Survey' and Section 'B' a case study. First, I describe the use of methodology and relevant issues, related to the selection of two statistical approaches, the qualitative method and the quantitative method. The techniques used in data collection are a structured questionnaire, open and structured interviews, and observation.

The study, therefore, examines the growth[1] of Christ Groups in a relational context, based on research undertaken in India, with particular focus on the State of Karnataka, using two main research tools: field research and analysis of the data. The field research was to gather quantitative data to test various hypotheses, and the data were then analysed by the use of statistical techniques. The data were collected both by a structured questionnaire and orally in an open-ended checklist. These methods included five types of questions: characteristics of the respondents, their introduction to Christ Groups, their perception of Christ Groups and their participation in and for the Christ Groups. The data included these variables.

The research has not solely used a quantitative approach because of limitations to the quantitative survey method in developing countries, especially where literacy is not high and people in rural areas find it difficult to follow questionnaires. As Weller argued, those who are moderately educated can follow questionnaire samples but it will be better if they are simplified as much as possible in the oral interview.[2] Many of the rural respondents can be classed in this category so questions were repeated and explained.

---

[1] 'Growth' here means what was it that helped Christ Group to continue in spite of hurdles it faced.... but those elements are taken to see how they affected or contributed towards their continuity

[2] Weller,S., 1998, *Structured Interviewing and Questionnaire Construction*, in B. H. Russell Handbook of Methods in Culture Anthropolog,y 363-407

Though there may be some limitation to quantitative research in developing countries like in India, yet it was necessary to use this approach to collect data in a practical way. This was the first time this kind of approach was used in these four Christ Groups. The research results arising from the questionnaires give an initial understanding of the phenomenon of the Christ Groups in Karnataka. The qualitative method with its open-ended questions[3] helped further to identify and clarify the questions used in the questionnaires. This means of using two approaches served the objectives of this research and were appropriate for rural India. It will be hard to separate out the two methods, that is, quantitative and qualitative methods, as exclusive to each other. Though two methods are used to get adequate results, the research can be seen primarily as qualitative in nature because of the limited resources which made it necessary from the outset to choose a small number of four Christ Groups for the case study. A random survey fully representing a larger number of CGs would have needed more time and money.

Combined Methodology

As Weinreich[4] remarked, 'In an ideal social marketing program, researchers use both quantitative and qualitative data to provide a more complete picture of the issue being addressed, the target audience and the effectiveness of the program itself'. He further emphasizes that each approach has positive attributes, and that combining different methods can result in gaining the best of both worlds. Holman[5] writing on the use of two approaches in research concluded, 'good ... research recognises the complementarities and interpretations of quantitative and qualitative methods of inquiry'. Furthermore, on the use of a combined methodology, as CDS (2002) observed that the quantitative approach may help to identify 'what', 'where', and 'whom',[6] while the qualitative approach may help to explain 'why' and 'how'. In addition, the quantitative approach may provide 'breadth' and the qualitative may offer 'depth'. As remarked by Bouma and Atkinson[7] 'the quantitative method focuses on measurement by applying statistical procedures whereas the qualitative is primarily

---

[3] Ann L. Casebeer and Marja J. Verhoef, Department of Community Health Sciences, Faculty of Medicine, University of Calgary, Calgary, Alberta, http://www.phc-aspc.gc.ca/publicat/cdic-mcc/18-3/c_e.html, accessed on 2006-11-07
[4] Weinreich, Nedra Kline, accessed on 2006-11-07, Integrating Quantitative and qualitative Methods in Social Marketing Research, 1996-2003, Weinreich Communications / webmaster@social-marketing.com
[5] Holman H.R., Qualitative inquiry in medical research *Journal of Clin. Epidemiol.*, 1993:46(1):29-36, op.cit., in Ann L. Casebeer and Marja J. Verhoef, Department of Community Health Science, University of Calgary, Calgary
[6] This was accessed on 21:12, 6 November 2006
[7] Bouma, G.D., & Atkinson, G.B. 1995, *A Handbook of Social Science Research*, 206

concerned with non-quantifiable aspects of peoples lives, their stories, and behaviour and can also investigate structures, relationships and movements in society'.

There is a continued debate to assess how far each approach is reliable. Bryman,[8] while contrasting the features of the two methodologies in *Quantity and Quality in Social Research*, stated that the qualitative researchers may assume that the quantitative research will produce superficial data. They view the survey research as a source of information, which will relate to the social scientist's abstract categories. It can be counter-argued in Liebow's words (1967) that the quantitative researcher will be suspicious of the limited generality of a study of two dozen men in one area of one city of which the data collected may have been heavily influenced by the researcher's specific emphases and predispositions.

To show the strengths and weaknesses of these two methods, Carvalho and White [9] in their paper '*Combining Quantitative and Qualitative Approaches to Poverty Measurement and Analysis*' discussed the following:

Table 6A.1 Strengths and Weaknesses of Quantitative and Qualitative Methods

	Strengths	Weaknesses
Quantitative	*Makes aggregation possible *Provides results whose reliability is measurable. *Allows simulation of different policy options.	*Sampling and non-sampling errors *Misses what is not easily quantifiable. *Fails to capture intra-household issues.
Qualitative	*Richer definition of poverty *More insight into causal processes *More accuracy and depth of information on certain questions.	*Lack of generalisability *Difficulties in verifying information

Haralmbos, Michael and Holgorn argue that the case studies need not depend only upon a qualitative method. They stress that the differences between the quantitative and qualitative methods is not as wide as alleged, but rather at times it seems to be overstated.[10] Cook (1984) and Haralmbos

---

[8] Bryman, A C., 1999, *Quantitative Data Analysis*
[9] Carvalho, S., & White, H., 1997, Combining the Quantitative and Qualitative Approaches to Poverty Measurement and Analysis: The Practice and The Potential (World Bank Technical Paper no 366) Washington D. C., www.worldbank.org
[10] Haralambos, Michael, R.M. Heald, Martin Holborn, 1995, *Sociology: Themes and Perspectives*, 856

and Holborn[11] advocated that both approaches are combined in a single study. Weinreich[12] remarked that social marketing researchers recognised that each approach has positive attributes and that combining different methods can result in gaining the best of both research worlds. Aron and Aron (2002:35) observed that those who lean on the qualitative approach prefer the combined method for better results. 'Important categories through quantitative approach...then determine their incidence in the larger population through quantitative methods'.[13] Then the aim of qualitative approach as raised by Bouma and Atkinson[14] is that it is not to prove a hypothesis but to show that the hypothesis is seemingly reasonable.

There are a greater number of research studies that assert the advantages of the fusion of the research approaches. Steckler et al. (1992) have suggested four possible models of integrating qualitative and quantitative approaches in research. In the first approach, qualitative methods contribute to the development of quantitative instruments, such as the use of focus groups in questionnaire construction. The second model consists of a primarily quantitative study that uses qualitative results to help interpret or explain the quantitative findings. In the third approach, quantitative results help interpret predominantly qualitative findings, as when focus group participants are asked to fill out survey questionnaires at the session. In the fourth model, the two methodologies are used equally and in parallel to cross-validate and build upon each other's results.

Further, Bryman[15] suggested that the data generated from both methods may be used, firstly, to test the accuracy of the conclusions reached on the basis of each to provide 'a more complete picture of the subject being studied or produced'. Secondly, qualitative data may be used to generate hypotheses, which may then be tested using the quantitative method to 'illuminate why certain variables are statistically correlated'.

Rossman and Wilson[16] suggested three general reasons: One is to enable confirmation or corroboration of mutuality via 'triangulation'; secondly, to elaborate or develop analysis, providing greater detail, and thirdly, to initiate new lines of thinking through attention to surprises or paradoxes, providing new insights.

Ravallion[17] pointed out in his paper, *'Can Qualitative Methods Help Quantitative Poverty Measurement?'* that there are two ways of mixing in

---

[11] Ibid.

[12] Ibid.

[13] Ibid.

[14] Ibid. 213

[15] Ibid. 127-56

[16] Rossman, G.B., & Wilson, B.L, 1984, Number and Words, Combining Quantitative and Qualitative Methods in a single large-scale evaluation study, *Evolution Review* , 9(5), 627-643

[17] Ravillion, Martin, 2001, 'Shaohua Chen', a file, World Bank, 40

'qual' and 'quan' approaches, that is, 'sequential and simultaneous'. Remarking on 'sequential', he suggested that it entails integrating methods sequentially for largely independent samples but within one well-defined context.[18] It means using open-ended questions asked in unstructured surveys of non-random samples as a preliminary step in formulating questions to be addressed by a structured sample survey. In a similar way, the 'simultaneous' method utilizes the traditional sorts of questions asked in the existing sample survey data drawing on the more subjective questions and participatory approaches. Casebeer and Verhoef[19] remind us that any study design, or combination of research methods selected for use, should be responsive to the particular research problem or question. Though Ravallion says 'that there are advantages in combining 'Qual' and 'Quan' approaches, he warns of its downside that its integration with Quan studies will influence constraints on all this by dictating where the work is done, what topics are covered and how questions are asked, while pilot Qual studies, in which the agenda is left more open, might help to decide some of these issues'.[20]

However, whether ignoring or defending a particular research approach, it will be possible and more instructive to see qualitative and quantitative methods as part of a continuum of research techniques, the end mix depending on the research objective. Shaffir and Stebbins, [21] for instance, have modelled this continuum in a way that challenges the notion that qualitative methods are solely exploratory and inductive, while quantitative methods are only explanatory and deductive. Guba and Lincoln offered this comment: both qualitative and quantitative methods may be used appropriately with any research paradigm.[22]

With such growing acceptance of a combined approach, the two traditions can be used together, instead of arguing for one or the other with appropriate purpose and procedure. Corner[23] suggested that the use of different research methods within a single study can provide a richer and deeper understanding of the area under investigation than would otherwise be possible. As Bouma and Atkinson[24] observed, the selection of subject

---

[18] Ibid.
[19] Veerhoef, M.J., Casebeer, A.L., & Hilsden, R.J. 2002, Assessing Efficacy of Complimentary Medicine, Adding Qualitative Research Methods to the 'Gold Standards', *Journal of Alternative Medicine*
[20] Ibid. 41
[21] Shaffir W.B., Stebbins R.A., editors, 1991, *Experiencing Fieldwork: An Insider's View Of Qualitative Research*
[22] Guba, E.G. and Lincoln, Y.S., 1989, *Fourth Generation Evaluation*
[23] Corner, J., 1991, In search of more complex answers to research questions: qualitative versus quantitative research methods: is there a way forward? *Journal Adv. Nurs.,* 16,718-27
[24] Ibid. 208

may decide the approach; there may be subjects who are appropriate for quantitative investigation and in others, the qualitative method.

Quantitative Method: Descriptive Survey

The use of quantitative method was not limited to the precise use of the statistical techniques as per the rules as such, but to provide indispensable information in the analysis of the Christ Groups and understanding of its members in relation to change factors. The study starts with two hypotheses, focused on the respondents' introduction to Christ or Christ Groups and their perception of, or participation in the Christ Groups. The chapter contains the following: the method of measurement used in the survey, hypotheses, research method, data collection method, data selection and tabulation method, data analysis method and demographic data in the sample.

Measurement of Institutional-heads and
Individual Dimensions of Change Development Factors

In order to assess the institutional-heads and the Christ Groups members' attitudes towards Christ or Christ Groups and perception of and participation in the Christ Groups it will be necessary to find out who, how and what are the factors involved in leading to those changes. Religious change has been seen differently by different theorists. For contemporary sociologists, religion is a system of beliefs and pattern of behaviour,[25] for anthropologists, religion in some sense seen as reasonable to follow its beliefs and practices.[26] For Karl Marx, religion was the 'opiate of the people', which upholds the ideologies and cultural systems that foster oppressive capitalism.[27] For Emile Durkheim, religion was a social cohesion factor.[28] After World War II, many classical theorists and sociologists claimed a decline in religiosity, but religion has continued to play an important role in the lives of individuals, families, as well as in communities and societies worldwide. In the US, for the past 40 years, church attendance has remained the same. In Africa, South America and in some parts of Asia, for example in South Korea, Christianity is the fastest growing religion. At the beginning of 1900, Christianity in Africa was roughly estimated 10 million Christians, but at present the number is estimated at over 360 million.[29] This suggests that the presupposition of

---

[25] Geertz, Clifford, 1999, A Life of Learning, 'Thick Description', Lecture Charles Homer Haskins, USA

[26] Ibid.

[27] Weber, M., 1904, *The Protestant Ethic and the Spirit of Capitalism* (2nd ed), 126, 127

[28] Durkheim, Emil, 1912 (1915), *The Elementary Forms of the Religion Life*, translated by Joseph Ward Swain

[29] Jenkins, Philip, 2006, *The New Faces of Christianity*, 9

secularization is a myth that depends upon its definition and the definition of its scope.[30]

India, after attaining independence in 1947, was leaning more towards the Communist ideology of Soviet Russia, because of its rejection of the capitalistic ideology of western countries. Many wondered what would be the effect of that on religion. Though it looked for a while that socialism may make a deep impression on the India's religious stance, with 'Ayodya Yatra' in 1992, and its aftermath India saw a greater religious awakening, starting with Hindu fundamentalists, which eventually spread to other religious groups, like, Muslims, Christians and others. As Joseph D'Souza of AICC (All India Christian Council) said, 'Indians are spiritual people'.[31] The Christ Groups movement, which was started much earlier than the above mentioned period, in 1978 (officially, unofficially in 1968), may help us to understand why the spiritual hunger of the rural populace of India was positive towards Christ and his message. Table 6.2 below shows the various labels that were used for analysis of the content items.

Table 6A.2 The Various Labels Measuring Members' Priorities, Involvement and Purpose in joining Christ Groups

Various Labels	Contents
Priorities to Join Christ Groups: What made you to follow Christ and join the Group?	Message, Miracles, Healing, Family, Friends, Worship, Nearness, Leadership, Social links, Love and Equality
Change Factors: To become a Christian do you need any outward change?	Name, Religion, Dress, & Family-Life Pattern
Church's Ordinances: How important for you to adhere to the ordinances of the church?	Baptism & Sacraments
Concept of Change: Whether the concept of God changed when you became a Christian?	God
Cultural Observances: What have you done with your past festivals?	Past Festivals
Social Bonds: Do you have to sever your previous social bonds when you become a Christian?	Ties with Relatives, Christening, Marriage, & Funeral
Personal Profile of the Members	Age, Gender, Education, Occupation, Civil status, Income, Caste

---

[30] Ibid.
[31] D'Souza, Joseph, 2006, public address came when Christians in India were protesting against screening of a controversial film 'Da Vince Code' in India. His interview was on 'Times Now', a news channel

Social Involvement: Do you partake in social change after you became a Christian?	Rural Problems, Helping the Poor, Attitude Towards Others
Personality Development: Does, the group provide you any opportunity to develop your personality?	Leadership, Evangelism

The focus of the study is to show how the western individualistic and market driven (mass evangelism) approach was received in the relational context and the reaction. The reaction of these persons in the context was in the formation of Christ Groups and their functioning. (Section B, illustrates both aspects of Christ Groups and their continuity).

The study starts with three hypotheses, focused on the respondents' introduction to Christ or Christ Groups and their perception of, or participation in the Christ Groups. The chapter contains the following: hypotheses and research method, data collection method, data selection and tabulation method, and data analysis method.

Hypotheses and Research Method

Perception of members

Central to the thesis is those queries about whether there is a difference in the perception of the members about themselves or the Group from the originators of the Groups. As Weber[32] once stated referring to Calvinism, the ethic adopted by ordinary members of the church in their day to day lives will differ from the values propounded by theologians. Though this may seem right in the lives of regular church goers, the members of Christ Groups are beginners in every sense; they may not have come directly under such outside influence, only their own and immediate surroundings. The hypotheses to be tested here are: People when they were introduced to Christ or Christ Groups and the factors involved in this process will illustrate, why and how they responded to the Gospel in certain ways. What reactions do people have when they come into contact with a western individualistic driven approach? Will these people come under the influence of this western approach and respond accordingly or will the people respond to such an approach according to the context in which they live? Relevant questions are whether they have severed ties with their relatives, are they tolerant to others 'faith'; what have they done with their past festivals? The members stated that their own personal experiences helped them handle those issues, when they first became Christians.

---

[32] Ibid.

Are cultural changes required for people to become Christians?

Christianity in India is seen as European Christianity. When people became Christians during colonial times, they took English or other European names, dressed like them and followed their liturgy and worship. Today, it is seen as an urban Christianity because it has settled in cities for employment, education, and the cosmopolitan atmosphere.That type of Christianity may still be prevalent in some traditional churches. However, the hypotheses to be tested here ris to whether people coming to Christ require a change in specific cultural ways in order that they may be called Christians. Such factors will be analysed to see to what extent they influenced people when they made a decision tobecome Christians.

The following analysis describes changes the members themselves desired rather than any changes imposed upon them by the 'outsiders'. It also indicates how the Christ Groups provided the space for members to find out the true meaning of Christianity in their own context and become followers of Christ.

Geographical Locations and Christian Response

The four Christ Groups selected for the field studies are located in four different parts of Karnataka: North (Bijapur), South-East (Bagepalli), South-West (Hosadurga) and North- East (Pavagada). Except for Bijapur, where a Basel Mission Church existed, no other places had any church buildings or worship-groups in any form. Though Bijapur is larger in size and population than the other places, it wasjust as backward in development as Pavagada, Bagepalli and Hosadurga, Economically, Bagepalli was a backward place followed by Pavagada and Bijapur. Hosadurga was economically a more progressive place in comparison to the others. The education levels of these places vary though not to any high degree. Bijapur has both graduates and non-literates. More non-literates are found in Bagepalli and Pavagada. The caste differences seem high in Bagepalli, followed by Pavagada, Bijapur and moderate in Hosadurga.

Relevant hypotheses that are tested here state that despite these variations, there are no significant changes in their response to Christ and Christ Groups. What common aspects are found in these places? What was the perception of the Group? Were their felt needs met or do they see their fulfilment in the Group? Do they see themselves as leaders and agents of change in society?

Criteria, Purpose, Survey Design & Interview Methods:

EHC-I, in 1999, reported that they have formed over 28,000 Christ Groups and over 15,000 in India alone. This growth is remarkable in the post-independence period, considering the upsurge of Hindu fundamentalism and the intention to make India a Hindu nation. As far as the Gospel is concerned, Karnataka is known as 'South India's North India'. This means that Karnataka resembles North India, culturally and religiously, as it was never a happy hunting ground for Christian mission enterprise. During the Mass Movement, the response of North India was minimal in comparison to some southern states of India.

In a similar way, Karnataka always resisted the Gospel. In the 1991 census, the Christian population in Karnataka, including all denominations was 1.93 percent of the total, while the Christian population in the neighbouring states of Kerala was 18 percent, Tamil Nadu 11 percent and Andhra Pradesh 8 percent.[33] In such a prevailing situation, the statistical records of Karnataka IEHC show that in 1998 a total of 1400 [34] Christ Groups. An estimate of its total members would come to 150,000 to 200,000. This means the Christ Groups have become the third Christian denomination in Karnataka by the number of adherents, the other two being the Church of South India and the Methodist Church.

This study covers a span of twenty years from 1978 to 1998. The year 1978 was selected because the Hosadurga Christ Group began in Karnataka. The IEHC in Karnataka placed more emphasis on the Christ Groups during its Second Coverage, which was known as 'Evangelism in Depth'[35] to form Christ Groups and to nurture them. The year 1998 was chosen because the emphasis on Christ Groups ended at that time. From 1999 onwards, the IEHC moved towards promoting literacy work in India.

Purpose of the Survey

The purpose was to establish what relational matters influenced the rural people to become Christians over and against the western individualistic-driven mass literature distribution through a Christian agency. Other factors, social, economic and cultural will also be observed to discern through quantitative assessment, their influence on people to become Christians in the four sample *talukas* of Karnataka State. This could provide a reliable basis for strategic planning in future for the Christian missions to work in rural India meeting the needs and aspirations of the people.

Survey Design and Interview Methods

The research focused on the four *talukas* of the State. A total of 200 people were interviewed from four different fields, 50 from each field. The State

[33] www.censusindia-1991
[34] Statistical Report, 1998, A Statistical Report of IEHC Karnataka, Bangalore, India
[35] Louis, Robert, 1978, A Report on Karnataka IEHC, presented in a meeting arranged by the Bible Society of India, Auxiliary, Bangalore, India

of Karnataka was selected due to my acquaintance with the State and its *talukas*, almost from the beginning of the Christ Groups' work there.

The primary data were collected orally. The participants spoke openly, while what they said was recorded on tape. Data were collected from each individual participating in the discussion through the efforts of the evangelists-cum-pastors of these fields, who also helped to fill the data for participants for the non-literate and semi-literate, so as not to create any suspicion in the minds of the congregation due to the presence of anti-Christian elements in those areas. All the data collected were in the local language, Kannada. Some oral data were collected in the Telugu language (especially in Bagepalli and Pavagada) because for some participants this was their mother tongue. Questionnaires and interviews were employed to find out the perception of the members of these four different groups in different locations about their introduction to Christ and Christ Groups and their role in the Group and society.

The research explored the nature and extent of the perception of the Group and the activities in the Group. As a worshipping Group, what is the theological and philosophical framework used, and was it imposed on them from outside or did it come from within the context? What are the goals and purposes of their involvement? How have the traditional and other church denominations or movements perceived the development of the Groups? As individuals or groups, what are the contributing factors that generate their conviction to participate actively in spiritual and social issues and activities? Factors influencing involvement- religious, social and personality development- are considered.

The four regions were chosen where significant numbers of the Christ Groups members lived, to provide a range of geographical characters, social settings and differing points related to the Christ Groups formation and their functioning. As a whole, they represented the region of Karnataka State, where the sponsored body of World Literature Crusade was located, where the work of India Every Home Crusade's Christ Groups was carried out. Overall, this gives a better overview of the Christ Groups' impact in response or reaction to the agency's work in Karnataka State. These areas are listed below after a brief introduction to the State of Karnataka and its districts.

State of Karnataka (Map)[36] and Its Four Selected Taluks

Figure 6A.1 State of Karnataka and its Districts

Karnataka is one of the States in southern India. In the local language, it is called 'Karu nadu' which means an elevated place. It nestles between the Western and Eastern Ghats of the southern plateau. It is the sacred land of holy men, the unique land of great warriors, a glorious land, which has witnessed many achievements in religion, culture, literature, education and the arts.

Districts of Karnataka

Karnataka has 27 districts (counties): Bangalore Urban; Bangalore Rural; Bagalakot; Belgaum; Bellary; Bidar; Bijapur; Chamarajanagar; Chikkamaglur; Chitradurga; Kodagu; Davanagere; Dharwad; Gulbarga;

---

[36] www.karnataka.com accessed on 19-12-03

Gadag; Hassan; Haveri; Kolar; Koppal; Mandya; Mangalore (Dakshina Kannada); Mysore; Raichur; Shimoga; Tumkur; Udupi; Uttara Kannada.[37]

The four *talukas* (shires) chosen for the study and the districts they represent: Hosadurga Taluka of Chitradurga District; Pavagada Taluka of Tumkur District, Bagepalli Taluka of Kolar District and Bijapur Taluka of Bijapur District.

Demographic features of the locations:
Hosadurga: (Map)
Figure 6A.2 District Map of Chitradurga

Hosadurga ▶

Location

Hosadurga is one of the *talukas* of Chithradurga District. Hosadurga is the main town and the administrative centre of this *taluka*. This *taluka* is surrounded by different *talukas*, Holalkere on the north, Hiriyur on the east, Tarikere of Chickkamagalur on the west. Kadur of Chickkamagalur District and Chickkanayakanhalli of Tumkur District on the south. Apart from Hosadurga Madakere, Srirampur and Mathodu are hoblis (sub-towns) in the *taluka*, which has 225 villages. The *taluka* is 1372.3 sq.kms in area.[38]

---

[37] www.karnataka.com accessed on 22-12-03
[38] *The Karnataka Encyclopaedia*

Population

The total population of the *taluka* is over 200,000 according to the 1991 census. This includes those belonging to Scheduled Castes at around 45,000, Scheduled Tribes over 17,000 and the rest of the population of others about 150,000 [39]

Mountains and hills

Hosadurga is a place of hills and mountains such as 'Halu Rameshwar' Hill, the highest mountain in the *taluka*. Limestone fossils, iron-ore and coloured clays are found. Historical records reveal that 'Budimaradi' of this *taluka* was once known for gold mining.[40]

Forests and pastures

This *taluka* has a forest of 'Karachi' timber (like wild timber). This forest is always green, spread along the 'Kamari', a tributary of the 'Vedavathi' river. In other parts of the *taluk,a* palmolive, mango, tamarind and acacia are grown. The *taluka* also has good pastureland.[41]

River and reservoir

'Vedavathi' is the main river in this *taluka*. The river enters from the north-west and flows alongside the northeast side of it. A reservoir is built in 'Vanivilaspura' of Hiriyur taluka, called 'Vanivilas Sagar'. The backwaters of this reservoir are used on the farming land in Hosadurga *taluka*.[42]

Rainfall and the food-produce

The weather is pleasant throughout the year. The average rainfall is 511.86 mm. The total cultivable area in hectares is 95265.[43] The main crops produced are jawar, raagi (malt), paddy, lentil, chilli, coconut and cotton.[44]

Occupations

Agriculture is the main occupation. About 85 percent of the population depend on agriculture. The other occupations are animal husbandry and fisheries. Apart from these, people are also engaged in handloom, coir (jute) and cottage industries. Economically, the majority of the people are in the lower-middle class and come from a poor background.[45]

---

[39] www.nitpu3.kar.nic.in/samanyamahiti accessed on 22-12-03
[40] Ibid.
[41] Ibid.
[42] Ibid.
[43] www.karnataka.com accessed on 22-12-03
[44] Ibid.
[45] Ibid.

Industries, transportation, communication and financial institutions
Handloom industries are found here. Banks, post-office, electricity, public and private transportation and a rail-station are available. The population of the town is around 15,000. All the basic amenities are available in the town and it is a commercial centre. There are district roads and sub-roads that connect to all its villages and neighbouring towns.[46]

History

Once Hosadurga *taluka* was known for manufacturing glass bangles. The Palyegar-dynasty which was established by Giriyappa Naya' ruled here. Doddanna Nayak of this dynasty embraced the 'Veerashaiva' religion (Lingayat). Later in this dynasty, Halappa Raj Nayak built in 1707 a Mutt (a Lingayat-shrine) for Murgharajendra Swami (name of a Lingayat guru) and built a provisional food store and a lake. 13kms to the west of Hosadurga, there is a place called Neergunda, which was once the capital of the Jains, ruled by Neel Shekhara son of Parmeshwarappa, who built this place in 160 BCE and named it as Neelavathi. There is another place, Boodhihal, which is 26kms South East of Hosadurga, which has a fort, built in the 15th century.[47]

In 1676, the Palyagar dynasty's Chickkana Nayak built a fort here to defend the place against the Muslim rulers of Bagur. In 1708, a Hindu Jangum (saint) with the help of Palyagars built a marketplace and made it convenient for people to dwell in Hosadurga. This place for brief periods was under the rule of Hyder Ali, a Moslem ruler, as well as the Marathas, after which it was under the rule of Mysore's Maharajah (King).[48]

Religion

Hindus are over 90 percent. The majority of them are Lingayats (Virshivas). As it was under Vijayanagar-rule, Brahmanism was not encouraged under the Palyagar's, who, though they were originally Jains, in the 17th century embraced 'Virashaiva' (Lingayat) religion. The influence of Murgharajendra's shrine at Chitradurga is widespread in the districts of Chithradurga and Tumkur. A good number of Muslims live here. A large number of outcastes and tribals are in this *taluka*. There are very few Christians in the *taluka*. Christ Groups have produced more Christians than Christians who existed here.

---

[46] Ibid.
[47] Ibid.
[48] Ibid.

Pavagada: (Map)
Figure 6A.3 District Map of Tumkur

Pavagada
▼

Location

It is one of the *talukas* in Tumkur District and a main town of the *taluka*. Andhra State, except Chitradurga *taluka*, is on the west mostly surrounds the *taluka*. It is in the sub-division of Madhugiri taluka and has 144 villages and four towns: Niedugulloo, Pavagada, Hosakote and Nagalamadike. Taluka's size measures 1,856 sq. kms.

Population

The total population is over 225,000.[49] This includes the Schedule Caste population of over 65,500, Schedule Tribes 35,000 and other population of over 110,000.[50]

Mountains and hills

On the east side of the District towards the north-south, the hills contain granite and pass through the *taluka*. The hill of Pavagada is about 918 meters high. Two more hills in the *taluka* are Kamanadurga and Niedugallu

---

[49] Kannada Vishwa Kosh, 1990, 903
[50] www.nitpu3.kar.nic.in.samanyamahiti accessed on 22-12-03

and are 1077 and 1149 meters high respectively. Granite is found in some places of the *taluka*.

Rainfall and food produce

On the east of the *taluka* the 'Uttar Pinakini' river flows and joins the neighbouring Andhra Pradesh State. The average yearly rainfall in the *taluka* is 556 mm, which is the lowest in comparison to the other t*alukas* of the Districts. The *taluka* has 14,517 acres of forest area, 33,766 acre of pastureland and 163,405 of agriculture land. There are 64 open tanks and 3606 open wells in the *taluka*. Some bore-wells have been installed in the *taluka* but with little success. The *taluka* also produces ragi (malt), rice-paddy, jawar, dal, peanuts and other grams. In a few places sugarcane and coconut are produced.

Occupations

The majority of the population is engaged in agriculture. Only the affluent own land, but they are mostly agricultural labourers.

Animal husbandry

Animal husbandry is a widely practised trade and a cattle breeding is encouraged. Towards their development and protection, the government has established veterinary hospitals on the *taluka* and village levels.

History

Niedgull is one of the historical places in the *taluka*. It was an important centre of the Palyegar dynasty. Many historical remains exist here. In the hill of Bangar Nayak there remains and old fort and a building. Pavagada was once known as Pamu-Gonda. It was another important town of the Palyegar dynasty. Balappa Nayak then his dynasty ruled for a hundred years. In 1776, Hyder Ali (Tipu Sultan's father) captured it and imprisoned Timmappa Nayak, the ruler. In 1790-92 during the third war against Mysore according to Cornwallis' suggestion, Marathas who had captured Madhugiri again installed Timmappa Nayak as the ruler of Pavagada and he ruled for a short time. After a truce between Tipu and the British rulers, Pagagada was once again was given to Tipu and the dynasty of Palyegar come to an end. Today, whatever is remaining of the fort was built during the time of Hyder Ali and Tipu Sultan.

On the hill of Bangar Nayak there is a 13ft high stone column, which is worshipped like an idol in the temple of Kadambram. In Gundalahalli, the temples of Shiva and Anjaneya are well known in the *taluka*. Pavagada has a temple called Gopal Krishna and a temple of Shani. There is also a mosque and a few Muslim shrines as well as a Christ Groups church. Just as the Palyegar dynasty embraced the Lingayat religion in Hosadurga, the same was the case with the Palyegars of Pavagada. A strong Lingayat community lives here as well as some high-caste Brahmins, Marathas, and Muslims. Due to the lack of rain, a large number of people who live here are poor belonging to the outcastes. A Protestant Church, which is the fruit of the work of a Christ Group has been mainly successful among these poor people. A small percentage of the population may be Christians.

Bagepalli: (Map)
Figure 6A.4 District Map of Kolar

Bagepalli

Location

It is one of the *talukas* of Kolar District and its main town. Andhra Pradesh State borders to its north, east and west. On the south Gudibanda, Sidalghatta and Chintamani *talukas* are surrounded. It is a sub-division of Chikballapur. Miettemari, Chelur, Pathpalya and Golur are its other towns. This *taluka* has 228 villages; the total area is 932.9 sq.kms.

Population

The t*aluka*'s population is around 150,000. This includes the population of Schedule Castes of 40,500, Schedule Tribes which is 8,500 and the rest of the population numbers over 100,000. Bagepalli is considered as the poorest in the whole of the State.

Mountains and hills

This *taluka* is mostly covered with granite stones. It has some hills, which contain granite. Towards the east of Bagepalli, mountain strips called, Dongalkonda spread from the north to the south and divide the valleys of the Chitravati and Papagni rivers.

Rivers and reservoirs

On the northwest side of the *taluka* the 'Papagni' river flows. A reservoir called Vyasya Samudra has been built to store the water from the river. To the west of the *taluka*, the Chitravathi river flows. The Vandaman'stream, a tributary of the Papagni, originated in the hills east of Itkal Durga and flows for 25kms within the taluka, then joins the State of Andhra Pradesh.

Rainfall

The *taluka* receives less rainfall. The average rainfall in the year is only 676m.m. Usually this *taluka* experiences an excess of heat.

Forest and agriculture produce

This *taluka* has 45,576 acres of forest and 46,216 acres of pastureland. Agricultural land measures 232,831 acres but cultivated land is only 78,319 acres. There are some open tanks and wells found in the *taluka* providing water to the agriculture land. The water of Reddihalli tank and Ramsandra tank, which benefit from the Chitravathi River, is used for agricultural purposes. Ragi (Malt), rice-paddy, peanuts, chillies, onions and other grams are grown here.

Occupation

Due to the scarcity of water and low rainfall, only a few rich people are found (as landlords) and the majority of the population is agricultural labourers.

Animal husbandry

In order to compensate the income of the population the government encourages cattle breeding. With this in view the Government has established several veterinary hospitals.

History

A place called Gummu Nayakanhalli is a part of the *taluka* and was once an important place for the Palyegar dynasty, which ruled Pavagada and Hosadurga.

Religions

About 3kms from Bagepalli in Devargudipalli there is a famous temple called Venkatraman Swamy. Muslims have built a mosque there. The Christian presence can be traced only from the late 1960s. Though there is some presence of Protestant Christians in the town, there is no sign in the villages, except for some house churches or Groups that meet together on a regular basis.

Bijapur: (Map)
Figure 6A.5 District Map of Bijapur

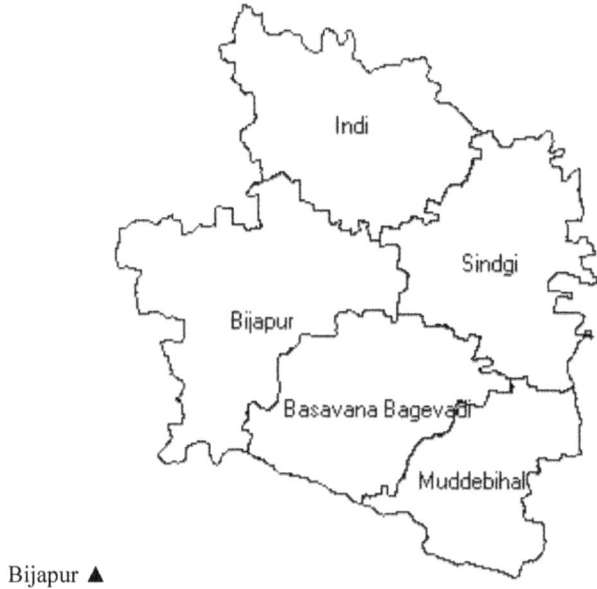

Bijapur ▲

Location

Bijapur is the District's headquarters and centre of the *taluka*'s administration. It is 96kms south of Sholapur and 576kms northwest of Bangalore. The city measures 1450 sq.kms. The total population is over 2,53,307. The *taluka* is comprised of 105 villages and measures 2659 sq.kms.[51] The total cultivable area is 2400 sq.kms.

Population

The total population of the *taluka* is over 300,000.[52]. This includes the population of Schedule Castes around 75,000 and Schedule Tribes 4500. The rest of the population numbers 220,000.

---

[51] Samanya Mahiti data of ZP, www.bijapur.net accessed on 19-12-03
[52] Ibid.

Rivers and reservoir

The Doni river flows towards the north of the *taluka* and the Krishna river in the south. Many open tanks are built in the *taluka* and in Bijapur there is a huge 'Hinkal Tank'. Due to meagre rainfall throughout the whole year the District and *taluka* faces a water shortage.

Forest

Bijapur taluka has a small area of forest, which measures 6.8 sq.kms.

Rainfall and food produce

The district and *taluka* received an average of 565m.m rainfall for the year 2001-02 that is, against the normal rainfall 768m.m. The main products are cotton and peanuts. Jawar and other grams are also grown.[53]

Occupations

Except for some urban dwellers in Bijapur most of the population is engaged in agriculture and many of them are agricultural labourers. Due to the lack of rain and water resources, the land is in the hands of rich people. Because the *taluka* produces good cotton crop there are many hand and machine looms. Urban dwellers mostly engage in trade and such other jobs.

Animal Husbandry

To underpin the income of the common people, the government encourages cattle and sheep breeding. The *taluka* exports meat to the Middle East.

Financial and educational institutions

Bijapur is a fast growing city. There are many government establishments. It has many colleges including a medical college. All the conveniences are available here: post, telephone, and electricity. Bijapur is also a trade centre and it has many commercial and co-operative banks.

History

The foundations of this historic city were laid during the reign of the Chalukyan dynasty of Kalyani between the tenth and eleventh centuries. They called it Vijayapura or the "City of Victory" from which its present name Bijapur is derived. Bijapur came under the Muslim influence, first under Allaudin Khilji, the Sultan of Delhi, towards the end of the 13th century, and then under the Bahamani kings of Bidar in 1347. In 1481, Mohammed III, one of the Bahamani Sultans, appointed Yusuf Adil Khan as the Governor of Bijapur. One of the sons of Sultan Mahmud II of Turkey. Yusuf Adil Khan fled his country on the death of his father, to escape the massacre of the crown prince in the battle for the succession to

---

[53] Ibid.

the throne. He was purchased as a slave by Mahmud Gavan, the Prime Minister of Mohammed. With the decline of the Bahamani power at Bidar, Yusuf declared his independence in 1489 and thus became the founder of the Adil Shahi dynasty, which survived as a kingdom until it was annexed by the Mughal Emperor, Aurangzeb, in 1686. Bijapur experienced a great burst of architectural activity under the Adil Shahi dynasty. The Adil Shahis encouraged building activity to such an extent that Bijapur itself has over 50 mosques, more than 20 tombs and a number of palaces. An interesting feature was the employment of large numbers of Indian craftsmen in contrast to the earlier Muslim rulers of the Deccan who deployed Persian craftsmen and architects.

Religions

Mostly Lingayats are the majority here but the population is comprised of a large number of Muslims. The Caste system is still strong in the rural parts. It is a land of contrasts where there are a few extremely rich people and a large number of poor people mostly coming from an outcaste background. Marathi speaking people are found here and other religious groups; Sikhs, Jains and Lamanis. There is a small number of Christians, living here dating back from the days of missionaries. Missionaries from the Basel Mission worked in this place, and since converts from a higher caste background were not available, families were brought in from neighbouring mission fields to run their mission in Bijapur. Around 150-200 Christian families are found in Bijapur. A Basel Mission Church has been built. For a decade or so, there is a good response from people and some of them have become Christians through the evangelical missions.

The study on the four areas encompasses a wide-ranging sample, in relation to one's exposure to western individualistic influence and experience or reaction coming out of such contextual settings. The World Literature Crusade, which sponsored IEHC's Christ Groups within these areas, was selected for the study in various rural and semi-rural contexts. These areas were intended to represent similar rural and semi-rural regions, based on the IEHC's leader's assessment of the overall Christ Groups' context and factors involved in their development. Thus, the sample was intended to represent a true picture of the work of the Christ Groups carried out by IEHC in Karnataka.

Data collection, description, procedure and data sample

The data were collected in two stages. An average of 8 Christ Groups members of a particular field were invited to their main Christ Group centre. Eight Christ Groups were selected on the basis of their proximity to the base. After conducting a Christian meeting, each participant was given time to share information about themselves, their Christian experience and group. During the interview, some relevant questions were asked: their perception of the group, personal development, theological base, social position, past beliefs and practice. The results were recorded on tape, some in Kannada and some in the Telugu languages. Participants were aware of their participation in collecting the information and all of them willingly co-operated. Since I had a personal knowledge of the local languages, interpretation was not required. A structured questionnaire was avoided at this stage in order to get the respondents' open feedback.

In the second stage, a structured questionnaire was given to the evangelists cum pastors of these fields to collect the relevant responses of the respondents: age, education, income, caste, festivals, and number of children and size of the family. The data were verified with the evangelists for the way in which they understood the questions and vice-versa, for my own understanding of the material they provided. This was to avoid any ambiguity on either side. The objective of exploring these characteristics was to examine how the religious experiences, civil status, caste-system, demographic and socio-economic factors influencing the members' response to Christ and Groups and their view of the Group to their felt needs that is, social, spiritual, religious, moral factors and role in nation-building.

The interviews addressed the views of the participants on their religious experiences, the role of the Group in personal development and community life. The interview was divided into four parts: Introduction and Perception of the Group, Continuity and Discontinuity with the Past and Present, Personality Development in the Spiritual and Social Sphere, Importance of Adherence to the Institutions of the Church. The following Table shows the questions.

Table 6A.3 A Sample Questionnaire

Introduction & Perception of the Group	Continuity and Discontinuity with the Past & Present	Personality Development in Spiritual and Social sphere	Importance of Adherence to the Institutions of the Church
How and who introduced you to the Groups? What factors helped you to join the Group?	Did your concept of God change after having this new religious experience and to what extent?	Do you participate in the praise and worship of the church? Do you share the good news with your people? Whether in your group you have a collective or single leadership?	Do you think 'Baptism' is necessary to join the Group? Do you prefer to have a Christian wedding and funeral?

What did you find in the Group which you did not find in your community?	What have you done with your past cultural and religious observances? Have fully you abandoned them or do you still observe them?	Whether you or the Group actively want to participate in social issues? Do you still maintain ties with your relatives and friends who do not have the same religious experience as yours?	Do you want your children to be christened in the Group or church?

In the second stage, a structured questionnaire was used to collect the data. The information was furnished by the individuals with the help of the evangelists cum pastors. More detailed information was collected to create scales and indices of the factors. The Table below explains the outcome of the process.

Table 6A.4 Sample of Structured Questionnaire Item

A. What are the priorities which helped you to join the Group?
01. Appeal of the Message of the Christ
02. Healing Experience- Self or Others
03. My Family and Friends attend the Group
04. The Worship Place Closer to my House
05. The Exemplary lives of the Leaders Impressed Me
06. I Found Music and Songs Lively
07. I Found Love, Acceptance and Equality in the Group
08. I was Helped by the Group in my Needs
09. The Group Participates in Social Issues
10. The Group Provides me a Space to Develop Myself

Sample Description and Procedure of Survey

The four Christ Groups were selected on the basis of the following criteria: The four Christ Groups represented four different locations of the State, which have different demographical, religious and lingual characteristics. Bijapur in the North, a district place, semi-developed, populated, historically Muslim ruled, a Lingayat dominated with Dalits oppressed, economically backward and dominantly rough Kannada mixed with Urdu and Marathi speaking. Hosadurga, in the South-West, a *taluka* place, semi-developed, Muslim, Maratha and Nayak (Ksihatriya means Warriors) ruled, Lingayat majority, Dalit not openly oppressed, economically better, soft Kannada speaking. Bagepalli, in the South-East, a *taluka* place, poorly developed, poverty stricken, poor exploited, ruled and dominated by Reddis, a business community, Dalits openly oppressed, terrorized by the Naxalites (who work against the government and the rich people, like the Maoist groups in Nepal), dominantly Telugu speaking place. Pavagada, in the Central-East, a *taluka* place, low-developed, poverty stricken, ruled by the Nayaks, a Kshatriya (warrior) community, dominated by the rich land-lords, poor exploited, Dalit oppressed, mainly Telugu spoken. Though the comparisons of these factors are not paramount, yet it will be another area for future researchers to look into. Nonetheless, it will be interesting to find what sort of impact people had when they received the Good News.

Data Sample of the Respondents

Weller[54] notes that the necessary sample size for both qualitative and quantitative research is a function of variability: 'the less variation there is (that is, the more homogeneous the responses), the fewer informants are necessary. With high agreement and repetitive responses across informants a small sample size may suffice'. As mentioned earlier in the chapter, the equal numbers of respondents, 50 each, were selected from the target groups of the four Christ Groups. The data indicates the three main characteristics of the respondents: gender, age and education. The distribution of respondents according to age indicates that respondents tend to belong to all age groups.

Table 6A.5

Names of Four Christ Groups		Number of Respondents	Percentage of the Respondents
Hosadurga	.00	50	25
Bagepalli	1.00	50	25
Pavagada	2.00	50	25
Bijapur	3.00	50	25
	Total	200	100

As mentioned above, an exact number of respondents was selected from each of the four Christ Groups. Table 6A.5 shows the names of the Christ Groups selected and the number of respondents chosen from each Christ Group.

---

[54] Ibid. 365

Table 6A.6

Gender Representation of Four Christ Groups		Number of Gender Representation	Percentage of the Gender Respondents
Male	.00	114	57
Female	1.00	86	43
	Total	200	100

Table 6A.6 provides the sample of gender breakdown of male and female at 57 percent and 43 percent, which shows a balance for gender representation.

Table 6A.7 Age Distribution of Four Christ Groups

Age-Group of Four Christ Groups Respondents	Number of Christ Groups Respondents	Perecntage of the Christ Groups Respondents
12-15 years	9	4.5
16-25 years	81	40.5
26-35 years	52	26
36-45 years	33	16.5
46-55 years	8	4
55-65 and above	17	8.5
Total	200	100

Table 6A.7 shows overall that the sample had an age breakdown of 87.5 percent below the age of 45 years, and 12.5 percent above the age of 45 years, it is a fair sample representing India where an average life expectancy is about 45 years.

Table 6A.8 Education Background of Four Christ Groups Respondents

Education Background of the Respondents		Number of Respondents	Perecntage of the Respondents
Illiterate	.00	64	32
Literate	1.00	136	68
	Total	200	100

Table 6A.8 indicates that the percentage of non-literates is 32 percent that is, within the State literacy percentage, which is between 40 percent and 50 percent. Literate percentage includes the semi-literate. The breakdown is discussed in the next chapter.

The survey was conducted after obtaining permission from the concerned officials at the national and regional levels, from the executive director on the national level and the regional manager on the regional level. Prior to the visit, a letter from me and from the regional office in Bangalore was sent to the evangelists cum pastors of the four study places asking them to organize the meeting for the believers at the respective places to come and gather in a central place, near where the evangelists lived.

The purpose of the visit was clarified to the concerned officials, the evangelists and the respondents.

Qualitative Research: Interviews, Observations and Documents

As stated, the research is primarily qualitative in nature because from the outset a small number of Christ Groups was chosen as the study population, 50 each from the each of the four Christ Groups. As Bouma and Atkinson[55] observed:

> Qualitative research makes use of two particular techniques. Participant observation requires the researcher to analyse what is happening in a particular setting, if possible, viewing events through the eyes of the participants. Similarly, interviewing involves finding out the life stories or world views of the subjects being interviewed.

How qualitative research methods such as interviews, observation and documents were used in the survey is described here. As discussed before, most of the respondents, who hailed from rural or semi-rural areas, would not have followed the main concepts asked in the questionnaire. Hence, the structured questionnaire was not administered in the beginning.[56] Rather, initially interviews were used to get the needed information. Personal interviews gave opportunities to clarify any difficulty encountered during the discussion in getting their own response from them. As described by Bouma and Atkinson[57] 'it can help us to understand what lies behind any phenomenon about which little is known and to gain fresh slants on things about which quite a lot is known'. I had personal knowledge of the places and people, but it was still helpful for him to check he was getting the right information on the things he had asked from the participants.

Observations and Documents

The four Christ Groups, chosen for this study represent four decades: Bagepalli, which started way back in 1967, Hosadurga in 1978, Pavagada in 1988 and Bijapur in 1992. The present study focuses on the period 1978 to 1998 because during that period IEHC had given more attention to the formation of Christ Groups. The selected four places represent four

---

[55] Ibid. 216
[56] The structured questionnaire was used only in the Second Stage, ref 199
[57] Ibid. 208

different locations and characteristics. The study's main focus is on the response of the people to the Good News irrespective of variation in places and people. All the four evangelists cum pastors are appointed staff of India Every Home Crusade, who also represent the four decades: Jayananda of Pavagada from 1966, Jayarajan of Hosadurga from 1976, Manik Peter of Bijapur from 1992 and Gangaraj of Bagepalli from 1996 (who himself being a fruit of IEHC ministry, grew up in his faith and took over the leadership when former leaders moved away). The spiritual activities in all these places, except for language and songs looked the same. In Bagepalli and Pavagada, believers used Telugu as the main language for their worship, but in Hosadurga and Bijapur people used the Kannada language. All four have different styles of leadership but worship, prayer and other spiritual activities were of a prototype. By the time of the survey, except for Bijapur, the other three Christ Groups met in a centralized place of their own for worship and prayer. In Bijapur, believers met in two different centralised locations.

Interviews with IEHC and WLC Leaders

The information from IEHC and WLC leaders was collected in two stages: one in 1998 with the IEHC leaders in India and another in 1999 with the WLC leaders in the United States of America. These leaders were chosen on the grounds of their position previously or presently held in the organzsation. The information collected from them is invaluable to the study due to their involvement in various stages of the ministry and their experience. A structured questionnaire was prepared, except for Dr. Yohann (Johnny) Lee, who was not available for interview, and used to get the information from the leaders. The leaders were aware of the questionnaire, and willingly answered the questions and agreed to answers being taped. Dr. Yohann (Johnny) Lee sent the questionnaire with his answers.

Separate interviews were conducted for IEHC and WLC leaders. In 1998, after collecting data in the field, a meeting was held with Mr M. M. Maxton, Executive Director of IEHC in Lucknow, which is 2-3 days journey by train from Bangalore to Delhi, and from Delhi to Lucknow. After coming back from him, with Mr. Albert Sudershan, Regional Manager of IEHC Karnataka and Mr. G. Guruprasad, former director and a founding board member of IEHC, were interviewed and interviews were recorded on tape. Earlier interviews with Mr. B. A. Prathapkumar and Sam C. Samuel were taken into account.

In 1999, during March, a visit was made to Colorado Springs and Pasadena to interview the former and present leaders of WLC. I spent nearly two weeks in the USA to meet these leaders and get other records for the study from the WLC headquarters. Interviews were conducted face to face with the Rev. Dick Eastman, the present President of WLC, and Mr.

Wes Wilson the Vice-President of WLC, also over the phone the Rev. Paul Goodwin, a former President and a board member of WLC. Then, in Pasadena with the founder, Mr. Jack McAllister, the First President of WLC, who took meto his house in the Los Angeles suburbs and the interview was conducted there along with his wife, Hazel McAlister. Then I interviewed Dr. Dale Kitzman, the former President of WLC, at the Centre for the World Missions. All these interviews were recorded on tape. Interviews were mainly concerned to gather information on their personal and organizational opinions and policies regarding the formation, continuation and closure of Christ Groups work in India. The information, which was collected from these interviews does not help to determine the impact of Christ Groups in the State of Karnataka, hence it is used to design the study but not in the results of the study.

Data Set, Selection, Tabulation and Analysis

The questionnaire divides into six parts. The first part consists of the characteristics of the respondents : age, marital status, education, occupation, income, caste, mother tongue, family size, family composition, Christian or non-Christian background and gender, listed in order to discern the social, economic, and religious backgrounds of the respondents.

The second part includes the perception of the respondents and their priorities for becoming members of the Christ Groups. This contains nine items similar to seven used in Bass's Charisma scale (1985a),[58] which were adapted and altered to the present context. 'The life and teaching of Jesus Christ impressed me', 'I attend because of my relatives' and such other views were some of the responses received.

The third part includes the social involvement of the members to discover whether they are involved in nation building as good citizens of India: helping the poor, concern for rural problems, such as drinking, gambling and their attitude towards people of other faiths.

The fourth part contains the leadership development aspect to see whether Christ Groups provide space and position for this, such as, who are the leaders of Christ Groups and who lead others to Christ?

The fifth part shows the dynamism of rural evangelism. What impacted them and how the rural community should be approached, e.g., Christians through message or healing, Christians through family evangelism or literature.

Lastly, the sixth part explains how to live as a Christian in a rural place, whether the change factors are necessary, taking into consideration that in the past the western mission enterprise insisted upon its converts being

---

[58] Bass, Bernard M., 1985, *Leadership and Performance Beyond Expectations* , in Yongi Hong, 1999:123

called Christians. Such factors were: change name/religion/dress/family life pattern, baptism, sacraments, and concept of God, past festivals, severing ties, Christian wedding/funeral/christening.

Selection and Tabulation of Data

The exact number of the respondents was not fixed for each field. A free hand was given to the evangelists to collect as much as possible. Manik Peter of Bijapur provided for the 50 respondents. This led to fixing the 50 numbers to select from other fields. Excess data collected by the evangelist were not tabulated. The collected data were initially entered in the SPSS version 8 programme. Now a version 9 has been installed in the same programme.

Data Analysis Method

The data collected were then analysed, using the representative sample described. The breadth and direction of the hypotheses and the amount of data collected were such that a statistical technique was needed to address the questions raised. Descriptive Statistics were used to analyse the data. As Trochim[59] stated, 'Descriptive Statistics are used to present quantitative descriptions in a manageable form'. He added, 'Descriptive statistics helps...large...data in a sensible way and...reduces lots of data into a simpler summary'. Descriptive Analysis is used to understand the nature of data and to provide an assessment of the hypotheses. There are four measures used to analyse the data through descriptive analysis: tables, bars, table and bars, and pie-charts.

Section B' will deal with a Field Survey II, especially focussing on a case study to make an impact analysis of the field study on the emergence of Christ Groups in Karnataka.

---

[59] Trocchim, 2002, 1, trocchim.human.cornell.edu

Field Survey Section B: A Case Study of Pushpamma of Hosadurga Christ Group, Karnataka

Background and Hosadurga Christ Group

This section proposes to analyse a case study of Pushpamma of Hosadurga Christ Group and to locate how the Christ Groups are formed and developed. How did the relational factors influence the forming Christ Groups? Why and how did the evangelists play an important role in forming the groups? What is the role of literature in forming Christ Groups? Why is family evangelism important in a relational context like India, especially in rural and semi-rural areas to form groups?

The section limits its study to Pushpamma and to some extent to her husband Rama Reddy. The section will not look into her other family members and other members of the Hosadurga Christ Group that is the testimonies of her sister Shivamma, and husband Ramanna Reddy, brother-in-law Appanna Reddy and the evangelist Jayaprabhu. At the end of the section, I will draw out the implications of the case study.

Some explanation of terms: Pushpamma (a young woman), Rama Reddy (Pushpamma's husband), Jayaprabhu (name of the evangelist), Hosadurga (name of a town), Karnataka is the State in southern India. Lingayat and Virashiva are two words that refer to the same sect of the Hindu religion. The words IEHC and EHC are abbreviations and stand for India Every Home Crusade and Every Home Crusade; WLC for World Literature Crusade.

Hosadurga

In 1998, I surveyed four Christ Groups fields of EHC. Hosadurga was one of the Christ Groups visited. A case study of the first member of this Christ Group assesses the formation and development of a Christ Group, where no church existed before or no mission had carried any tangible work there among non-Christians before 1978.

Hosadurga means New Fort, which is situated 180kms north-west of Bangalore in Karnataka State. Hosadurga is a historical place, a fort built around its mountain recalling its glorious past. Hosadurga was ruled by the Palyegars of the Chitradurga dynasty.

Location

Hosadurga is one of the *talukas* (shires) of Chithradurga district of Karnataka State. Hosadurga is the main town and the administrative centre of this *taluka*. It is surrounded by different *talukas*, Holalkere on the north, Hiriyur on the east, Tarikere of Chickkamagalur on the west. Kadur of Chickkamagalur district and Chickkanayakanhalli of Tumkur district to the south. Apart from Hosadurga, Madakere, Srirampur and Mathodu are *hoblis* (sub-towns) in the *taluka*. The total population of Hosadurga *taluka* is around 200,000 and it consists of 225 villages. The *taluka* measures 1372.3 sq.kms.[60]

Religion: Virashiva or Lingayats

Hindus are over 90 percent. The majority of them are Lingayats (Virshivas). As it was under Vijayanagar-rul', Brahaminism was not encouraged under Palyagars, who, in the seventeenth century embraced Veerashaiva (Lingayat) religion from Jain religion. The influence of Murgharajendra shrine of Chitradurga is widespread in the districts of Chithradurga and Tumkur.

Linga

The word Lingayat means bearer of the *linga*. The word *linga* has a dual meaning, for Hunshal it is 'phallus'[61] but for Nandimutt it is a column of light. [62] Scholars have some disagreement about the worship of the phallus. Gopinath Rao traced its antiquity to 200 BCE.[63] However, for Lingayats, the *linga* is the energy of Shiva, which divides itself into the lord which manifests itself in the guru and into the *linga* which is in all souls. A small *linga* (amulet) is worn always on the body by every Lingayat who has to pay homage to it three times (some scholars say twice) a day.[64]

Origin of Virashivaism

Virashiva or Lingayat religion was founded by Basava or Basavanna, by birth a Brahmin, who took the main reformist role when India in the twelfth century was experiencing the Bhakti Movement.[65] According to Nandimutt,

---

[60] *The Karnataka Encyclopedia*, 1978
[61] Ibid.
[62] Ibid.
[63] Hunshall, S.M., 1947, *The Lingayat Movement, A Social Revolution, The Ethics of Lingayatism (Bhaktisthal)*
[64] *The Encyclopaedia of Religions*, 1987, Hinduism, Eliade, Mircea and Adam Charles (eds.).
[65] Ibid.

'Basava did not found Virasaivaism but only revived it'. The traditional origins of Virasaivaism were the five traditional prophets of Virashiva in each *yuga* (time period), the prophets of Kaliyuga being Revan, Marula, Ekorama, Panditaradhya and Visvesvara, who founded gotras (sub-sects) and established *mutts* (shrines) which continue to this day.[66] Professor Sakhare traces the ancestry of the Lingayats to the Keshin and Vratyas mentioned in the Atharva Veda, who attached greater importance to a life of austerity and meditation than to the performance of sacrificial rites. It is interesting that Chinmayananda classifies Virashaivites under non-Hindu new religions or non-religions.[67]Lingayatism is rooted in Hinduism but, is opposed to Brahmanism.

Location of Lingayats

The Lingayats are mainly spread in the Karnataka State. Their population is around 22 percent of the total population of the State of 55 million. Also they are found in the neighbouring states of, Andhra Pradesh, Tamil Nadu, Kerala and Maharashtra.

Philosophy of Virasaivaism

Virasaivism or Lingayatism is a non-Vedic religion. In principle, it opposed the Vedic and the domination of Brahmanic religion andcondemned temple worship, sacrifice, and pilgrimage. The caste system is rejected, the sexes are declared equal, child marriage is forbidden, and remarriage of widows is allowed. However, in the course of time, the system tended to reappear.[68] All ritualism is condemned by Lingayats but some rites are practised. These rites are performed by *Jangamas* (Lingayat priests) rather than by a Brahmin priest. There is a rite-like initiation for male children and all pay homage at least twice a day (Nandimutt says thrice a day) to the small linga they wear. They observe *Astavarana* (eight rituals) to gain their salvation: the guru, who is more revered than God; the wearing of the small *linga*, the *jangamas* (priests); holy water (*padodaka*); returned offering (*prasada*); holy ashes (*vibhuti*); the rosary (*rudraksha*); and the mantra '*Om Namah Shivaya*'. Lingayats also believe in reincarnation, except for those who attain a certain degree of holiness in this life. However, the Lingayats do not believe in the cycle of rebirth. They believe that the strict observance of Lingayat doctrines to ensure the *mukti* (release) in this life. Virasaivism lays emphasis on both knowledge and good works for achieving salvation.

---

[66] Ibid.
[67] Hiebert, Paul, 2000, in Chinmayananda (1998:33), *Missiology*, 'Missiological Issues in the Encounter with Emerging Hinduism', Vol. xxviii, No 1, Jan 2000, 50
[68] Ibid.

Virasaivism lays more stress on the ethical and spiritual, rather than on the philosophical, aspects of religion.[69]

Lingayats think *Maya* (illusion) is the cause and origin of the material world. *Maya*, which is also known as *Sakti* (power) of Siva, though it is an illusion but real as it comes from the Real, the Supreme God; but it holds that *Maya* is real in the beginning of the soul's journey and unreal in the end. Liberation from this world is obtained not only by knowledge (*Jnana*) of the Supreme Self, but also by *Kriya*, that is through strict regime of six practices. The six phases (*sthalas)* are: *Bhakti sthala* (devotee phase), Mahesh sthala (god's phase), *Prasadi sthala* (sacrament phase*), Pranalinga sthala* (spirit of linga phase), *Sharana sthala* (fellowship with devotees phase) and *Aikya sthala* (eternal union phase), which will finally bring the devotee to union with Shiva (united with energy). This union is not, however, complete identity with God.[70]

Sacred books of the Lingayats

Agamas, which include Virashaiva elements, some doctrine and the most important and popular *Vachanas* (sayings). These are sermons, poems, and mystical utterances of the great Virashaiva saints like Basavanna.[71]

Concept of God

Virashivas firmly believe in God, Shiva. As the 'One' without a second. Lingayatism protests against polytheism. It is a monotheistic sect. Shiva is presented in the *Vacanasahitya* (sacred sayings of Lingayat gurus, like Basavanna) in more attractive colours than in the ancient Puranas. Shiva is visualized as a personal god so that the 'unknown' may be approached through the 'known'. Virashivism insists on understanding as well as achievement. In the later stages, the Virashiva realizes the unfathomable nature of the Infinite. Shiva is all pervading and all transcending. Virashivism believes that all-things are not God though God pervades them all. In the final stage, the Virashiva goes further and views all objects as God. The final stage is to be experienced, not comprehended and described.[72]

Concept of sin

Unlike Vedic religion, the Virasaivaism emphasis on sin mainly takes the form of *avidya* or ignorance or not knowing or not having knowledge. *Avidya* is caused by entanglement with *Samsara* (world). However, it differs from the other Hindu understanding of attaining release from *avidya*

---

[69] Ibid.
[70] Ibid.
[71] Ibid.
[72] Ibid.

(ignorance). For Lingayats, the entanglements of the world are real and one has to face them. They believe that the world is a creation of God Shiva. How can God's creation be unreal? Virasaivas describe this stage as *Bhakti sthala*, where there is complete duality; in that stage, the soul understands duality better than unity with God. Virasaivas maintain that strict observance of the Virasaiva doctrines that leads the soul, step-by step, to complete liberation from *avidya*. The Virasaivism has devised six stages, one above the other, and by rising through them, step-by-step, it is possible for the soul to reach realization. *Bhakti*, devotion, is the means by which the soul rises. In this way, duality gradually vanishes and unity is attained.[73]

Virasaiva morality prohibits polytheism. It does not have any gods other than Shiva nor make any images except the *linga* – not to steal, not to lie, not to kill, not to covet another's property or wife. Lingayatism rejects Shankara's view of *Maya*. Shankara taught that wealth is *Maya*; woman is *Maya*; earth is *Maya*, and man's greed is *Maya*. This is similar to Buddhist teaching that 'Greed' is the main cause of human sorrow and pain.[74] The wearing of a small *linga* on one's body always cleanses the wearer from all impurities. The *linga* is equal in reverence to the guru. Although the *linga* is offered by the guru, it represents Shiva. There is also the belief that if any one commits sin, one should go to a believer's house and eat food and drink water that will cleanse away all the sins of the sinner and purify him.[75] Today, Lingayatism is not well known. Its influence is largely restricted to the northern part of the State. Common people are not fully aware of Lingayatism or its teaching. Today, the majority of people have more of a leaning towards popular Hinduism.

Popular Hinduism

The main current of living Hinduism is popular Hinduism. This is affected by every change the tradition has gone through. It is assumed to have ancient roots, in some aspects traceable to the Indus Valley religion, in other aspects to Sudra (a lower caste or a fourth place in the caste-ladder but not outcaste), village, and tribal forms of religion that were never more than alluded (to- and then negatively-) in the ancient and classical sources. Bhakti (devotion) and Tantra (esoteric) are two movements within Hinduism that draw inspiration from this broad current, and popular Hinduism today remains dominated by Bhakti and Tantric expressions. Popular Hinduism is an attempt to reconstruct its Dravidian, pre-Aryan, or non-Brahmanic components. However, some scholars observe that popular

---

[73] Ibid.
[74] Ibid.
[75] Ibid.

Hinduism and Brahmanic forms of Hinduism are integrated at the popular level.[76]

Popular Hinduism, on the one hand has the elements of Bhakti,[77] and on the other hand, it has the elements of 'idol worship, festivals, and pilgrimages'.[78] This is the popular scene in India today. Hosadurga is dominated by Lingayats. Though Lingayatism is an off-shoot of Hinduism, like the Bhakti movement, it adopted a more radical approach, in respect to idol worship, which it rejected in its initial stage. Over the centuries, Lingayats took over once again the form of 'Popular Hinduism',[79] especially the worship of idols. Lingayatism has its own influence at large, especially in the area of tolerance to other religious beliefs.

Other religious (Hindu & Muslim) groups

Apart from Lingayats, some belong to Marathas, Devadiga and out-castes. Muslims are 4 percent, which is the second largest minority group.

Christianity

There are a few Roman Catholic and Protestant families found in and around Hosadurga, but no church buildings. Hosadurga Christ Groups built their own church building in 1992.[80] The Seventh Day Adventist mission has established a primary school in Hosadurga town that is now managed by a Protestant Christian family. Before EHC's work started, Hosadurga was not under any Christian influence. Christianity in India did not spread in rural parts for various reasons. One reason i, that the congregation fully depended upon missionaries or clergy to meet their physical and spiritual needs. Today, the same scenario is present among many mainline churches in India. As Houghton remarked, it bred a dependency whereby converts were not able to share the Gospel with others.[81] Vinay Samuel is also of the same opinion that the mainline church members from birth to death heavily depend upon the clergy to do everything for them.[82] Thus, Christianity lived in cities and became an urban Christianity and never fully penetrated into the rural areas.

---

[76] Ibid.

[77] Ibid.

[78] Ibid. 52

[79] Ibid.

[80] Jairaj, P., 1998, personal interview, February, Pastor of Hosadurga Christ Groups Church, Hosadurga, India

[81] Houghton, Graham, 1968, *The Impoverishment of Dependency*

[82] Samuel, Vinay Kumar 1998, personal interview, Oxford, UK

Hosadurga and the Gospel

In the 1960s and 1970s, Hosadurga was hostile to the gospel work.[83] IEHC, in its first coverage, met severe opposition from the upper-caste people. Their main opposition to Christianity was that the Hindu religion is an eternal religion (*sanathan dharma*), but Christianity is a foreign religion.[84] They argued that the spread of Christianity would help colonisers to rule India again. Christ and His message was very much misunderstood and identified with British rule and missionary enterprise in India. There may be other reasons like conversion, inducement, demonizing the Indian culture, derogative remarks against Hindu gods and goddesses, and the westernized and urbanized look of Christianity. Opposition to Christianity continues in Hosadurga and India from some Hindu fundamental groups, but the larger population is in favour of the good news.

The majority of the population in India have an interest in the person of Christ and his teachings.[85] His selfless life, His act of forgiveness to all people and His power to heal the sick attracts them. People also like to hear the good news when it is brought to them by their own people[86] not by 'missionaries, who worked not only for the Kingdom's sake but for the sake of their colonial powers'.[87] This Gospel as St. Paul says, 'is the power of God' (Rom 1:16) and is able to translate into any soil or culture without changing itself.[88] Although the Gospel is powerful enough to change anything that comes into contact with it, missionaries and Indian churches in the past have failed to penetrate into the rural areas.[89] Important questions are how best to present it and what are the means to be used.

Beginnings of Hosadurga Christ Group and its Key Players

In 1978, the Second Coverage of IEHC aimed at in-depth evangelism, that is, evangelism and Christ Groups formation. The team of EHC came to Hosadurga to begin its work there.[90]

Pushpamma and the EHC team

In 1978, Pushpamma was 15 years old, a daughter of Perumal and Jayamma Reddy. Permal Reddy, a father of five children worked in the

---

[83] Guruprasad, G., 1998, personal interview (a former Director of IEHC Karnataka and founding Member of IEHC), Bangalore, India

[84] Ibid. 48, 51

[85] Ibid.

[86] Vinay Kumar Samuel, 2003, Personal interview, Oxford, UK

[87] Pityana, N, 1973, *What is Black Consciousness?*, 59

[88] Sanneh, Lamin, 1989 (2002), *Translating the Message*

[89] Ibid.

[90] Jayaprabhu, B., 1999, Personal interview, February, in a Discipleship Training, Yellapur, India

Government sector as a road-roller driver, owned a house, 4 acres of agricultural land and five goats. Pushpamma was betrothed to her mother's brother, Rama Reddy, when she was eight years old.[91] Permal Reddy was considered economically sound. He sent his children to school. His children were able to read and write, if not well. The EHC team rented a room from Permal Reddy, which was adjacent to his house. The team consisted of four members: Jayaprabhu, the team leader, Jayaraj, Pundlik and Vijayakumar. Except for Jayaraj, the other three were Hindu converts to Christianity. Jayaprabhu was older and the more experienced member in the team. He was 36 years old, married and had 12 years experience in the ministry. Every morning around 4 o'clock the team members spent at least an hour in prayer and Bible reading before they went to villages for the ministry.[92]

Pushpamma's background

By Hindu caste, Pushpamma came from the Sudras the cultivators of the land or farmers. There are many sub-castes in Sudras. Pushpamma's family comes from the Kammareddy caste. Kammareddys in Hosadurga followed popular Hinduism that was heavily influenced by the Lingayats. Pushpamma said:

> We worshipped Shiva and other Hindu gods and goddesses. I worshipped idols with intent and immense zeal. My favourite shrine (mutt) was a Lingayat's. I visited the shrine regularly and worshipped zealously. I offered everyday 'poojas' (a Hindu form of ritual) with flowers and coconuts, and burnt fragrant sticks and incense. I fasted every week and made pilgrimages with my parents and relatives. Although I led a good devoted life, as a young person I lived with some guilt of my own. I often felt helpless to get away from these guilt feelings, in spite of my increased devotion towards the gods.[93]

Popular Hinduism advocated idol worship and devotion. Pushpamma tried to unify herself with the eternal one by increasing her devotion. However, her increased devotion did not lead to deliverance. She was left with emptiness and hollowness in spite of it. Popular Hinduism brought some revival into traditional Hinduism, and tried to integrate a large Hindu population into the mainstream of Hinduism. Pushpanna did not find an answer to her inner search for how to be free from guilt and sin.Some may sincerely search until they find it and some who reverse their thinking may find something of their own creation, like in the west where 'cultural

---

[91] Pushpamma, R., 1998, personal interview, Hosadurga, India
[92] Report., 1980, A Report on Karnataka IEHC, Bangalore, India
[93] Ibid.

Christians'[94] are looking. Pushpamma was neither interested in other religions nor tempted by any inducement to be converted to another religion. It was her inner soul (*atman*) that was prompting her to find the inner peace and deliverance. Christian missionaries may try to meet such spiritual needs of people rather than making any harsh remarks on other religions or their deities as in the past[95] (Houghton:1968) and now by some evangelical groups.

Pushpamma and her proposed wedding with Rama Reddy

Pushpamma was young and beautiful. She came to the age to get married. The marriage was fixed for some time during the year. Pushpamma remarked:

> I was rather nervous to think about my marriage with Rama Reddy. I was betrothed to him when I was a child. Rama Reddy led a very violent life in the community and loved pleasure and violence. I cannot break my proposed wedding on my own. I have to obey my parents. Betrothal meant to me that I was already married. My family members, community leaders and religious leaders had tried to correct him, but he heeds no one. This may be my fate. This might be punishment for my previous life. I might have done something wrong or it may be my 'Karma' (fate). My only hope remains in my gods. But, which one will change him? If they fail, I have no choice but to bear all that will come to me.[96]

There is no individualityfor a Hindu woman. In her childhood, she will be under her parent's custody. In her wedded life, she will be in the custody of her husband. In her old age, she will be in the custody of her children (sons).[97] Fatalism or *karma* is such that an individual recognises a lack of ability to control their future.[98] In India, *karma* is thought to be predestined and as something that cannot be altered in any way.[99]

The doctrine of *karma* reflects the Hindu conviction that this life is but one in a chain of lives (*samsara*) determined by actions in a previous life. *Karma* is accepted as a law of nature, not open to further discussion.[100] This calls individuals to be responsible for their lives.[101] The acts of a previous life influence the circumstances of the next life. They also determine one's happiness or unhappiness in the hereafter between lives, where one will

---

[94] Peck, M. Scott, 1978 (2003), *The Road Less Traveled: A New Psychology of Love, Traditional Values and Spiritual Growth*. Richard Dawkins in an interview with BBC One in 2006 uses the term, that is before his debate with Alister McGrath.
[95] Ibid.
[96] Ibid.
[97] Desai, Neera, and Maithreyi, Krishna Raj, 1987, *Women and Society in India*
[98] Studdley, John, 1992, in Banfield 1958, Levi 1947, Bista 1991, 'Fatalism'
[99] Ibid.
[100] Ibid.
[101] Samuel, Vinay Kumar2000, Personal interview, Oxford, UK

spend a time in either one of the heavens or one of the hells until the fruits of his *karma* have been all but consumed and the remainder creates a new life.[102]

Karma binds individuals completely. In Hinduism there is no doctrine of atonement (except one should pay for one's own sins) when someone already paid for the past, and the price of the future is secured. This belief would bring a new identity to people who are forgiven and restored despite their past, because of the cross.[103]

> Pushpamma said, 'that whatever is happening to me now is destined from the gods because of my previous life. How can I change it'? She says, '…that for us (Hindus) husbands are a god (patiye divum), how can I separate from my god'? Pushpamma also remarks, '…I am a woman, weak and helpless because of my position in the society, I have no other way than to accept whatever is given to me from my parents and elders'.[104]

In a Hindu society, the birth of a boy child is considered as a divine blessing, but not the birth of a girl child. In society, their position is not highly regarded for having a female child is preferred only to remaining childless.[105] Women like Pushpamma are not given the same understanding as males. However, in the Christian faith, they are created in the image of God. God wants to call them His sons and daughters.[106] Though officially legislation brought equality to women,[107] in fact their status in the society remained same. Women in such a society have to accept their status as it isgiven to them.They need to be taken out of such a false understanding to a true awareness of themselves.[108]

Hindu society requires women to be subservient to their husband.[109] The wife has to please her husband at all times.[110] A wife not only serves her husband, but also his parents and other older people who live in the family.[111] Whether the husband is good or bad, his wife has to seek his welfare always if she wants to see her husband live long and that she will die as a married woman. That is considered as the blessed status of a woman. Widows are considered as non-propitious (un-blessed) and they are not allowed to participate in any ominous occasions, like marriages.

---

[102] Ibid.
[103] Sugden, Chris, 1997, *Seeking the Asian Face of Jesus*, 355
[104] Ibid.
[105] Ibid.
[106] Ibid.
[107] Wolpert. Stanley A., 1993, *A New History of India*
[108] Ibid.
[109] Derne, Steve, 1995, *Culture In Action: Family Life, Emotion and Male Dominance in Banaras India*, 22
[110] Ibid.
[111] Ibid.

Women in a society ruled by 'superior males'[112] do not have any personality of their own, unless they come to understand God's love for them and His desire to crown them with His glory.

Pushapamma's new reality

Pushpamma was now faced with a new reality, when she met EHC team members as her neighbours:

> I was greatly impressed when the team members spent their early hours of the day in singing spiritual songs, reading the scripture and in prayer. When Jayaprabhu prayed, he used to cry as he prayed. The prayers of the team members were offered not only for themselves, but, they prayed for her and her family, the neighbours and for all the people of Hosadurga and the world. This way of prayer was new to me. I never prayed like that, my 'poojas' were offered to appease the gods and the desires I made known to gods were mostly concerned of me and my family.[113]

The devoted Christian life of converts coming from the Hindu faith of a rural community suggests to Hindus like Pushpamma some resemblance to Bhakti (from Sanskrit *bhaj*, 'to allot,' 'to revere'), a devotional movement emphasizing the intense emotional attachment and love of a devotee toward his/her personal god. This way is superior to achieving salvation than through knowledge *(jnana-marg)*, ritual and good works *(karma-marga)*. This way is open to all, irrespective of sex and caste. Bhakti (devotion) includes the recitation of God's name, singing of hymns in praise of him, wearing his emblem, undertaking pilgrimages to sacred places associated with him, and serving him in a variety of ways.[114] Jayaprabhu and the team members sang popular Christian songs like Indian popular songs, but not traditional hymns. Their prayers were offered in simple tones and words not in a traditional bishop's way. They talked to God as their friend in an intimate way often crying. This appealed to Pushpamma. Christians living in their local context brings meaning to their message.

What appeals to a Hindu, like Pushpamma, is a true Christian life, that is a selfless and sacrificial life. Recently, a Roman Catholic priest from the Kalaghatgi constituency was elected to the Karnataka State legislative Assembly, defeating an upper-caste candidate.[115] What appealed to people to elect him was his concern for others and a selfless life. Pushpamma listened to their prayers and songs everyday and became curious about them. She thought it was not at all like her *pujas*. Pushpamma commenting

---

[112] Ibid.
[113] Ibid.
[114] Ibid.
[115] Prasad, Rao, 1998, personal interview, Pastor of an independent church, Kalghatagi, India

on those prayers says that through such prayers 'I can pray to God, as if I am speaking to some one who is in front of me'.[116]

She wanted to ask the team members about their prayers, but felt shy to ask any such thing. One day, taking courage she asked Jayaprabhu, 'What you do every morning?' Jayaprabhu replied 'We worship the God who created everything, including you and me'. Pushpamma, for the first time, heard that she was not an inferior creation, but created by God. She felt there is equality between men and women in His creation. For a Hindu-woman when she realizes that she is God's creation, that she is made in His image and that she belongs to Him it brings self-esteem and self-worth to her. Such a place was denied to Pushpamma in her own religion. Samuel suggests: 'for centuries women have been exploited and oppressed in India'.[117]

Samuel wrote, 'The image of God in humanity, has spiritual (to represent God as steward), intellectual (to reflect God's mind and communicate with him), social (dominion over God's creation to structure human society according to God's plan), and physical dimensions (relationship between men and women)'.[118] The Christian message brings self-esteem and self-worth to its hearers and followers. It transforms ones understanding of oneself. The term 'transformation' was adopted at the Wheaton Consultation on the Church in response to human need.[119] Transformation speaks of a total change in one's life and in all relationships with others. This change offers the individual personal development in terms of self-esteem and self-worth. These benefits are not earned by the individual, but are bestowed upon humankind by a loving God through His grace:[120]

> Pushpamma asked further, 'Where is the idol'? 'Where are the flowers'? She felt very strange about everything the team did in respect to God.[121]

Then Jayaprabhu explained to her about the true nature of God, true worship of God, and the story of Jesus coming to this world, His death and resurrection. Jayaprabhu explained to her the way to salvation and forgiveness of sins through faith in Jesus' name and not by works. Pushpamma's understanding of God was confused by coming to her from Popular Hinduism, which encouraged idol worship and *Bhakti-marg*

---

[116] Ibid.

[117] Ibid. 166

[118] Ibid. 353

[119] Samuel, Vinay Kumar, and Chris Sugden, 1987, *The Church in Response to Human Need*

[120] Sugden, Christopher, 1986, *Witnessing to The Living God in Development in Contemporary Africa*, David M. Gitari and G.P.Benson (eds.)

[121] Ibid.

(devotional path), and Lingayatism. Lingayatism, though it was once a monotheistic religion, later became polytheistic. Lingayatism believes that all things are not God though God pervades them all.[122] It also insisted on understanding and achieving a good life.

The Christian understanding of God to Pushpamma looked strange yet impressive. She saw a Christian community living a simple life of faith in God without boasting about any achievement. She saw in the lives of the community how their trust in God was relevant in them. They were not disengaged with the world in their pursuit of the spiritual life like her Hindu saints. They were young and simple folk like her who had found meaning and direction in their lives. The Christian way looked a simpler and easier way to her than *Bhakti marg* (devotional way).

For Pushpamma, the Christian message was impressive. Jesus' life and death and miracles impressed her. She was deeply touched to know that Jesus died for her sins and He is able to forgive all her guilt and sin. Christ's selfless and sacrificial life always attracts Hindus. Hindus have similar stories of their saints. However, Christ's crucifixion for others' sake brings new truth to a Hindu. Hindus use different types of sacrifices, including animal sacrifices. However, these sacrifices are meant to appease or to fulfil vows to gods and the concept one dying for the sins of all is not found in Hinduism. Hinduism makes individuals responsible for their own good and bad deeds. The consequences of such deeds must be met by the individuals themselves in this life or in their next life.[123]

The resurrection of Jesus brings another new truth to a Hindu. Jesus' victory over death gives them hope for their present and future life. Not submitting to their 'fate', but faith in Jesus gives them the confidence to overcome their fear of *karma*. The miracles of Jesus bring another truth to Hindus. Many of their holy men have performed miracles. For a Hindu, to accept the miracles of Jesus is easier than a 'rational' Westerner:

> Pushpamma said, '…though it was strange to hear all about Jesus and His way, it felt good to hear that my sins and guilt can be forgiven now and I can become a child of God. For the first time, I heard that Jesus had concern for me and for my problems. Especially, about my forthcoming wedding with Rama Reddy'.[124]

At this point, Pushpamma could not make a decision to follow Jesus. As an individual and as a woman it seems it was difficult for Pushpamma to take the decision on her own..

---

[122] Ibid.
[123] Samuel, Vinay Kumar, personal interview, Oxford, UK
[124] Ibid.

Pushpamma and miracles

Meanwhile, her family lost their goats in the forest. Many efforts were made to find them, including her father inquiring of the sorcerers, but to no avail. This problem was brought to the notice of Jayaprabhu who comforted the family members and prayed with them. He gave them the assurance that within three days their lost goats would be found. For the next three days, Jayaprabhu and the team members prayed for this and miraculously the lost goats were found. A stranger brought back their goats. This brought great joy to the family and their trust in the words of the team members grew strongly.

Pushpamma remarked 'that these people and their God are not ordinary, they are truly special ones. These people are God's true messengers and their God is a powerful one, who hears the prayers of his people, even without offering anything to Him'.[125]

Loss to a Hindu is considered as an unpropitious sign. They believe that all their prosperity will vanish away. Goats have good economic value. It was an economic loss to the family. The family was perplexed and lost hope. It was time for the family to ascertain whether their gods were angry with them or not, because of some improper poojas or failure to observe some rituals. In a time like this, the prayers of Jayaprabhu comforted the family. Christian witness came openly to the family now. Along with the family, other community members came to hear Christian witness. Prophetic words endanger Christian witnesse, but God intervenes into a situation and His name triumphs. Miracles, signs and wonders seemed to play an important role in effective Christian witness.[126]

What if such a miracle had not happened? Would Pushpamma have become a Christian? For Pushpamma, the miracle was just one of the factors. She was already attracted to Jesus for other reasons. Miracles certainly add more trust in a person who seeks Christ. She recognised the power of His name when she realised that her gods were not able to help her family.

Pushappamma and her family's decision for Christ

A few days later, when Pushpamma noticed that the team members had not cooked food for three days (the team members had no money to buy food), and moved with compassion, she invited them for meals. (Hindus like hospitality. Feeding the hungry is a noble thing to do). The team gratefully accepted that and ate their fill. After the food, Jayaprabhu asked Pushpamma whether they might be allowed to pray with them. Before prayer, Jayaprabhu presented the gospel message once again to Pushpamma, her mother and brother. In his message, Jayaprabhu asked the

---

[125] Ibid.

[126] Bayard, Taylor, 1984, op.cit., E.D.Ashwal, *It Can Be Done*, 75

family to seriously consider the question, 'If you die today, where you will go'. [127]

For sometime, Pushpamma had questions about life and death. This had become a very serious question to her when her aunt had died. She did ask others about it but no one was able to answer her convincingly. Although among Hindus, there is belief in rebirth, real questions of life and death are a challenge to them. An average Hindu does not wish to go through the cycle of rebirth but struggles to find a real way to god. A Hindu does not easily talk about death. But Pushpamma and her family had experienced death in the family. For some time, thoughts about death bothered the family. So, an opportunity was created in the family to talk about it. Jayaprabhu's question neither put the family off nor did it bring fear in their hearts. This means people do struggle with questions over life and death. An appropriate Christian message in this context has meaning.

Pushpamma asserted, 'This was an important question but I had no answer. I felt absolutely helpless and all my religious beliefs and practices seemed to fall short in giving me clear understanding about my future life with God. Along with this, other questions about the true God, the forgiveness of sins and Christ's crucifixion came back to me again. Then I made a decision to follow Christ. It was a new experience for me. Along with me, my mother and my brother made decisions to follow Jesus'. [128]

Pushpamma countered her fate with faith. The idea of fate brought agony and despair in her life. Faith brought hope and change to her life. Faith assured her that all her guilt and sins were washed away. Pushpamma had thoughts of fatalism pervading her present and future life. Faith promised to bring change to her life. Pushpamma made up her mind to move away from a fatalistic attitude to life to a faith life. It was a new venture altogether, but, she was not alone because her family-members were with her. This new adventure was not displacing her either from her place in the society nor was there any demand on her to change her religion or name. Christian missions in the past and the present have made such demands on new converts. Are these outward changes important for one to be called a Christian? Is Pushpamma seen here as a Christian, who did not try to change her name or religion to be called a Christian? This suggests people of other faiths are looking for real changes in their religious beliefs rather than just outward changes.

Christian witness may also see the importance of conversion of a family, or families in rural areas rather than leading people individually to the Lord. It may be possible to lead individuals to Chris, but in the long run such converts find it hard to live as Christians due to family and community pressure, especially if they are a joint, extended or large family because

---

[127] Ibid.
[128] Ibid.

these bonds seem stronger than their change. It may be the demand of the relational context rather than following any ideology or methodology.[129]

Pushpamma understood that it was not *karma*, but sin and guilt that bothered and burdened her. Through *karma* nothing would change her, not even her gods whereas he Christian message brought hope in her life. She realized her new allegiance would certainly bring changes in the things she had no hope to change in the past. Though it was a new belief, it meant a change for the better. Pushpamma felt that she was drawn to Christ than to the Christian religion. This suggests people are more willing to be drawn to Christ rather than to the Christian religion.

Rama Reddy

Pushpamma bought a Bible and read it everyday and prayed regularly to God. It was all a new experience to her, but she says 'it was really worthwhile to me, and I found joy, which was more than satisfying to me'.[130] Day by day, Pushpamma grew stronger in the Lord. Christian witness empowers people not only with experience but with knowledge and wisdom and leads them to a Spirit filled life. The holy books are revered by Hindus. Through Bible reading, or seeing herself as she was, the truths Pushpamma had heard became real to her through the written Word of God. This enlightened her more and built her faith life more strongly. This shows Christian witness empowers the powerless and the oppressed.

Meanwhile, the EHC team moved to another place and she faced another challenge in that her would-be husband Rama Reddy had fallen very ill, seemingly fatally. Family members all made efforts to save him, they even took him to the Davangere Medical College but nothing seemed to heal him. All the people in the town felt happy about this. Rama Reddy had caused so much distress in the town through his violent behaviour. For Pushpamma, it was important moment; she was not prepared to lose him. She prayed for him and sent word to Jayaprabhu and requested him to come over to Hosadurga and pray for Rama Reddy's speedy recovery. Jayaprabhu, taking that opportunity, shared the gospel with Rama Reddy and asked whether he was willing to put his faith in Jesus for healing. The tears rolled from Rama Reddy's eyes and he willingly prayed for God's forgiveness for his sinful life and for healing. To everyone's surprise, Rama Reddy was miraculously healed, and Pushpamma and the family members were very deeply impressed. After some time, Pushpamma got married to Rama Reddy and later both were baptized.

Pushpamma's faith day by day, grew stronger and stronger in the living God. As a woman in Indian society, she was a weak link to be used to establish God's work.Howevert as Paul reminds to Corinthians, 'God chose

---

[129] McGavran, Donald A., 1988 (1970,1980), *Understanding Church Growth*, 395-400
[130] Ibid.

the weak things of this world to shame the strong. He chose the lowly things of this world and the despised things' I Cor 1:27,28. She believed in Jesus, His Word, healing power and in prayer which helped to win her would-be husband for God and herself. She was now able to see her life filled with hope and God's glory.

Aftermath

Pushpamma's marriage took place according to the Hindu custom. When I asked her whether she was uncomfortable about her Hindu wedding, she said:

> No, not at all. It was a social gathering. The religious significance was minimal. My community met together. Our community elders and our parents blessed us. Our belief in Christ was not shaken because of that. We testified to our community how Christ blessed and changed our lives. If we had opted for a Christian wedding, we would have lost our family and community. Today, some of our families have become Christians. Though they took time to follow Jesus, they have made a decision to follow Him. We need patience and perseverance.[131]

Pushpamma's story continues. Some of her family members, friends and neighbours have put their faith in Jesus. Christ's empowerment helped her to believe that not only is He able to change her present and future life, but also to believe in change for her fiancée's life, however wicked or hopeless it was. Pushpamma is a living testimony to true Christian change.

Implications of the Study

How are people led to Christ? How does the formation of a Christ Group take place in a land like India? The case study of Pushpamma states that it is because of the decision of her and her family members, or a group's decision for Christ, led to the formation of the Hosadurga Christ Group. The people are not led to Christ, nor form a Christ Group, just by receiving or reading a tract, nor through any such impersonal mass evangelistic methods, especially in a land like India, where the relational context exists.

As Prasad commented, while writing to Kietzman on use of 'only literature', which Kietzman was insisting for IEHC to adhere, India needs a 'total evangelism'. That meant the distribution of tracts to every home will not help to complete the evangelism in India, because of its context, which needs a different approach, if tract distribution is to be effective. Prasad further adds, 'campaigns (open air or gospel meetings) and word of mouth methods' and combining them with tract distribution are equally important for effective work to reach every home, that could help to complete the

---

[131] Ibid.

evangelization of India.[132] Prasad commenting on 'literature evangelism' wrote, 'if the basis is only 'literature evangelism' we will miss 64 percent of India's population' That includes the rural people, illiterate or people who need more explanation and more time to understand the message rather than needing to read a tract on their own and understand it. Prasad's 64 percent was the proportion of illiterate as 36 percent literate was the national figure of that time. The 36 percent literate includes those who only knew how to sign and but were not able to read and write. This means more than 64 percent or between 70 to 80 percent of the population could be missed 'if the basis was on literature evangelism' alone. Though there may be claims from some mission agencies in India about such happenings, those claims need to be a separate study. Prasad, who is a seasoned mission strategist, over four decades, called for 'total evangelism' in a context like India, rather than employ a 'sole idea' conceived as 'the method' strategy of western missions. Such strategies, ideas and methods are driven by the sponsor or partner agencies to follow and implement without giving any considerations to the contexts of their partners' regions.

The case study of Pushpamma suggests that people is coming to Christ, and the formation of a Christ Group, is a process which require patience on the part of the good news' bearer. The listener goes through a period of careful observation of the bearer's life and message. At this stage, the role of the evangelist becomes crucial. Prasad emphatically asserted that 'Christ Groups were not formed due to reading the printed page, but through the earnest efforts of field evangelists'[133] and further compares evangelists to fishermen and says, '...his heart is more on the fish than the net'.[134] Alongside the efforts of evangelists, as Pushpamma's story suggests, there is a need for some kind of response from the hearer. As the bridge builds up between the parties, they need a time and occasion to engage themselves in further dialogue for more information and clarification of the message. At times, especially in critical stages, like goats and health lost and prayer answered in case of Pushpamma's story, such divine interventions in real life situations are important in the lives of both parties, and to have an impact and influence of the message they have received or shared. Though the response of the hearer was delayed until the end, the family came forward with deeper convictions and took a step of faith for Christ.

What changes are necessary in order to be a Christian? Change the past names of new believers and give them a Christian name? Rename Pushpamma as Priscilla? Does that make any difference? The study shows

---

[132] Prasad, B.A.G., 1986, A Letter written to Dale Kietzman on 22nd December, Secuderabad, India
[133] Prasad, B.A.G., 1999, *Prayer Bulletin*, 17, November, Secunderabad, India. This wasan earlier article of Prasad, which was used even after his death in 1995
[134] Prasad, B.A.G., 1991, *Prayer Bulletin*, 14, December

that unless a person truly encounters with Christ and realises a need of Christ, there is no change. In the past and the present, some Christian missions emphasize outward changes.[135] New converts were not allowed to visit their relatives.[136] Christian mission threatened the existing religious communities. New converts, when they became Christians, excluded themselves from others. McGavran observed, 'converts become detached from the natural communities to which they belong, and become attached to the foreign mission and its institutions, and are required to conform to ethical and cultural standards which belong to the Christianity of the foreign missionary'.[137]

The story of the Christ Group in Hosadurga presented the 'Christ of the Indian way' to the people. Though Christ's message brought a different perspective to their lives, it did not threaten their identity and their culture. If the message had come to Pushpamma by alien missionaries, they would have forced their culture on her which would have hampered the story of Pushpamma. Walls argued 'that such controlled power on converts is 'proselytisation' rather than 'conversion' which he interprets, 'simply and wrongly is forced to repeat a foreign cultural form of belief and practice', and for him 'conversion' means, 'not to add something new to something old'.[138]

Christ's message was presented to the families and groups rather than a Western driven individualistic approach. The personal and relational approach became effective rather than mass evangelism driven with an impersonal and so-called efficient approach. Young and old were attracted towards Christ. Their experience of Christ became their own experience rather than being imposed. They owned Christ in their lives. Christ's presence brought change within them and externally. Though it took time it did not exclude them from others. They continued to live in their own culture and context, but they are not bound by it. They seek Christ's glory and the good of their communities. They want to live as true followers of Christ as well as being true Indians.

Pushpamma and Rama Reddy are now in their forties, and have a grown up daughter and son. Both daughter and son are believers in Christ. Their daughter married a believer and their son serves the Lord in a Christian mission, and Pushapamma leads the worship group in the church. She has become a leader in the church, a position she had not dreamt of in her past religion. Rama Reddy is an elder of the Hosadurga Christ Group. They want to remain faithful to Christ and have a burden to share the good news with others. Alongwith sharing the gospel, they share their food and time

---

[135] Fernandes, Walter, 1981, *Caste Conversion Movements in India*, 2
[136] Goudies, 1983, in Graham, Houghton), *The Impoverishment of Dependency*, 115, 118
[137] Neill, Stephen, ed. 1971, *Concise Dictionary of the Christian Mission*, 479
[138] Walls, Andrew F., 2009, a profile, from 1910 to 2010, accessed from the web

with others. One of the aspects which became a stepping stone to Ramanna and Pushpamma to continue and grow in their Christian faith whatever the situation they went through was their past religious experience and the influence of Lingayatism.

Now the Hosadurga Christ Group has become a full-fledged church with its own building and a full-time pastor. The pastor and his members actively take part in evangelism. Today, there are six established churches of different denominations which function here and hundreds of believers have become Christians from other faiths.[139] Though the glory may be given to the Lord for extending His work in Hosadurga, it is appropriate to give credit to the Hosadurga Christ Group for the impact and influence which it has left over the years on the larger community of this area, and which now has become a stepping stone for many churches and mission to develop their work.

Prasad envisaged from the beginning about the Christ Groups work in India when he said 'a total evangelism' to Kietzman and other WLC heads, who failed to understand the need of the context and effectiveness of the work, rather than insist IEHC to stick to their (WLC's) 'original' vision or method. Prasad tried to convince WLC leaders over and against their so called 'vision and method' by saying, 'we were caught up with the rush of reaching the last home...forgot...the ultimate goal...which is the saving of souls and adding to the church'.[140] Though his statement seemed appropriate it went unheard by the idea and method driven WLC heads.

Another important point to come out of this study is that though the IEHC team which worked for three months in Hosadurga *taluka* and distributed ten thousands of tracts to thousands of homes, except for Pushpamma's 'family', they failed to establish any other real contact per se. As the study shows 'one family' over a period became a church and influenced its immediate and surrounding communities and became a stepping stone for other churches and mission to establish and develop their work. On the whole, this sounds like a 'ripple effect' and indicates how the Gospel work can be carried into the rural places of India and what is the better, or effective way, to work there.

---

[139] D'Souza, George Steven, 2007, personal interview, Pastor, Calvary Sharon Church, Hosadurga, India
[140] Ibid.

Chapter 7
Research Results:
Christ Groups Members and their Identity

The research results of this chapter are based on the different sources mentioned in the previous chapter. The first part of the chapter contains primary data of the four Christ Groups and interviews held with WLC and IEHC officials and the later part focuses on a case study. This chapter is divided into three sections. 'Section A' examines whether the relational context approach will react differently to the western individualistic approach or not. If it reacts differently, then questions arise of by and to whom, why and how it reacts differently and to what degree. What are the factors involved in influencing such reactions? The results presented support or falsify the first hypothesis concerning the reaction of the relational context to the western individualistic approach, the response of the Indian rural populace to the distribution Christian literature on a mass scale.

This section proceeds by describing who the members are, especially looking into their identity. This is to ascertain whether Christianity was only for the outcastes or for members of the other religious groups. Some Hindu fundamentalists in India have alleged that Christianity is for the outcastes, poor, non-literate, or weaker sections of the people only. Such cases took place during the Mass Movement, when those who became Christians came from outcastes. Who and how they were led to Christ or a Christ Group and what was their family context? Alongside that, what were other factors that influenced them to take such decision? This study is based on the four Christ Groups: Bagepalli, Hosadurga, Pavagada and Bijapur. Sources of survey data include questionnaires and interviews with the members and evangelists cum pastors. Moreover, certain magazines and reports of IEHC have been verified to see whether the accounts either in the mission fields or testimonies of the individuals with whom interviews were conducted tally or whether any important things are missed out. The first domains treated by the survey focussed on the identity of the membersunder the headings: Backgrounds of Members, Gender Representation, Income, Occupations and Caste Representation.

The second grouping relates to Family Context: Married or not Married, the Size of the Family, Family Evangelism or Other Evangelism. This second grouping helps especially to understand the family context in rural evangelism.

Study on the Identity of Members

Some of the key issues that the identity of Christ Groups members are vital to establish are who they are and why they are there. If the findings help to clear up such age-old allegations that Christianity is only for the outcaste, not for all, they may be of great help to many mission practitioners in India.

The Christian presence in the rural parts of Karnataka State is negligible or nil. During the Mass Movement, those who became Christians came from villages but they became city dwellers for many reasons. As Sunder Raj, who is a leading missiologist, argues, 'the individuals who became Christians are alienated from their families and communities.'[1] There may be other reasons why missionaries contributed to this, like giving better education to those new believers and making them to stand on their own feet to support their families without seeking help from their landlords and dominant communities, who were hostile towards Christianity. Today, Christians predominantly live in cities and hence it is seen as an urban or city Christianity. Samuel remarks that today 98 percent of evangelism takes place in India mostly among urban Christians.[2] This is to suggest that the Gospel instead of going to therural areas stayed in the cities.

In the post-independence period, the reaction to the Christian Gospel changed to a great degree, if not totally. When questions were asked and data gathered, there was just one family, which came from a Christian background,whereas all others were from a non-Christian background. That one family was in Hosadurga, on a job transfer. Though Bijapur has some Christian presence, non-Christians responded to the Gospel. IEHC did not intend to create any divisions or disturbance among existing churches.[3]

Table 7A.1 Respondents' Background of Four Christ Groups in Karnataka

Respondents Background		Number of Respondents	Percentage of Respondents
Non-Christians	.00	199	99.5
Christians	1.00	1	.5
Total		200	100

In the rural context, people of other faiths have deep appreciation and interest in the person of Jesus Christ and his good news.[4] They sincerely

---

[1] Sunder Raj, Ebenezer, 2001, *National Debate on Conversion*, 15

[2] Samuel, Vinay Kumar, 2004, personal interview, Oxford, UK

[3] Sudershan, Albert, 1998, personal interview, IEHC, Bangalore, India

[4] Houghton, Graham, 1983, *The Impoverishment of Dependency*, 133

desire to follow Jesus and want to live in their own context. Sunder Raj asserted, 'Christian mission must enable persons to maintain full family ties and social harmony.'[5] During the Mass Movement, the Christian mission may have feared that the converts would go back to their past beliefs and practice, if the converts were allowed to stay in their own contexts and hence the believers were detached.[6] Here Christianity appeared to be overprotective of its converts.

However, Christ Groups, which were formed in the context, did not detach people from their context and community allowing them to grow in their own environment. This may have drawn people of other faiths to come to Christ. This suggests that some in rural India will follow Jesus if the new believers are helped to grow in their own context. Christian mission conducted in India without fear or becoming overprotective of its converts, needs to test the power of the Gospel and the Holy Spirit in the lives of those believers to see whether the change is real and rooted in the Gospel or is temporary only. Christian mission need not to be too concerned with numerical or population growth of Christians in India. Rather, it may allow that the good news of Jesus Christ to bring needed change in those lives of people, who may then live as better citizens of India.

The members of these Christ Groups have lived for the last two to three decades as Christians in their own context and continued as changed human beings without labelling themselves as belonging to any distinct religious community. Yet they were rather happy to call themselves members of a Christ Group. Often sociologists and some religious fundamentalists allege that Christian mission presents its Gospel to the vulnerable section of the society, that is, women, the illiterate and the poor.[7] Though the good news of Jesus Christ does not make any distinctions based on gender, status and education to present the Gospel, it was felt necessary to check whether such claims match reality in these areas.

In the four Christ Groups, from observations and data, there were almost equal number of men and women present, including children. In India, people want to partake in social and religious gatherings as a family.[8] When conducting these surveys, I observed in all Christian meetings the presence of the family members rather than individuals representing the family.

---

[5] Ibid. 15

[6] Ibid.

[7] Augustine, John, 1998, personal interview, a sociologist, professor in UTC, Bangalore, India

[8] Vinaykumar, Stanley, personal interview, an elder in Brethren Assembly, Bangalore, India

Figure 7A.1 Representation of the Members of Four Christ Groups;
CG Survey in Karnataka State

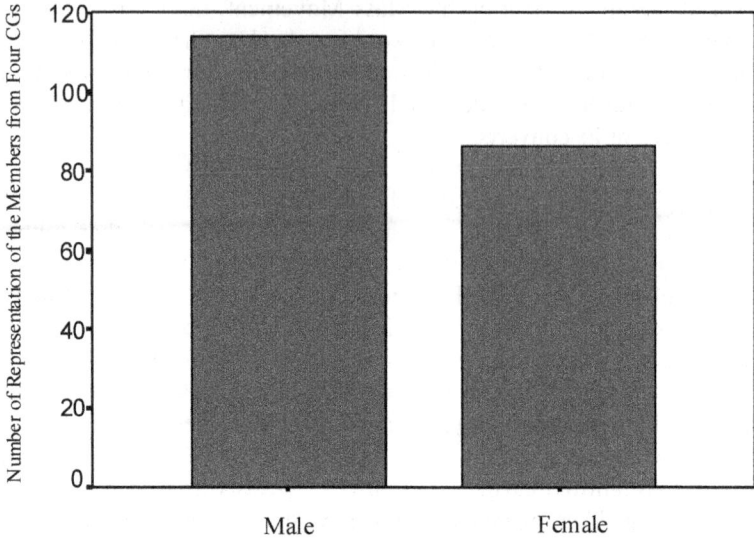

There were variations in male and female representation among these four Christ Groups. In Bagepalli and Pavagada, the female representation was slightly more than male; not so in Hosadurga, it was almost equal, but male representation in Bijapur was more than female. Although Bijapur in the context of Karnataka State is a male dominated area, it was surprising to see that more males had responded to the Gospel. Similar variation was present among literate and non-literate people in four of the Christ Groups. Bagepalli and Pavagada showed more illiterates, but not so Hosadurga, where there were more semi-literates than illiterates. Bijapur showed more college degree holders than in the other places. During the interviews, I observed that none of the participants representing the four Christ Groups made any point regarding their education, whether it hindered or helped them to know the good news. Yet, they were happy to state how the Gospel touched them when they first heard it.

Figure 7A.2 Educational Background of the Members of Four Christ Groups; CG Survey in Karnataka State

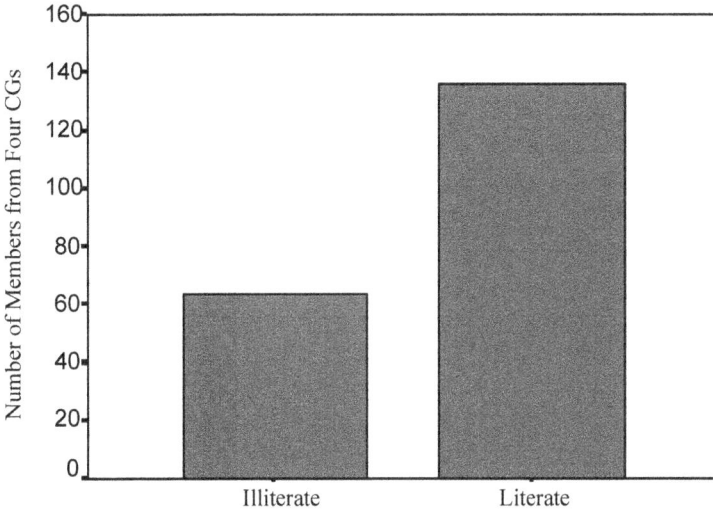

During the Mass Movement (1890-1930), it was estimated that about 80 percent of the converts were illiterate.[9]. After independence, India gave more emphasis to literacy programmes. 'Free education' was provided to the rural masses to improve literacy. In the last decade, the Government of India and non-governmental organisations (NGOs) invested a lot of money and training in increasing the literacy rate in the country. In Karnataka State, the literacy rate has risen to 50 percent. This suggests that there may now be fewer illiterate people in the rural areas compared with illiterates during the Mass Movement. Christ Groups, during this period, due to their simple structure recruited and retained both the literate and illiterates. Moreover, the members of the four Christ Groups did several different kinds of job: farm labourers, farmers, housewives and other manual jobs. The Group cannot be considered rich, upper class, or even high middle class. The Group consists of the poor and lower middle class people. The interviews and data showed that there were variations in such classes in the four Christ Groups. Bagepalli and Pavagada had more from poorer backgrounds. Hosadurga had more economically strong members, if not rich. Bijapur showed a contrast, that is, some had more and some had very little. Overall, an equal number of people, that is, poor and lower middle class people had responded to the Gospel.

---

[9] Samuel, Vinay Kumar, 2003, personal interview, Oxford, UK

Table 7A.2 Distribution of Occupations of the Members of Four Christ Groups; CG Survey Karnataka State

Occupations of the Members of the Four Christ Groups		Number of engaged in occupations	Perecentage of the memebrs engaged in occupations
Students	.00	8	4.0
Agricultarilists	1.00	38	19
Civil servants	2.00	3	1.5
Small business holders	3.00	4	2.0
Clerks/teachers	4.00	23	11.5
Labourers	5.00	68	34.0
Industrial workers	6.00	9	4.5
House wives	7.00	39	19.5
Others	8.00	8	4.0
Total		200	100.0

Table 7A.3 Distribution of Income of the Members of Four Christ Groups; CG Survey in Karnataka

Income levels of the Members of Four Christ Groups	Number of Members in Each Group	Percentage of the Each Income Group
Rs 0000-1000	46	23.0
Rs 1001-2000	54	27.0
Rs 2001-3000	29	14.5
Rs 3001-4000	21	10.5
Rs 4001-5000	14	7.0
Rs 5001-7000	7	3.5
Rs 7001-9000	4	2.0
Rs 9001-11000	18	9.0
Rs 11001-25000	2	1.0
Rs 25001-40000 and above	5	2.5
Total	200	100.0

This indicates that the 'poor' and those who live 'below to poverty line' are more often attracted to the gospel. In the words of Jesus, 'The Spirit of the Lord is on me, because he has anointed me to preach good news to the poor' (Luke 4:18). As Sugden remarks, 'Yes, the Gospel is indeed for the poor'[10] as now among the poor in Karnataka State. During the interviews when I asked the question what did they receive from evangelists-cum-

---

[10] Sugden, Chris, 1991, 'What is Good About Good News to the Poor', *AD 2000 and Beyond: a Mission Agenda*, Samuel, Vinay Kumar & Chris Sugden (eds.)

pastors when they became Christians, the answer was simply, 'Jesus'. Some added that we know how to live in this poverty, and we are not worried about our conditions, but after coming to Christ we had a wonderful experience of knowing His power and blessing in our lives.

The poor here were not coming to Christ because of 'rice or rupee',[11] a phrase coined by Mahatma Gandhi while commenting on poor outcastes becoming Christians during the Mass Movement. Though the members of Christ Groups may have received some physical benefits like healing and deliverance from alcohol addiction or demon possession, none of them received 'rice or rupee' to become Christians. The evangelists-cum-pastors received meagre material support from their mission, lived in small houses and used bicycles for their work. Neither they, nor their mission, had anything to spare to give these believers. While the poor may have a desire for their basic needs to be met, that does not stop them looking for much deeper answers to their spiritual thirst and hunger. The Good News meets the needs of the simple rural Indian population and gives meaning to their lives in Christ and in their Christ Group.

The poor and the lower middle-class people are the majority population of India, though India is a land of contrasts, where both very rich and very poor people live. This indicates the emergence of a core group, which represents the majority of the population of India which has responded positively to the Gospel. Predictably, the upper income group and rich people have not responded to the Gospel. The Good News has been presented to all without making any distinction on gender or section of the society lines. If a certain section of the society takes a decision to become Christian it shows their interest in the Gospel rather than that it has been accompanied by use of force or inducement.

When Christianity in India is seen as a religion of outcastes, this is because a large number of Christians today are the converts and their descendents from the Mass Movement period, who mainly came from the outcaste groups. This Christian movement was a liberation of the outcastes from their past oppressive Hindu caste system. Some interpreted it as the poverty stricken situation of the outcastes that made them become Christians, others said that it was for material benefit and social mobility.

In Karnataka State, Christians are often called in the Kannada language 'Kiri Stanaru', meaning 'Kiri' is 'small' – and 'Stanaru' – 'status'. A certain section of society coined this phrase when they saw outcastes becoming Christians, as a way to demean the status of Christianity in the eyes of larger religious groups.

---

[11] Ibid. 186

Table 7A.4 Caste Distribution of the Members of Four Christ Groups;
CG Survey in Karnataka

Classification of Caste of the Members of Four Christ Groups		Number of the Members Each Caste Background	Perecentage of the Members of Each Caste Background
Upper Caste	.00	70	35.0
Backward Caste	1.00	34	17.0
Out-Caste	2.00	92	46.0
	Total	196	98.0
Total		200	100.0

During the sample interviews, I saw everybody sitting together, singing, praying and worshipping. I asked them whether they minded sitting together even though they come from different castes and sub-castes. Most of them said that after becoming Christians such caste differences are not required anymore. Only on certain occasions, when non-Christian community people are around, to please them they may show such language and attitudes, otherwise they feel that all of them are God's children and Jesus loves them all.I observed that there was almost an equal number of different caste people gathered together. The outcastes comprised almost half and the other castes together comprised the other half. Surprisingly, there were no Brahmin converts, that is, from the highest caste.

Upper caste includes Kshthriyas (warriors, second in the caste-ladder after Brahmins, see Appendix-4), Lingayats (agriculturists) and Vaishyas (business community). Some suggest that 'Lingayats' are 'Sudras' (lower-caste) due to their occupation, which is agriculture. However, in Karnataka they are the ruling caste comprising one quarter of the State's population and are viewed alongside Kshathriyas in importance. The backward caste, or class, includes Muslims and Lamanis. Though Lamanis (Gypsies) are a tribe they are considered as a backward community.

The Gospel has no social boundaries, such as castes and cultures that it will not cross. It has ability to penetrate into all sorts of places, whether it is hard or easy going. Indians in general have a high regard for the teachings of Christ. Physical blessings such as healing and deliverance have a great impact on the lives of all caste people. The view of some that Christianity is a religion of the outcastes is ageneralization, though the Gospel of Christ may appeal to them most. The sufferings of Christ, which may be similar to their own sufferings and His liberating power giving them a better hope for the future, may have drawn them to accept the Good News. Other caste people told their stories of conversion, about how the power of Christ helped them to overcome their falling and failures and the blessings they received from Jesus Christ.

Study of the Family Context of Members

Whether the response of the Group members to the Gospel was made individually or as a family, a group or a community, gives some helpful insights into how families function in a rural or semi-rural context of India. The study focused on the individual and family and did not look into how a group or a community responds to the Gospel. Respondents were asked: 'How did you arrive at a decision when your son's or daughter's wedding was taking place? Do they have any say in it? Do you allow them to make a personal choice about their wedding'? It was an open-ended question though data were collected through a structured questionnaire. The response of the members of the Christ Groups was similar in all the places with little variation. In Bagepalli and Pavagada, the respondents said that parents take the decisions and children do not have any say. In Hosadurga and Bijapur, due to their semi-rural context and better education, they said that though it is the parent's decision, they do ask for the consent of their children. However, overall, the headman's or husband's or father's decision is honoured. Sara Hobson[12] who did research on how the family functions in a rural context in Karnataka in a village (Palahalli, near Krishnapatna about 80kms from Bangalore) entitled her book 'Family Web'. She explored how a family in a rural area took decisions on important issues. Though she agrees that the headman of the family takes the final decision, other members of the family are involved in that process amidst agreement and disagreement.

There may be some individual conversions in India, such as Sadhu Sundar Singh, Pandit Ramabai, Keshubchandra Banarjee, Bhakthsingh and many others. However, such converts have to face a lot of opposition from their family, relatives and community. The evangelist of Bijapur Christ Group told me about an incident with one of their converts, Srimanth Chalavadis who, after his wonderful conversion to Christianity, faced continued opposition from his family, community and finally political pressure, which made him go back to his first faith. Many of the individual converts have succumbed to such pressures and have returned to their past faith. When asked, 'When you made a decision for Christ, was that your own or by your family? Which one do you think was easier, whether to become a Christian on your own or as a family?' The answers of the respondents in all four Christ Groups were similar when the decision was made with the family, they felt at ease, protected from any outside pressure and found space to grow in their faith along with their family members.

---

[12] Hobson, Sara, 1978, *Family Hub: A Story of India*

However, those who had made the decision on their own expressed the struggle and opposition they had to go through due to their Christian faith.

The community in the villages closed boundaries; it may be rather for individual converts to stand-up against that when the culture expects them to be obedient to their parents and elders. If they are not, the dominant culture may damage the relationships between them. Ultimately, the Christian (Faith) Mission will be blamed for this. All four Christ Groups without much variation showed that it was mostly families that joined. However there were variations in age groups among families. Whole families (consisting of, husband, wife, and children with other members of the family) were in those groups. In Bagepalli and Pavagada, couples were in their forties with older children; in Hosadurga and Bijapur, the younger couples, in their twenties with young children predominantly in the Groups. Interestingl,y there were only a few older couples with grown up children present in the Group. This indicated that the young and slightly older couples look for social progress in their newly formed families. They are looking for a better direction for their family life. It is an Indian concept that when they receive blessings from God, like healing, deliverance and success, those are the result of a divine person living within. Now, with all reverence, they feel obliged to follow Him and receive more blessings from Him. Also, these families found the true meaning of the Gospel: forgiveness, reconciliation, peace, and hope, for example, in the family like Pushpamma, who have stood the test of time and continued to live as Christians for over 30 years.

Table 7A.5 Marriage Status of the Members of Four Caste Groups

Marriage Status of the Four Caste Groups Member		Number of Members Marriage Status	Percentage of Members Marriage Status
Unmarried	.00	54	27.0
Married	1.00	125	62.5
Widow	2.00	9	4.5
Widower	3.00	12	6.0
Total		200	100.0

Table 7A.6 Distribution of Households' Family Composition of Four Christ Groups Karnataka State

Christ Groups Members Family Composition		Number of CG Members Family Composition	Percentage of CG Members Composition
Single Parent	.00	2	1.0
Parent and Children	1.00	31	15.5

Parent, Children, Other	2.00	167	83.5
Total		200	100.0

WLC claimed that individually people are won for Christ. A question was put to the evangelists, 'How were families led to Christ, when you distributed tracts to every home?' The evangelists from Bagepalli and Pavagada explained that though they were asked only to distribute tract,s they found it useful that since people would not understand it just by reading it, to sit in the homes of those families and explain the Gospel to them. The members of Hosadurga added that Jayaprabhu, who led Pushpamma and Rammanna Reddy to Christ, regularly followed them up and wrote to them about matters concerning spiritual things. He visited them to encourage and exhort them in studying the Scripture. The evangelist from Bijapur said that when he started his work in the 1990s, IEHC had launched the 'Final Thrust-5000', under which, 'Family Evangelism' was emphasized and he straightaway started his ministry with that sort of evangelism.

Figure 7A.4 Responses of the Households of the Four Christ Groups to Family or Other Evangelism; CG Survey in Karnataka

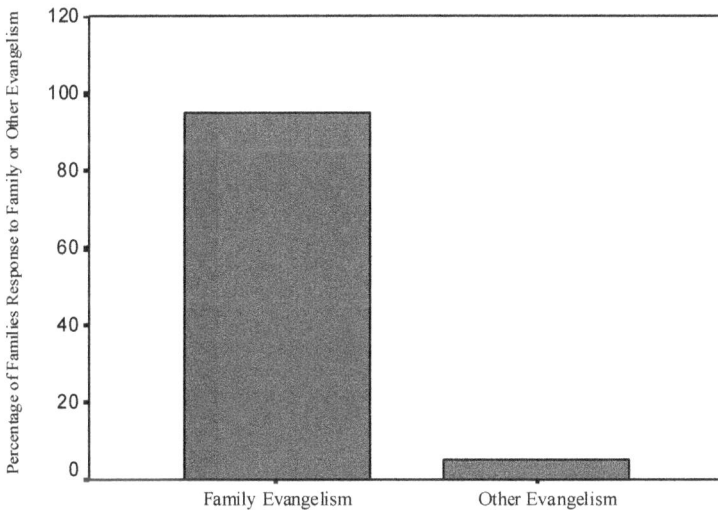

Bringing families to Christ and helping them join Christ Groups was appropriate in these areas. Thisindicated that the rural and semi-rural communities in India will respond to the Gospel, if it is presented to the families. The claim by WLC that only through the distribution of tracts were people won was far from the reality.

From the Analysis of the First Section Two Important Points emerged

1. A view of the 'Whole' that is, reaching the entire rural community, without giving any room for suspicion that society is threatened with the Christian message. Though there may be some variances of response shown from one family to another and one member to another, the entire community, with some exceptions, indicatds the nature of the response.

2. There emerged a 'Core Group', which shows a good response pattern and represents the main population of the rural community. However, it is an economically and politically weaker group but because of its numerical strength in the community it is a decisive channel through which the others in the rural context can be reached.

The next section will deal with 'what change factors are needed and whether those changes are necessary or not in becoming Christians.'

Christ Groups Members and the View of Christian Mission

This section examines what makes a member of Christ Group call themselves a Christian. From the time of Christ, Christianity is making attempts to define itself and to determine version of Christianity is true. Whether it is of the East or West, in the Gospel, 'the Pharisees asked him, walk not thy disciples according to the tradition of the elders, but eat bread with unwashed hands?' (Mk 7:5 KJV). In the times of the Apostles, we read in the book of Acts that certain Christians of the Pharisee background wanted Gentile believers to be circumcised and keep the Law of Moses if they were to be save (Acts: 15:1-23). Some missionaries wanted their converts to live in the tradition of their home countries. As David Livingstone said, he wanted to take colonization, commerce and Christianity to the places where he went for exploration in order to replace Arab slave traders. It will be interesting to see what marks the members of Christ Groups as Christians, and whether they were forced on them or if they willingly took them as their own.

Christ Group Members and their Christian Marks

The domains treated by the survey are: the change factors in tangible ways, the theological stance, church traditions and social bonds. In the four Christ Groups, it was necessary to discover what sort of Christianity they followed, – traditional, western, Scriptural or contextual. As stated earlier in the survey, except for Bijapur, in the other Christ Groups places no or very little Christian presence was evident. Even in Bijapur, nominal Christianity existed, where Christian faith is for the name's sake only and in an isolated way, that is, where Christians live in mission compounds.

An open-ended question was asked: 'Would they want to change their names, dress, family life pattern, religion, since they have become Christians'? 'The family life pattern' not only looked at adoption of other lifestyles but also different relationships in the family (with those who are not yet Christians), and ceremonies (like weddings). The traditional view of past western missions, or some of the present Christian missions in India expected to see some tangible changes when people of other faiths became Christians. It may also indicate the role of Christ Groups: how they provided the space for members to find the true meaning of Christianity in their own context and become committed followers of Christ.

Table 7B.1 Distribution of Members of Four Christ Groups' Opinion about 'Change of Name' to become a Christian; CG Survey in Karnataka State

Representation of members		Number of members represent	Perecentage of representation of members
Strongly agree	1.00	1	.5
Disagree	2.00	108	54.0
Strongly disagree	3.00	86	43.0
Neutral	4.00	5	2.5
Total		200	100.0

'To change names', most of the members of these Groups did not agree. Some said, 'we have put our faith in Jesus, not in Christian religion'. 'Becoming a Christian' and 'Christian Religion' seemed to have two different meanings. On the one hand, 'becoming a Christian' means having faith in Jesus and following him. On the other hand, 'Christian religion' means something to do with the Christianity of the traditional churches. They believe that they are Christians as followers of Christ, but they did not think the same way about the Christian religion. This seemed partly due to the teaching of the evangelists, who in their sermons emphasized that it is enough for them to have faith in Jesus and accept Him for their salvation and there is no need to change their names, religion, etc., when they become Christians. Evangelists explained that it seemed appropriate for them to emphasize this because of the context where they lived, which showed much interest in Christ and His message rather than the forms of Christian religion. It was interesting to note that most of the evangelists themselves were converts from other faiths and felt that they (evangelists) understood what the people of other faiths are really looking for in Christianity, that is, for Christ and his message rather than any outward form of Christian religion. The evangelists themselves were examples of how they followed Christ without practising any outward form of the Christian religion; rather they had become the bearers of that Good News.

They wanted the members of Christ Groups to follow their way, which they (evangelists) thought would be appropriate for the members.

Some members suggested that changing one's name might hinder them from sharing their testimony with others. If they retained their own name it would be easier for them to testify about their Christian experience to others, giving them an open opportunity to share the Gospel. Some expressed fear of their community and relatives if they chose a Christian name. One of the members from Bagepalli, namely, Venkatswamy said, 'he would change the names of his children rather than his own'. Venkatswamy did change the names of his children and called them, Samson, Elisha and his daughter Suvarthamma (a word for the Gospel in Kannada language, like Evangeline). Another person, Muniswamy from Bagepalli, called his children by Christian names, like Timothy and Immanuel. Ramanna Reddy of Hosadurga has also named his son Immanuel. This suggests that the first generation Christians are not willing to change their names for the reasons mentioned above. There is no need for the Christian mission or community to be apprehensive about their faith or following Christ. What the Christian community at large needs is forbearance and continued prayers for such Christians that they (members) may give a strong witness for Christ. This also indicates that the second generation of these converts are willing to change, taking upon themselves some form of Christian religion as such.

Most of the other members of the groups have named their children using some common names. One member from Hosadurga has named his sons Guruprasad (God's gift) and Prabhudas (God's servant). In Pavagada, one named his son Prakash (Light). Such names may have a closer meaning known to God but do not sound like Christian names to the people. In Bijapur, members were happy to retain their former names and did not show any interest to changing either their own or their children's names. This indicates that the members who have come to faith want to move further on in their walk with God and live to His testimony. Although in Bijapur, members were hesitant to opt for any change, their faith was not stagnant, but growing.

Missionaries in the past, and today among some Christian circles, prefer changing the names of converts during their baptisms, though there are only a few incidents in the Bible when certain names of people were changed. The Lord God changed the name of Jacob to Israel. (Gen 32:28) Jesus changed the name of Peter to Cephas and Saul's name was changed to Paul. (Acts 13:9) There is no indication in Paul's ministry to changing the names of his converts. William Carey did not approve of this. He said, 'Our duty is not to change the names of the native converts'.[13] Some converts liked to be called by their own names instead of alien names.

---

[13] Smith, David, 1996, A Report: William Carey and Religion in Europe and Asia: An Enquiry into The Founding and Early Influence of the Baptist Missionary Society, a

Sugden argues that there are demeaning names in India when converts wanted to change names to give them a new status in the society.[14] In 2009, I came to know an evangelist who works in Nargund for the Gospel for Asia mission who stopped using his family (surname) name, that is, 'Madar'. He said that if any one hears that name they will not allow him to step inside their homes. 'Madars' are like 'Madigas' of Andhra Pradesh who in large numbers converted to Christianity during the Mass Movement. 'Madars' are the lowest sub-caste of the outcastes. Among the outcaste,s no one closely associates with or allows them to have a meal..

Table 7B.2 Distribution of Members of Four Christ Groups' Opinion about 'Change Dress' to become a Christian; CG Survey in Karnatake State

Representation of members		Number of members represented	Perecentage of representation of members
Strongly agree	1.00	3	1.5
Disagree	2.00	160	80.0
Strongly disagree	3.00	34	17.0
Neutral	4.00	3	1.5
Total		200	100.0

On whether to 'Change Dress', it was observed that except for Hosadurga and Bijapur, which are semi-rural places, people wear pants and shirts and tuck them inside. This style was not present in Bagepalli and Pavagada, where people wear traditional dress, white *lungis* (wrap-around), long-sleeved shirts, and towels on their shoulders. Men in Bijapur wore *pethas* (head-guards) and *dhotis* (like wrap- around material, but separated between the legs, to look like pyjamas). Women in all four places wore saris, and the young girls wore long skirts, medium tops, and *dhavanis* (like stoles, but longer). The exceptions were the sons of Venkatswamy and Muniswamy, of Bagepalli, who were sent to Christian hostels and schools, wearing pants, shirts, suits and ties.

Some Christian missions, during the colonial period, had forced converts to wear 'Christian' dress (pants and shirts for male and skirts for female) by the baptism,[15] so that they may be called 'Christians'. Fernandes further suggests that the converts listened to whatever the missionaries told them to do, but followed their own customs without the knowledge of these missionaries. This indicates that Indian Christians during the colonial period and now show 'greatest resistance...to the change of dress".[16]

---

former head of the Whitefield Institute, Oxford, UK

[14] Sugden, Chris, 2009, personal interview, Oxford, UK

[15] Fernandes, Walter, 1981, *Caste Conversion Movements in India*, 10

[16] Webster, C.B., 1976, *The Christian Community and Change in Nineteenth Century*

Though, today it, such forced practices are not be prevalent in Indian missions. In Christ Groups, such practices had not been introduced to its members.

'Changing Dress' in the case of 'the bare breast' or 'the upper cloth' controversy of 1829[17] in Travancore of Shanan women was practiced for centuries to honour the higher caste people. Christian missionaries, especially Rev Charles Mead,[18] actively took part to fight against it and faced stiff resistance from the high castes but succeeded in bringing the law against such a demeaning tradition.

Table 7B.3 Distribution of Members of Four Christ Groups' Opinion about 'Change Family Patterns', to become a Christian Family; CG Survey in Karnataka

Representation of Members of Four Christ Groups		Number of Members Represented	Percentage of Representation of Members
Disagree	2.00	152	76.0
Strongly disagree	3.00	47	23.5
Neutral	4.00	1	0.5
Total		200	100.0

Were the members of Christ Groups far from realizing what a western pattern of family life is? Were they fully aware about what sort of family life traditional Christians live in India? Most of the members said it is their duty to look after the elderly and those who are dependent (immediate relations) upon them. For their faith's sake, they do not want to shrink from their responsibilities. They want to show care and love to their family members. There was no place for individuality in the rural society, rather it was a family or group which was in-charge to run the family, especially fathers, elder brothers or some aged, experienced family persons. In Bagepalli and Pavagada, mostly extended families lived together, where parents, children, elderly and other family members, like a widowed sister with her children, married and unmarried brothers and sisters, all under one roof. In Hosadurga and Bijapur, husband and wife, children with or without elderly parents lived together, but not the families of married brothers and sisters. Not many nuclear families were found in the groups, that is, parents with young children or only a husband and wife. Children live with their

North India, 80

[17] Rudolph, Lloyd I., & Susanne Hoeber Rudolph, 1984, *The Modernity Tradition: Political Development in India*, 39

[18] Mead, Charels, 1829, *A Report of the Neyoor Mission*, July 1829, dated 30 June 1829, CWMMSS (SI(Trav), in Robert Eric Frykenberg, 2003, *Christian and Missionaries in India: Cross-Cultural Communication since 1500, with special reference to caste, conversion and colonialism*

parents until they get married. Sons or one of the sons live with their parents, even after their marriage. On the death of the father the elderly son, or sons, will take charge of running the family. Though this system from the point of view of westerners may look strange and complex, those who live under that tradition regard it as routine and an ongoing matter for them.

After leading the family head to Christ, it was easier to bring other members of the family to Christ. In the rural parts, 'the family evangelism' may be the answer to effective evangelism. In the past, many missionaries wanted to see the converts in their own 'model'[19] making Indian Christians follow them. Later, many Indian Christians tried to imitate the western missionary's lifestyle. They became aliens in their own homelands. Such outer signs seemed unnecessary to seal one's Christianity. Christ Groups, as in the above cases, did not attempt to threaten their rural community. The family-life pattern of village community is strong and deeply valued. Christian missions rather than trying to change the family-life pattern, as William Carey suggested, help the families to have 'divine change and moral values'[20] that the village community would deeply appreciate.

Changes of family patterns after becoming Christians, mean whether to follow western family life style as some Christians in India without discerning 'the difference between Christian life and a pseudo-western culture'[21] Kushwant Singh comments that, 'it is sad to see Christians in India look foreign to their own people because once they become Christians they try to adopt the western style of living rather than their own'.[22] It may be apt to have some Christian distinctiveness but it might not be appropriate to adopt another's culture as their own. Rather than an imitation becoming a stepping-stone to share the Good News, it may become a hindrance.

Table 7B.4 Distribution of Members' Opinion about Change of Religion to become a Christian; CG Survey in Karnataka State

Representation of Members of Christ Groups		Number of Members Represented	Percentage of Representation of Members
Strongly agree	1.00	2	1.0
Disagree	2.00	132	66.0
Strongly disagree	3.00	62	31.0
Neutral	4.00	4	2.0
Total		200	100.0

---

[19] Ibid. 14
[20] Ibid. 30
[21] SunderRaj, Ebenezer, 1998, *Confusion Called Conversion*, 38
[22] Kushwant Singh, 1974, *Kushwant Singh's view of India*, in Roger, Hooker, 1979, 85,86

As discussed earlier in this chapter, members have different views about being a Christian and Christianity. 'Christian' for them means following Christ without changing their religion. Christianity is a religion with which they do not want to associate. Members valued highly the place of Christ in their lives and his teaching but they did not give the same place to the Christian religion. Mostly, members opposed the idea of changing their religion to the Christian religion. As Joseph D'Souza said, 'Indians are spiritual people'. It seems that the members want to have such a spiritual attitude and feeling towards the Christian faith and practice, but outwardly do not want to identify themselves as someone belonging to the Christian religion. Evangelists explained that as Christianity in India is the religion of the outcastes, the converts, those who became Christians from upper castes, would not dare to label themselves. Though it was interesting to note that Venkatswamy, Muniswamy and Surya Narayana of Bagepalli, Appanna Reddy and Ramanna Reddy of Hosadurga, Ramanjaneya, Prakash of Pavagada (from the upper and the lower castes) allowed or granted their children to change the status of their religion as Christians, either during a wedding or birth of their grand children. The members of Bijapur (except for Subbanna's family, which allowed their daughter to be married in a Christian way) stated that they wanted to follow Christ rather than go for any outward changes.

This indicates that for the Christian mission it is better to present the Gospel in an appropriate way to the rural populace. There is no need to force any sort of change upon people but allow them to develop a deeper experience with Jesus and His word and then that message will bring any needed change in the people, starting from the inside. Christian mission in its agenda to 'Win India or the World for Christ' or in the cause of 'World Evangelism Now', or 'Harvest India' would do better not to force expectations upon these converts but rather allow things to happen at their own pace, especially in the case of rural India.

Traditional churches in India insist that converts declare in the civil court their willingness to change from the religion to which they belong to Christianity.[23] Mainly these churches are in the cities where people are educated and who would be willing to take a step forward to follow the rules. However, this procedure will shut off most rural people from becoming Christians. Rural people are not highly educated, so to declare their willingness to become Christians in civil courts would create a lot of fear and suspicion in their minds. This procedure may not be advisable in the current situation of India where the word 'conversion' has become contentious.

---

[23] Soans, Murphy, 2004, personal interview, Bijapur, India (an ordained pastor of CSI Church)

As Walls suggested, 'Christ took flesh in a particular family... member... with the tradition of customs... with that nation. Wherever He is taken by men in any time and place He takes that nationality, that society, that culture.'[24] Walls gives a broader understanding of what is meant by becoming a Christian.

Christ Groups did not force or advocate its converts to change their religion in order to be accepted as Christians. The evangelists teach their members to follow Christ and His teachings rather than to change their religion and to follow certain sets of religious traditions. This might indicate what kind of teaching the rural people want without threatening their social foundations and the approach for the future. According to Walls, one should allow Christ to sanctify 'all that is capable of sanctification by his presence'.[25]

Some new Christians desired to be followers of Christ without changing their religion.[26] Changing religion in civil courts is only a sort of paperwork formality otherwise it has no value per se. Should Christianity be outwardly visible to others, or a real change in one's own life, understanding the right values of life which God has bestowed freely on human beings through His Son Jesus Christ?. As Carey suggested, let us strive 'to produce a moral and divine change' in the lives of new converts.[27] Christ Groups should aim this in the lives of its members.

Christ Group Members and their Theological Practices

Christ Groups showed very high regard to Jesus and His message. It will be interesting to study whether these members have given Him the highest place in their lives, families and community. Do they consider the church's institutions important to them? Do they equate Christ with their other deities? Have they adopted their tradition into Christian faith?

Table 7B.5 Distribution of Members of Christ Groups' Opinion about 'Concept of God'; 'Changed' to become a Christian; CG Survey in Karnataka State

Representation of the Members of Four Christ Groups		Number of Members of Christ Groups Represented	Perecentage of Representation of the Members of Christ Groups
Changed	.00	151	75.5
Not changed	1.00	47	23.5
Neutral	2.00	2	1.0
Total		200	100.0

---

[24] Walls, Andrew, 1982, *The Missionary Movement in Christian History*, 97f:93-105
[25] Ibid.
[26] Jaganath Rao, 1998, personal interview, Bangalore, India
[27] Ibid.

For members, the understanding of most theological and doctrinal matters was not uppermost in their minds. They are happy that they are Christians, their sins are forgiven because of Christ's death, and if they die today, they will be with Jesus in heaven. Though they seemed to have heard the teaching on the Trinity and such complex subjects, the members were happier to speak more on what Jesus is doing in their lives. The name of Jesus was used for describing any matter concerned with God. Like Jesus hears our prayers, helps and protects us and provides for our needs. This may be due to the teaching content of evangelists, who did not wish to confuse their converts by talking more about subjects, like the Trinity, the gifts of the Holy Spirit and such basic doctrinal issues. Another influence was the kind of songs they sing. Mostly songs were about the love of Jesus, His death, suffering, forgiveness, healing, deliverance from demons and black magic. Some songs were on the Holy Spirit but the members hardly spoke about the Holy Spirit as they use the name Jesus for every spiritual matter. They know the importance of prayer in their lives, especially how Jesus answered them when they or someone in the family was unwell or provided for their needs and His protection over them. They all (men and women) openly worship God, especially thinking about Jesus and His work for them. About God they think that He is their creator and a holy God. As Hwa Yung suggested, for Indians, it is their experience of God which is important to them.[28] Along with their limited knowledge of the Scripture, their experience of Him may move them to grow in their faith.

When evangelists visit villages, they do not speak anything against the convictions of other faiths or their deities. Rather, they present stories of Christ, his teaching, miracles and healing of people. However, one member said that when he first heard the Gospel his concept of God was immediately changed. Most of the other members of Christ Groups stated that gradually their concept of God was changed as they grew in their faith and understood more from the Bible, either through listening or reading.

Shivamma of Hosadurga told of her experience after she became a Christian. Her husband Appanna Reddy, before he became a Christian use to offer *pujas* (worship and prayer) to their house god, Shani (trouble-maker) every Saturday. As a wife,, it was her bounden Hindu duty to keep all required things to be used or offered during the *pujas*. She had to sit with her husband until he finished his *puja*. All the while, she used to pray to Jesus, while her husband performed *puja*. It took nearly a year before Appanna became a Christian but her dilemma about doing what is right continued. All along, she prayed that the Lord would change her husband and waited patiently before God to answer her prayer. If she had done

---

[28] Yung, Hwa, 2000, op.cit., Samuel Jayakumar (1999, 97), op.cit., Neill (1972, 68), Forrester (1980, 83f), Kingdom Identity and Christian Mission, a lecture in OCMS, 31st August, Oxford, UK

contrary to this, such as a bolder witness or step, she may well have lost her family and husband and may well have created a lot of indifference towards Christ from Appanna and other family members.

This indicates that if new believers, without becoming apprehensive about the approval of their family members in regards to their faith, could patiently walk an extra mile like Shivamma and pray continuously for them they may in the end see the whole situation reversed in Christ's favour. This may be a situation which Naaman encountered: 'but may the Lord forgive your servant for this one thing: When my master enters the temple of Rimmon to bow down and he is leaning on my arm and I bow there also- when I bow down in the temple of Rimmon, may the Lord forgive your servant for this' (2 Kings 5:18).

Some Christian missionaries in the past and present have made some derogatory remarks against the deities of other faiths. Time and again this has been pointed out and severely criticized by the people of these other faiths. It is better to present Christ and his teaching rather than criticising others convictions and their deities. The rural masses have a sensitive understanding of their deities and temples. In the Groups there were members, who were 'not yet decided' whether the concept of God was changed since they became Christians. There was a willingness to change, but they were influenced by fear of the community, or desire to please someone in the family, or not being fully convinced on the subject observed. Evangelists of the four Christ Groups are of the opinion that most of these people who have not decided, would decide at a later stage and that then their concept of God would change. There were a few more members who said that they have not given any thought to that subject.

The Christ Groups Manual[29] strictly forbids evangelists speaking anything against 'other' deities, traditions and cultures. During the survey, I observed that the evangelists do not raise issues concerning 'others' deities. Rather, they share more about Christ and his teachings. Such teaching may help the members continue to grow in their faith and reflect upon the teachings they receive may help them to improve their understanding of the 'Concept of God'.

Table 7B.6 Distribution of Four Christ Groups' Opinion about 'Baptism' to become a Christian; CG Survey in Karnataka State

Representation of Members of Four Christ Groups		Numbers of Members Represent Four Christ Groups	Percentage of Representation of Members
Taken and willing	.00	150	75.0
Not decided	1.00	49	24.5
Neutral	2.00	1	0.5
Total		200	100.0

---

[29] Lee, Yohann, 1976, *Christ Groups Manual*

Table 7B.7 Distribution of Four Christ Groups' Opinion about 'Sacraments'
to become a Christian; CG Survey in Karnataka State

Representation of Members of Four Christ Groups		Numbers of Members Represent Four Christ Groups	Percentage of Representation of Members
Taken and willing	.00	151	75.5
Not decided	1.00	47	23.5
Neutral	2.00	2	1.0
Total		200	100.0

The traditional way to become a Christian and join a Church was through baptism [30] when they are allowed to participate in communion. These two are 'Church's Ordinances' or 'Institutions of the Church'. From the time of the Apostles, there are divided opinions for and against these institutions among Christian missions and churches. Whether or not new converts have to undergo such church practices to become 'Full Members' of their church is another matter for discussion. This discussion will attempt to show how the concept of baptism is seen by the members of Christ Groups in Bagepalli, Hosadurga, Pavagada and Bijapur.

According to the Christ Groups Manual,[31] any one can attend meetings of Christ Groups. Those who express their faith in Jesus can join the Christ Groups and become members. The Christ Groups Manual does not promote or force 'baptism' on anyone who wants to become a member of the Christ Group. Evangelists do occasionally teach on the subject, indicating the openness Christ Groups create for its members to join without undergoing baptism, though cautious teaching on the subject helped Christ Groups to attract the rural community to its fold.

Baptism is an important milestone for the members of the Christ Groups, who came from the other faiths, which may give them the feeling that they are now in Christ's fold and it symbolizes a 'holy dip'. This concept of 'holy dip' is embedded in their past faith, which is sacred to them. Whoeverdesires to follow some 'Guru,' goes through such initiations.

In my own ministry, I have seen the people of other faiths, who apart from expressing their faith in Christ, consider baptism is an important step and a sacred exercise. It is interesting to note that most of those who have willingly undergone baptism have shown continued growth in their Christian faith. Bagepalli stands first in the order, where hundreds of baptisms have taken place. On occasion, more than a hundred people took baptism.[32] In that place, Christ Groups started much earlier than in other

---

[30] *Prarthisu*, 1966, 2
[31] Ibid.
[32] A Report, 1968, a publication of IEHC, Karnataka, Bangalore, India

places. In Pavagada, fieldwork started later than in Hosadurga, but Pavagada stood second in the number of baptisms. It is a similar location to Bagepalli, which is poor and exploited, where people who came from the outcaste background and are Telugu speaking. During the Mass Movement, most of the people who became Christians came from Telugu speaking people. Hosadurga stands third in ranking order. Not many baptisms, unlike Bagepalli or Pavagada, took place here. Here people are educated, economically strong and came from the upper and lower-caste backgrounds, but not from outcaste backgrounds. Bijapur stood in last place for the number of baptisms where the field was started in the 1990s and people were still growing in their faith and not fully convinced about baptisms. Surprisingly, McGavran[33] viewed 'Church Growth' in terms of numbers without assessing what seemed important and sacred to the rural masses when they trust in Christ.

In the Groups, there were some still undecided people, including those who wanted baptism at a later stage or were in fear of the community, not fully understanding about baptism, nor yet convinced. Evangelists who worked among these Christ Groups stated that most of them in this 'not decided' group eventually took baptism. One person, in another Christ Group, (not in the study) took 16 years to be convinced and then he was baptized with his wife.

Like 'Baptism', the members of Christ Groups give the Sacraments a similar place. For people of other faith,s whatever is sacred they respect and revere. In Christ Groups, the 'Communion Service' is regularly observed on Sundays. Those institutions symbolize sacredness to the people of other faiths. In their former faith, when they visited temples a priest could perform a *puja* (worship) to gods and then would distribute 'Holy Things' to devotees who were present at that time in the temple. These holy things included rice crispy and coconut water or plain water, which is called *prasada* (God's gift). Those elements are kept before their deities until the *puja* is over.

The sacraments are not the same but gave similar meaning to the members who come from other faiths. After becoming followers of Christ, taking sacraments were an important step to them. Rural people are simple, looking more for visible expressions of faithThese sacred exercises may not only speak to their consciences but to their outward expression as Christians. Thus, Jayakumar speaking on Dalit conversions described how they viewed the 'holy things': 'the Bible gave them a new possession-previously not allowed to touch holy things.'[34] This is another reason why in Bagepalli and Pavagada more people became Christians and took baptism and participated in the 'Holy Communion'. This indicated that for

---

[33] McGavran, Donald A., 1980 (1970), *Understanding Church Growth*, 8
[34] Ibid. 15

rural people these sacred practices replace their own past practices and gave them new meaning. It also helped them to live as Christians in their own context and bring some change into it, as we see in the next section how the members of Christ Groups were involved in the social issues.

Throughout the year, the people of other faiths have one or more festivals.Household objects throughout the house will be cleaned, new clothes bought and worn, families and friends may be reunited, differences between members of the family or others are sorted out; one such event unites the whole community and village. In the pas,t new Christians were taken out of their traditional context, isolated from their people and asked to observe Christmas and Easter in the western style. These festivals in India are still regarded as foreign.

The Christ Groups Manual suggests that one should respect the other faith traditions and culture.[35] Without offering any worship to their past deities, they celebrate their festivals that help them not only to keep their social bonds but also to give them an opportunity to share their newly found experience. Evangelists suggested that during such festivals their members offer prayers instead of *pujas*. Christ Groups may have given this freedom to its members. This indicated the sentimentality of the village community in regard to their festivals and a way in which the rural community can be attracted to the Christian message.

Table 7B.8 Distribution of Four Christ Groups' Opinion about Observing 'Past Festivals' to become a Christian; CG Survey in Karnataka State

Representation of Members of Four Christ Groups		Numbers of Members Represent Four Christ Groups	Percentage of Representation of Members
Yes (without idols)	.00	178	89.0
Yes (with idols)	1.00	22	11.0
Total		200	100.0

Most members were in agreement that they observe their festivals without any worship of their former deities. Some admitted that they continue worshipping their former deities during festivals because of their difficult situation where the head of the family or some members of the family may have not yet have become Christians.

Interestingly, all the members of four Christ Groups expressed that they wanted to observe festivals, which gives them identity and belonging-ness to their context but not at the cost of the living God. This may allow believers to experience new life rooted in their own culture and context. The members may not become alienated from their own culture, since the whole exercise expressed unity and the reconciliation of the rural people.

---

[35] Ibid.

For Christianity to take deep root in the rural soil of India, it may have to go through these tensions, which is how to remain true to one's own culture and be distinct in some sense as a Christian. As Walls[36] suggested, 'Christianity in the West took a longer time to become Christian-fifteen hundred years! The fear of appropriateness may not dampen the spirit of experiencing true Christianity rooted in its own culture and context.'

The next analysis is in Section C. The analysis starts with the Christ Groups members' response to 'Social and Spiritual Issues'. Did the members of the Christ Groups see themselves 'heaven-bound' only, or were they able to take up some responsibility in nation building and personality development within or through the Christ Groups?

Role of Members in Christ Groups

This section focuses on whether the members of Christ Groups felt good about themselves after becoming Christians or made any effort to influence the wider society through actively participating in solving the rural problems, and thus contributed towards nation-building while playing their role in Christ Groups. The aim is to see how the members of these four Christ Groups participate in, or engage with, those matters that related to the social aspects and in the larger community and spiritual aspect, that is, the Christ Groups' communities. Sources of research data include questionnaires, interviews, reports and the Christ Group Manual.

This part begins by describing the views, perceptions and observations of Christ Groups members concerning their understanding of the role they need to play in social and spiritual spheres. However, in this study, the role of the Christ Groups in social issues is not discussed because the Christ Groups manual is silent on this issue. Moreover, WLC was not able to foresee the engagement issues of Christ Groups with the larger community. The target group in the study includes members of the four Christ Groups and evangelists. The domains used in the survey to focus on the social and spiritual issues are the larger and the local community. Here, the larger community represents the community of all faiths and the local community represents the Christ Groups' community. The perceptions of the members on these issues are the following: engagement with the rural problems, helping the poor, promoting communal harmony, evangelism and personal development.

---

[36] Walls, Andrew F., 1999, Seminar on 15 November, Oxford Centre for Mission Studies, Oxford, UK

Members' Involvement with Social Issues

The respondents of the four Christ Groups were asked, 'Do you think it is right for you as a Christian to be involved with the social issues of your community and promote communal harmony in your surroundings'?

The answer to the involvement in the social issues and communal harmony included: engaging in rural problems, helping the poor, and attitudes towards people of other faiths. These concepts were introduced to understand whether the members of Christ Groups were interested only in spiritual exercises or 'heavenly minded attitudes', or whether they recognized any responsibility and duty towards the world they live in. The interviews were conducted with the members and the evangelists-cum-pastors. After data collection, further clarifications and verifications were conducted separately with the evangelists-cum-pastors in case of any ambiguity. Rural problems refer to problems with alcohol or gambling; poor civic amenities, refers to lack of lighting and roads; 'helping the poor' means any needy person those who live below the poverty line. Promoting communal harmony means working towards the common good of everyone without making any absolute claims or worsening any existing divisions in society.

Though the Christ Groups Manual[37] does not specify the participation of the members in rural social involvement, some of the members are actively involved in solving rural problems. As members live in a relational context, mutual consent and cooperation are needed for the safety and security of the larger community. The members of the Christ Groups did not divorce themselves from their responsibility towards the larger communit but as good Christians they felt the need to share their love through being involved in rural problems. This suggests that such involvement would help the gospel spread and gain the goodwill of the wider rural community. For example, the Hosadurga Christ Groups site was freely given to it by the council as a result of its involvement in social issues like alcohol addiction.

In the following Table 7C.1, the response to the question about 'Participation in Rural Problems' shows that members who actively participate in rural problems number 54.5 percent. This is not high but is significant.

---

[37] Ibid.

Table 7C.1 Distribution of Four Christ Groups who participate in 'Rural Problems'; CG Survey in Karnataka State

Representation of Members of Four Christ Groups		Numbers of Members Represent Four Christ Groups	Percentage of Representation of Members
Active Participation	.00	109	54.5
Non-active, support active	1.00	91	45.5
Total		200	100.0

Rural problems like alcohol and gambling threaten the well-being of the rural communities. Civic amenities like roads, lighting and water are for the common good. As Christians, it is important to play a positive role in solving the problems of the rural community. Members after becoming Christians do not want the rural community to think that Christians are exclusive, who will talk only about spiritual matters and are not interested in common problems. The members as Christians showed a willingness to participate in the rural problems and were available to help the rural community. By doing so, the message of Christ is better understood by the larger community and room is denied for suspicion towards Christians and their message labelling the members as agents of a foreign religion. Speaking on the origin of Christianity in India Hedlund asserted, 'Christianity...an ancient religion of India... Christianity has been home in India from the earliest time... Christianity is Indian...' and it should continue to be an Indian (and world) religion.[38]

When the members became Christians, how far did they helped the poor? After becoming Christians, did they detach themselves from the responsibilities towards the society. While the Christ Groups Manual is silent on these issues, the members because of the relational context they live in, and as good Christians, have engaged in social issues. This indicated that as Christians they were aware of their responsibility towards their fellow human beings, particularly those who live below the poverty line.

In the following Table 7C.2, the respondents who helped the poor are 69.5 percent. This is relatively high and is significant. Most of the new Christians want to play a part in the community at large where they live. Because of their new-found faith they are not deserting their responsibility towards the community. Those who do not help live by themselves and are poor. This proportion is relatively low.

---

[38] Hedlund, Roger E., 2000, *Christianity is Indian*, 'The Emergence of an Indigenous Community', xiii

Table 7C.2 Distribution of Four Christ Groups who participate in 'Helping the Poor'; CG Survey in Karnataka State

Representation of Members of Four Christ Groups		Numbers of Members Represent Four Christ Groups	Percentage of Representation of Members
Helping	.00	139	69.5
Not helping	1.00	61	30.5
Total		200	100.0

This indicated that on becoming Christians, they should not be displaced from their context and should be encouraged to play a role in building their local community. In the Mass Movement, those who became Christians were mostly poor and displaced from their own context and developed a dependency upon western missionaries. They failed to take part in the development of their community. Mostly, they were kept in the mission compounds. Hence, they were isolated from the rest of society. They might have developed to rely on receiving from missionaries, who might not have taught them how to give. Often Christians in India are accused of not participating in nation-building. Although this may not be true, there may be some truth in it. Being Christians means they are to be salt and light to their community (Matthew 5:16).

Regarding the 'Attitude of Christians towards people of other faiths', during the colonial period, 'the failure of Christian mission in India' is attributed towards the 'superiority attitude' of the missionaries.[39] Such 'superiority attitudes' are now also present among many Christian missions or churches in India. In India, the Christian community is categorized as a 'forward' community, mainly based on their education and ability to earn more than others. There is a tendency among Christians who are better educated than their fellows to look down upon their immediate community. Such an attitude instead of helping the Kingdom of God to spread hinders it.

The Christ Groups Manual[40] does suggest the members to stay on the ground and share the gospel with others. Table 7C.3 shows the attitude of the members of the Christ Groups towards others in society.

---

[39] Houghton, Graham, 1983, *The Impoverishment of Dependency*, op.cit: 1983:19, 128
[40] Ibid.

Table 7C.3 Distribution of Four Christ Groups 'Attitude Towards People of Other Faiths'; CG Survey in Karnataka State

Representation of Members of Four Christ Groups		Numbers of Members Represent Four Christ Groups	Percentage of Representation of Members
Good	.00	158	79.0
Tolerant	1.00	42	21.0
Total		200	100.0

The attitude towards people of other faiths has good and tolerant features. 'Good' means to mix with the people of other faiths and maintain healthy relationships. The response of 79 percent is very high. The Christian faith made them not to think differently about others but willing to relate to others about the common good of the community and make the Christian message meaningful to others. 'Tolerant' means not to cause any rift in the community because of their faith and willingness to live together with the larger community for its common good, without making any superior claims about their faith or strong accusation against others' faith and deities. The response to this, 21 percent, is low. This indicated that when the new converts are allowed to live in their own context it helps them to be good and tolerant to others' faith without making any absolute claims on their own faith and to avoid any division in the community.

Members' Involvement in Spiritual Issues

Have Christ Groups been spiritual clinics of religious opinion where needs were met or treated? Have they helped the members to develop their personalities, especially in the case of Dalits and women, who are usually exploited and undermined by the larger society?

In this part, the question is asked whether the groups were led by males or females; also, how far Christ Groups were wholly dependent on evangelists as quasi-ministers to lead the groups like traditional churches. Or was there other leadership available in the group to lead? This may also suggest what would be the future of Christ Groups? Will they be dependent on the evangelists to carry the good news or will the members spread the good news on their own? What is the future and continuation of Christ Groups in India, particularly in the State of Karnataka?

The Christ Groups Manual[41] has provided the space for the members to develop their leadership qualities from the beginning of the Christ Groups. Most Christ Groups have multiple leaders. There is no distinction made between male and female to lead the group. Equal opportunities are provided to both. Table 7C.4 shows how many males or females led the

---

[41] Ibid.

Christ Groups. This may also indicate that when opportunities are given, women who are empowered by the Good News take up the leadership in the rural context.

The Christ Groups led by males are 70 percent. This is high but not excessively where male domination is prominent. Female led Christ Groups are 30 percent which is less, but significant. About one third of the Christ Groups were led by females in comparison to the males, which is significant in the rural context. Bagepalli and Pavagada showed even more female leaders, Hosadurga showed mixed leadership and Bijapur showed more male leaders. The reason why there were more women followers in Bagepalli and Pavagada, than in Hosadurga was that more couples were followers, so both genders were equally represented. It was same as Hosadurga in Bijapur, but due to the male dominated context and better education of males, more males led the groups. The message of Christ not only liberates a person from his or her sin but also, empowers them to overcome their own disability and fate. The Gospel develops leadership qualities in the lives of these ordinary men and women.

Table 7C.4 Distribution of Four Christ Groups who became the Leaders of their Christ Groups; CG Survey in Karnataka State

Representation of Members of Four Christ Groups		Numbers of Members Represent Four Christ Groups	Percentage of Representation of Members
Male	.00	140	70.0
Female	1.00	60	30.0
Total		200	100.0

The next spiritual aspect discussed is the 'Task of Evangelism', to see whether it rested only on evangelists or was shared by the other members of the Christ Groups. This is to establish whether the members of the Christ Groups became only the 'Gospel Hearers' or the 'Gospel Bearers' too. That will indicate something of the future of Christ Groups and their continuity in the future.

Table 7C.5 shows how the gospel was spread in and around the Christ Groups. It also suggests the effective way to further evangelize rural India.

The response to the question of the evangelist who led families or people to Christ is low at 21.7 percent. This suggests that the evangelist mostly led key families or people to Christ. The members' response at 78.3 percent is high and significant.

Table 7C.5 Distribution of Members Led to Christ by the Evangelist or Other Members Christ Groups; CG Survey in Karnataka State

Representation of Evangelist of the Members		Numbers of Members Led to Christ by the Evangelist or Other Members	Percentage of who Led to Christ by the Evangelist or Other Members of Christ Groups
Evanglist	.00	43	21.7
Other members	1.00	157	78.3
Total		200	100.0

The gospel receivers became themselves gospel carriers and their approach was effective. This also indicates that the relational factor is more effective in the rural context of India. The gospel is easily heard or understood by other people when it is conveyed by their own people in their own way. This also suggests that a gospel community created among the members, that is, multiple leadership, provided them with the space to develop those qualities. This method also shows it was effective to carry out the mission of Christ by its recipients, rather than the WLC's gospel tract as an economical and effective tool for world evangelization.

The next chapter deals with the implications of the study and research in the broader context.

Chapter 8
Study Results and Conclusions

Introduction

The purpose of the study was to find how far WLC, which had committed itself to literature distribution on a mass scale and so combined modernity and a western individualistic idea of evangelism, had succeeded in its attempt to evangelize India, where a social relational rather than an individual context was emphasized. WLC presented the Gospel in message form on the printed page through their systematic house-to-house distribution programme. To what extent was their method effective? The study also considered such factors as social, economic and cultural aspects by using quantitative assessment to assess their influence on whether people became Christians as a result. The study mainly examined the reaction of Indian rural people to an alien approach and any unplanned consequences of WLC's method. The study also examined what factors influenced the growth of Christ Groups. In this chapter, the major issues and findings that have emerged from the study are discussed, as well as the implications of the needs and aspirations of the people for effective mission practice in rural India.

In Part One (Chapters 1-5), the theoretical framework was based on the influence of modernity and its adaptation and effective use by mass evangelistic agencies in the USA and the way they commodified religion. WLC was born into this era, and commodified the gospel in message form: by distributing one message for all in order to claim that 'world evangelism' in this generation could be achieved. The present WLC's logo, 'It Can Be Done!' still claims this, although Dr. J. R. Mott's inspirational call in the nineteenth century and the call of Dr. Billy Graham, AD2000[1] and such movements in the twentieth century for 'world evangelization' have disappointingly failed to achieve the stated goals. The survey covers part of this historical period. The study demonstrates: 1. How people in this particular relational context responded to the non-relational approach of the

---

[1] www.ad2000.org accessed on 06-06-09. The Movement sought to ... establish a church within every unreached people group... by the year 2000, but the movement was not successful

American Christian mission agency and, 2. How the approach took root in the context, taking a different shape and subsequently spreading out. In Part Two, a case study and the study results assessed the response of the people to the western mass evangelism technique, intended to lead people to commit their lives to Christ.[2]

Summary of Research Findings

The main concern of the study was to see how and why the rural people in India responded in families and groups to this particular evangelization approach, which was meant to appeal to the individual conscience. Two other concerns of the study were to look at WLC's and IEHC's reaction to the formation and the phenomenon of Christ Groups. The research findings are mixed, and show some support to the hypotheses; they also raise questions because they contradicted some of the assumptions made at the beginning of the research and thus have suggested a new research direction.

WLC, an American agency under the influence of modernity, using mass evangelistic methods designed to encourage an individual to make the choice for salvation, converted the Gospel into a message form on the printed page so that it could be presented and received anywhere by anybody.[3] Its main goal was to reap the highest profit ratio, that is, 'highest number of conversions to the printed page' as expressed in their most acclaimed slogan, 'highest from the lowest' on 'fast footing' operations. The study identifies the basis for the expectations of WLC and its reactions to the formation of Christ Groups in western modernity. To WLC,the formation and growth of Christ Groups was an unexpected event,[4] requiring spiritual nurture, pastoral care and counselling, and seemed to be a time consuming and expensive approach.[5] It lacked marketing elements and especially the maximization of the commodity for the least spending. A key assumption made at the beginning of the study was that WLC could claim to have originated the vision of Christ Groups, but personal interviews with the leaders of WLC, which are rather complex, suggests that WLC went to the extent of disowning them.

The study examines the reaction of IEHC leaders to the formation of Christ Groups. The Indian leaders, who were from church backgrounds, knew the importance of church and its nurture. The study shows that they were excited to see the formation of Christ Groups in the rural parts of

---

[2] Stricland, Don, 'Charles Finney's assault upon Biblical Preaching'. The Founders Journal, main page, contents 9, accessed on 7th Sep 2006 (see Appendix)

[3] Samuel, Vinay Kumar, 2004, personal interview, Oxford, UK

[4] Lee, Yohann, 1999, response to questionnaire, Los Angeles, USA

[5] Sugden, Chris, 2002, personal interview, Oxford, UK

India,[6] which they saw as a leap forward in Indian church history, after the Mass Movement of the nineteenth century. Some of the leaders themselves were pastors and elders of their denominational churches, to whom the formation of the Christ Groups was like a 'milestone' in the history of Christian mission in India. The Mass Movement was as the beginning of a new era for 'church movement' in India, and a successful model for future church planting movements.[7] However, IEHC leaders failed to see that WLC's real underlying entrepreneurial interest was in the maximization effect of the printed gospel message rather than in the formation of the Christ Groups, for which WLC showed mere sympathy.[8] One thing the leaders of IEHC were able to realize was that the WLC's interest was in the 'number game', that is the statistical data of the distributed printed page and its maximum effect, that is the number of conversions attributed to it. Alongside this, they also came to realize how much Indian Christians appreciated and applauded the formation of Christ Groups. This may have put the leaders of IEHC in a precarious position, which may have forced them to play a dual role to satisfy WLC on the one hand, and to meet the expectation of the Indian mission context on the other. They provided required statistical data to WLC and to some extent tried to play a role in the development of Christ Groups. This dual role of the Indian leaders at times put Christ Groups' work off track, whenever they were assigned by WLC to work on some other literature distribution programmes.

An important assumption of the study was that IEHC officials might have adopted the vision of WLC. The official records, minutes, and personal interviews all show that this may be true in regard to distribution work but about Christ Groups work they did what seemed best in the Indian context.[9] Though the official records show how they struggled to continue the momentum of Christ Groups, yet in the end they failed to convince WLC of the importance of the formation of Christ Groups in the Indian context. The study focussed on Christ Groups on how the respondents reacted to an evangelisation approach that was not familiar to them and on the role of the distributors, who handed a printed form of the gospel to them. Were the members of Christ Groups seen as the consumers of the Gospel product? What was the role of 1400 workers who participated in the distribution? Did those workers see themselves only as distributors as the WLC termed them, or as evangelists?

The response of the respondents to the Gospel was spontaneous from families and groups and Christ Groups arose. Discovering the formation,

---

[6] Prabhakar, B.A., 1970, a Board Resolution of IEHC, New Delhi, India
[7] Samuel, Vinay Kumar, 2004, personal interview, Oxford, UK
[8] A Resolution, 1984, WLC Board on Christ Groups
[9] Guruprasad, G., 1998, personal interview, Bangalore, a founding member of IEHC and a former director of IEHC, Karnataka, India

function and expansion of Christ Groups brought pertinent insights on rural evangelistic work in India. The comparison of Christ Groups with other church movements like the Mass Movement, and McGavran's Peoples' Movement, and some Indian Christian Indigenous movements expands our understanding of church planting and provides a new pathway for the church planting movement in the rural context of India. Alongside this, a comparison is made with some Hindu pietistic movements like Bhakti, Lingayatism and Nudi, which have brought amongst a large rural Hindu populace a new way of thinking about attainment through 'devotion'.

An important assumption in the study was that the otherwise missing relational factor was the key to explaining the phenomenon of Christ Groups. AMoreover, another key factor that emerged was the evangelism of families. To work in rural India it might be better to focus entirely on the reachable population, to contact and affect them, and to work through the indigenous families. That in turn would affect their neighbours and the entire village community, rather than concentrate on certain groups or sections of the society such as women and children. This may create division and suspicion in the community and thus the effect of the Gospel would be less. Using the first approach creates a ripple effect.

In summary, Christ Groups brought great tension to WLC.[10] To some extent it forced them to rethink their strategy. The leaders of IEHC tried to swim in two opposite directions. Christ Groups saw themselves in a new role as changed and changing agents. In the same way, distributors changed their role and became evangelists. These responses were not what was expected at the beginning of the study. The descriptive statistical method has been the main way used to reveal these results. Consistency is obtained in all these results. The findings have not been distorted by any bias in the research tool. Further research in the area would be valuable.

Conclusions

To achieve this, the specific attitudes of the following three groups have been analysed, focusing on their most important aspects, beginning with the entrepreneurial WLC.

Entrepreneurial WLC

WLC universalized its methods, that is, the 'Systematic House to House Distribution' and the use of hired 'Distributors'. This process and practice was thought to be unique and perfect being applicable wherever the 'every home' programme was launched from the United States to India. This was a market strategy, which the WLC chose rather than finding a relevant pattern to fit Indian society and culture or learning from Indian Church

---

[10] Ibid.

history what was best for its context, or a pattern based on the Scripture. The market strategy wascapable for implementing world evangelisation. WLC assumed that 'every home', referred to where a single family lives, as in western countries. However, in India 'every home' consists of more than one family. Two, three or may be more families live together especially in rural India. As in the UK, Hindujas, an Indian origin family wants to build a 'palace', in order to house 38 of its family members, which may be consist of 7-8 families. This is very typical of Indian families, who want to live under one roof.[11] This may means WLC's pattern of just handing a pair of printed pages to a member of the family does not justify its claim that 'systematically every home' was covered or may be it was thought that a pair of tracts distributed to every-home whether it was a small or big was seen as a 'systematically reached' home. However, WLC method of every home was well suited to western countries rather than to India. In the Indian context the method on its own is seen as a 'Hit and Run' ministry. It is not really targeting the said populace, that is, every home, but the printed pages are just placed in those homes like a postman, without giving sufficient or even any explanation. Thus, it may it was a superfluous claim that 'Every Home' is visited.

WLC's 'Distributors' were seen as hired workers, who can be fired at anytime. Their job was simply to place the printed page systematically in every home, like paperboys.[12] There is no need for them to say anything, but the printed page will do everything needed.[13] WLC mistook 'Evangelists' for 'Distributors', many of whom for the sake of a sacred vocation had given up their secular and government jobs.[14] WLC underestimated the enthusiasm of the evangelists, who wanted to make use of the golden opportunity before them to share the good news with their fellow countrymen,[15] rather than to place the printed page in every home. WLC misread 'the literary context' of the west to apply to 'the oral context' of India,[16] where people needed more explanation of the printed page, which evangelists provided contrary to WLC's directives. The people believed in their words rather than in the printed page. WLC's pursuit of distributors is never going to end. They still look for them to carry out their

---

[11] *The Times*, 2006, 27th August, UK
[12] Lee, Yohann, 1978, *Everybody*
[13] Ibid.
[14] Solomon, B. G., 2000, personal interview, a former field staff of IEHC, who left the government job in Horticulture department to become an evangelist, lost his job in 1984 and now pastoring a Bhakthsingh church in Bangalore, India
[15] Louis, Robert, 1970 (PL), IEHC Karnataka, Bangalore, India
[16] A Manual, 2002, *Discipleship Through Story Telling*, 6

distribution work in India,[17] but paradoxically India has produced more evangelists and pastors instead.[18]

WLC universalized the Gospel in message-form, which is the same message from the United States to India. The Gospel is universal but it must take on particular form in a given culture as Paul informed the Jerusalem Council. The WLC message was written in the materialistic context of possessions and what satisfaction one gets from them.[19] WLC thought this to be an appropriate message for the people who had little or no material possessions. WLC thought the printed message was complete in itself, and did not need any human assistance to be easily understood by the reader. WLC's spirit of universalization did not need to know whether the 'consumer' was an American or an Indian, who would better understand the message through some plain talk rather than reading from a printed page. WLC failed to note the difference in belief systems, that is, what Indians understood by saying 'Sin', and 'Salvation' compared with Christian teaching on such doctrines. How would they understand those concepts by reading a printed page unless someone was to illustrate it for them? The Scripture itself makes this clear when the evangelist Philip asked the Ethiopian eunuch: 'Do you understand what you are reading? 'How can I, he said, unless someone explains it to me?' (Act:8:30,31). WLC's main interest was to maximize the effect of their universalized message-form, that is, to see more conversions to their message form rather than meeting the spiritual needs of the Indian people. WLC sought quick results of conversions to its universalised message-form rather than how long its fruit would remain.

WLC also saw the gospel as a message-form presented to anybody, to any national, and by anyone. It was shaped by a modern worldview. What sense of modernity shaped them? One aspect was commodification of the gospel.[20] The gospel was seen as a product. Those who were evangelized were seen like 'Coca-Cola' users. The gospel in literary form has modern market elements. WLC did not capitalize on their approach and ideas in India. Some 1400 employees of WLC were appointed as distributors of the gospel message in printed form. Distributors were the passers-on of the message. These workers themselves believed in the gospel. They saw themselves as evangelists and shared their experiences and convictions. Distributors, who are believers, shared their beliefs, convictions and experiences with others, which made people believe in the gospel rather than just reading the printed message. The people who believed in the good news shared the same in turn with others. This led to the formation of the

---

[17] Prarthisu, 2000, a publication of IEHC Karnataka, January, Bangalore, India
[18] India Mission Association, 2000, a publication of IMA, Chennai, India
[19] Lee, Yohann, 1966, *AP-1*
[20] Samuel, Vinay Kumar, 2004, personal interview, Oxford, UK

Christ Groups. Distributors became evangelists who did not want to give a tract as a product, but saw the tract as a tool. They did not want to claim the tract was a process for winning people, but they shared the gospel with conviction and burden. For the WLC the tract contained the message and the reader would understand and respond to that message. That response was a part of 'Conversion' process. In this process WLC failed to see the 'tract' making any change (5). Tension arose between mass evangelism versus evangelists; distributors versus evangelists; distributors versus sharers of the gospel; tract versus words. These tensions produced the 'Christ Groups'.

WLC universalized its Bible Correspondence Course,[21] so that the same lessons were taught in the United States as within India, without assessing whether the students benefited from these lessons or not. Indian students hardly had any background in Christian doctrine and teaching. WLC's interest was mainly in statistical data that would count increased student numbers enrolled on their course rather than seeing how far the student had learnt something from it or not.

Though WLC wished, burdened and prayed to 'win souls' of the heathen land, their crowning desire was the maximisation effect of it on their donor, that is, to raise 'maximum money' from their programme. In the 1970s, WLC amassed 70 million dollars a year,[22] out of which, 00.02 percent, like a 'widow's mite', was sent for their programme in India.[23] It may be the case that WLC had a preponderance of businessmen to serve on its board, which had almost changed the WLC from a literature agency to an investment, where it attracted deposits, endowments and managed people's wills. WLC's 'passion' for world evangelization and its 'crowning desire' for wealth creation may have led it to serve 'God and Money' at the same time.

WLC's unwelcome attitude, lack of interest and disowning spirit towards Christ Groups make clear that its claims of world evangelization were superficial,an advertising stunt, made to impress themselves, their supporters and Christians around the world. WLC's undying desire to continue its distribution programme in India is by and large unwelcome to Indians, especially to their own evangelists[24] because most of the Indian Missions have moved forward into the church planting tradition. This includes OM of India, which now claims to have over 700 churches all over India.[25] This process has sidelined WLC from the mainstream of the Indian

---

[21] Lee, Yohann, 1964, *AP-2*

[22] McAlister, Jack, 1999, personal interview, March, Los Angeles, USA

[23] Guruprasad, G., 1998, personal interview, Bangalore, India

[24] Peter, Manik, 1998, personal interview, a former Christ Groups evangelist of IEHC Karnataka, now works as an independent worker in Bidar

[25] Das, Madhusudan, 2006, personal interview, Bangalore, India

missions to the periphery and now WLC has become a mere spectator rather than the master of their programme.

Dual Role IEHC Leaders

IEHC's 'founding and some subsequent leaders' were either pastors or elders of their local denominational churches.[26] They were burdened to reach their countrymen and women with the Gospel message. However, for a time, they took up an alien ideology as their own and tried to satisfy themselves and WLC by just placing the printed page in every home. They were well aware of their context, that is, the importance of church planting and the nurture of converts. They knew how the church planting movement, like the Mass Movement in India, was a successful model to follow.[27] Some of the leaders themselves were second or third generation fruits of that movement.[28] They were sure of the fact that literature alone cannot reach the people of India unless someone explains it to them. They took twenty years to express this view to the WLC but by then the WLC officials had turned their backs on them. The fear to express their context, experience and conviction shows how the Indian leadership failed to play its due role in an appropriate and meaningful way. They were caught in playing a dual role to please themselves and their masters.

The IEHC leaders were criticized by the Indian Christian leaders during and after the first coverage, that is, between 1966-76, for the lack of concern for their new believers. The IEHC leaders made some effort to nurture the believers and thereby tried to impress the Indian Christian leaders but did not attempt to make their plans clear to the WLC. Thus, the leaders failed to echo the concern of their countrymen to WLC but rather played out this dual role to please the WLC heads on one side and on the other their own countrymen.

Though the IEHC leaders were happy to see the formation of Christ Groups, they painfully waited for 10 years, from 1968 to 1978 (the first Christ Group was formed in 1968),[29] to get directives from WLC, indicating what plans they had drawn up for the Christ Groups in India. They should have been engaging themselves during that period to study what was happening before their eyes and deciding how to nurture the converts with the help of Indian Christians or Churches or Missions. This shows how the IEHC leaders were utterly dependent upon their WLC heads. It is also an indicator of how much the leaders lacked self-confidence and motivation to carry out the opportunity which God had given to them. The leaders helplessly looked to WLC for their official stamp upon the future of the

---

[26] Samuel, Vinay Kumar, 2004, personal interview, Oxford, UK

[27] Ibid.

[28] Prathapkumar, B.A., 1998, personal interview, Secunderabad, India

[29] Taylor, Brayard, 1990, in E.D. Ashwal, *It Can Be Done*, 'Christ Groups Survey'

Christ Groups. However, in the end, nothing resulted but WLC's disowning of Christ Groups in India.

Nonetheless, IEHC leaders, during Prasad's period in the 1990s, woke up to their call and played a stellar role to keep up the momentum of Christ Groups in spite of financial cuts.[30] They tried to raise their own funding to keep the ministry moving and made efforts to build partnerships with other churches, missions and Christians for the development of Christ Groups.[31] However, the untimely passing away of Prasad in 1995 brought down a final curtain on Christ Groups' work. WLC made the subsequent leadership listen to them 'by rocking the boat' rather than running the ministry on their own. Again, IEHC leaders succumbed to the pressure of the WLC leaders rather than risk themselves to travel with the Christ Groups. Thus, they opted for a survival strategy[32] rather than to risk their future for the sake of the survival of Christ Groups.

Christ Groups: A New Vision of India

The mission tradition of India for the last 200 years was of 'Church Planting'. Missionaries were not sent to find converts to the response of the message but converts were to build up the church. From the 1950s onwards, the tradition of mass-evangelistic organizations like WLC and OM looked for conversion from the 'message'. Billy Graham held such an opinion for a long time but later changed it and supported the church tradition. In India, the mission traditions were of church planting, building the churches and following up and nurturing the converts. Cultural Church planting differs from the modern approach.[33] The WLC shared the message as a universal message and measured the results by the response to that. The WLC wanted conversions because conversion produces numbers,and the largest numbers were measured to the response to the product, that is, the tract. However, evangelists in India personally shared the gospel with others. The perception of the 1400 evangelists was to share the gospel, to disciple the converts and to form groups and nurture them. WLC under the influence of modernity driven with market techniques wanted to take the gospel to which the reader may respond. Why did not the IEHC field staff fit into the WLC's frame? WLC wanted the distributors to be players and themselves as stakeholders. The tension between modernity and church planting traditions, WLC versus IEHC, WLC versus Evangelists, IEHC versus Evangelists, Evangelists and people continued. The Evangelists'

---

[30] A Manual, 1992, Final Thrust 5000, a publication of IEHC, Secunderabad, India
[31] Ibid.
[32] Wilson, Wes, 1999, personal interview, February, a former vice-President of EHC-I, Colorado Springs, USA
[33] Samuel, Vinay Kumar, 2003, personal interview, Oxford, UK

tradition of church planting led them to form Christ Groups. The tension between mass evangelism and church planting continued.

In India the tradition of church planting was successful. McGavran's approach to mission was of conversion movements founded on the church planting tradition. The Mass Movement was also founded on the church planting tradition and became successful. However, the WLC wanted to produce conversions to their message where the tradition of church planting existed. WLC in its confusion allowed Christ Groups to continue and be successful. Mass evangelistic organizations' success depended upon modern means of communication and their effective and efficient use. Conversion numbers were the measure of its success. Church planting success was building church fellowships, helping the converts to become disciples and sharers of the good news. Mission agencies sending church planters saw success in the planting of churches rather than just in conversions and their numbers. Mass evangelism's main focus was on the message and the effective use of its language. Its focus on an intelligible response was the essence of conversion. Mission traditions' focus was on church planting, believers, and disciples. Others had a different focus. The tensions were between WLC versus IEHC (its precarious position while representing WLC) versus Evangelists. (The tension between IEHC leaders and Evangelists was ideological. IEHC leaders were particularly while strategically they seemed supportive of Evangelists but they were pressurized to implement the new vision of WLC and for their own survival they unwillingly distanced themselves from the Christ Groups which resulted in tension between them and Evangelists.)

Cross-cultural mission entailed traditional missionaries to work in an alien culture. When conversions took place, missionaries were faced with how to deal with the traditions of the believers. Missionaries even forced or imposed some of the culture of their sending mission. Cross-cultural mission faced these tensions. Peoples Movements were started by the evangelists, who were ordinary people, who used a simple approach. They shared with the locals who were looking for some spiritual answers, seeking answers to their spiritual needs from the facilitators, who enabled them to start the groups.. The locals owned Christianity, but did not abandon their culture or religion. Christ Groups were not under any such compulsion from any alien or local forces. Rather they were given freedom to make choices of their own. That to a greater extent enabled Christ Groups to be rooted in their soil and yet live as true witnesses of Christ. In Samuel's words, 'a person or communities ability to choose a desired outcome and act to achieve it is empowerment. Providing necessary knowledge... and creating opportunities to choose freely and act confidently and achieve desired outcomes is use of power to build capacity'.[34]

Christ Groups became rooted in the soil and established as a result of their past religious experience and the influence of the Bhakti, Lingayatism and Nudi movements. (5) Lingayatism stressed its followers to know God through their own and experiences of others, Bhakti's devotional life, and Nudi's expectation of the Messiah were all anti-Brahaminical and given a new meaning to them in Christ and his message. The new message did not come with the baggage of controlled power,[35] neither had it threatened their past religious experience but brought new meaning to the old.[36] This study may not be similar to Farquhar's and Ivan Sathyavratha's studies on 'Fulfilment Theology' where converts' convictions depend on 'Christ of Experience', whereas in Christ Groups converts' convictionsdepended on their 'Christ of the Scripture'. For instance, Narayan Vaman Tilak acknowledged 'that he has come to the feet of Christ over the bridge of Tukaram'.[37] Tukaram was a great poet-saint of Maharashtra, who was one of the saints of the Bhakti tradition, worshipped his family god 'Vitoba' and claimed to be experienced intimacy of Vitoba through his deep devotion. Tilak's words 'coming to Christ over the bridge of Tukaram' express the same. Tilak seemed to place the Scripture on a par with Hindu sacred books, in which he saw 'Christ has come, not to destroy but to fulfil'.[38] Tilak's words echo the words of Farquhar's of fulfilment (5). Tilak's main emphasis was on experience of Christ through deep devotion like Tukaram.

Meeting in the houses for worship, sharing their experience of Christ with others and facing opposition from the hierarchical system was not altogether new to them. The experience of their past religion and hope of the new message and freedom to make their own choices gave them immense strength to be rooted in their soil and established in their faith. WLC and IEHC did not wish to impose any of their ideologies on these groups because their task or aim was on the message and its response. Though some Christians disapproved of what was happening, the people accepted the movement's claim upon themselves. WLC and IEHC as catalysts without changing themselves, allowed the movement to fill this role. People took the movement forward by gathering on their own for prayer and worship, sharing their experiences with others, and, when they gathered together, the caste problem was reduced.

---

[34] Samuel, Vinay Kumar, 2009, Mission and Power, a seminar paper, OCMS, Oxford, UK
[35] Ibid.
[36] Ibid.
[37] Staffner, Hans, 1987, *Jesus Christ and the Hindu Community*, Narayan Vaman Tialk, *The Bhakti Marga as a Way to Christ*
[38] Ibid.

Cross-cultural missions (western missions who came to establish churches), on the other hand, found a problem with caste, which came as an outsider to impose its ideologies and doctrine upon the group. The group had started with the help of the outsiders. The Peoples' Movement (includes the Mass Movement, Church Growth and Christ Groups), did not find such tensions. The Peoples' Movement did not take away the identity and culture of the people. However, the cross-cultural movement, which imposed certain things on the alien culture, caused concerns over the identity and culture of the people. Christ Groups Evangelists were not cross-cultural missionaries but facilitators who shared the gospel. People opened up; communication took place within the peoples' own traditions. Evangelists were not cross-cultural missionaries bringing in the baggage of their own tradition in order to impose it. Evangelists were ordinary people, not missionaries or development workers who followed the Indian way. The whole idea of context was through the involvement of the people. Christ Groups themselves made their own decisions about the contextualzsation of the new, owning Christianity while following their religion and traditions. Evangelists took tracts as a tool but people were connected and guided by God. Their spiritual hunger found what they looked for and faith developed on that basis. People were attracted to the gospel that was shared with them by ordinary people like themselves. When people found their spiritual needs were met, Christ Groups formed. Evangelists shared the gospel because local people found answers to their own spiritual need through them. Tracts played a minor role; they were incidental. Discipleship was taking place. The Peoples' Movement started from within. Evangelists played the role of catalysts and provided the spark, while the movement expanded through the peoples' response. Any other such developments will occur when people are central to it. The idea that Christ Groups were started by tracts is a 'myth'. Through evangelists, evangelzsation took place. People took decisions and a bigger movement resulted. The success of the Christ Groups movement took place because of the effective interaction of evangelists, people, and IEHC. WLC was isolated in the process. The Mass evangelism tradition was dominated by its own ethos of numbers. The church planting movement is directed towards connecting and building religious communities, which focussed on the Peoples' Movement.

In contrast to the church planting traditions of India, Traditional Churches (started by western denominational churches), Peoples' Movement (the Mass Movement & the Church Growth Movement, and the Indigenous Movement (AK Banarjee and others), Christ Groups may have provided better options for the rural people which built up a 'New Vision for India':

    a.   Christ Groups saw themselves as the owners of the movement and became the bearers of the good news. In the process, they eliminated the traits of 'Traditional Churches' church planting movements, that is, an alien ideology, hierarchical order and dependency, western origins, clergy centeredness[39] and the label 'rice and rupee' Christians.[40] Neither were they started under any alien influence, pressure or inducement to follow Christ as some Hindu fundamentalist groups allege of the Christian mission in India, but through their own will and choice.

b.   Christ Groups created an equal platform for all castes and classes of people. They were not a divisive movement like the Peoples' Movement of McGavran, which in their zeal to provide a more suitable platform for every caste and sub-caste in India launched homogenous churches. This was seen by many missions in India and elsewhere as a divisive movement rather than a uniting and harmonizing one, when the country needed 'Nation-Builders' rather than dividers. There existed many internal communal forces threatening the unity of Indian society. Christ Groups were seen as 'sons of the soil', which were grown within the natural context and culture by people themselves unlike the 'Peoples' Movement' which was an alien ideology, built upon western perceptions adapted to the Indian context and culture.

c.   Indigenous church planting movements like A K Banarjee,[41] Subbarao,[42] Narayan Vamanrao Tilak[43] and Sattampillai (his real name is Armainayagam, but he was better known as Sattampillai),[44] were started in reaction either to western missionaries or organized churches; they took the essence of Christ rather than the Christ of the Scripture. Christ Groups were spontaneous and formed when the people heard the Gospel, who in turn became the Gospel carriers. They took the Christ of the Scriptures but not the Christ of the western or organized churches.

Looking at the emergence of Christ Groups, Sugden remarked that a theology from the below has emerged.[45] Sugden in his article, *'What is Good about the Good News to the Poor'*, explains how the Good News transforms poor people when they receive and are involved in it. That brings in them a sense of worth and dignity.[46] Christian Lalive D'Epinay noted how the theology from below emerged when the slum dwellers of Chile, who were rejected by the mainstream, got dignity, worth and a role

---

[39] Ibid. (Samuel)

[40] Ibid. (Houghton)

[41] Sathyavratha, Ivan, 2001, 'God has not Himself Without a Witness'

[42] Richard, R.L., 2005, *Exploring the Depths of the Mystery of Christ: K. Subba Rao's Eclectic Praxis of Hindu Discipleship to Jesus*

[43] Ibid.

[44] Kumaradoss, Vincent Y., 2000, 'Creation of Alternative Public Spheres and Church Indigenisation in Nineteenth Century Colonial Tamil Nadu: The Hindu – Christian Church of Lord Jesus', *Christianity is Indian*, Roger Hedlund ed.

[45] Sugden, Christopher, 2009, personal interview, Oxford, UK

[46] Sugden, Christopher, 1991, 'What is Good about the Good News', in *AD 2000 and Beyond, A Mission Agenda*

from the Pentecostal churches and that was the reason for the phenomenal growth of those churches.[47] This theology Gustavo Gutierrez terms 'Latin American Theology' while distinguishing it from 'English' and 'North American' theology.[48] Julio De Santa Ana[49] described how the 'Liberation Theology' was formed by people involved in fighting against the unjust structure of the society to bring peace and equality in the society.

Christ Groups did not need to look for any recognition from western mission, which has a limited scope of theology to apply on a country like India. Walls stated, 'Western theology is "in general too small for Africa (India)"; it has been cut down to fit the small-scale universe demanded by the Enlightenment, which set and jealously guarded a frontier between the empirical world and the world of spirit'.[50] Nor do Christ Groups require recognition of the mainline churches in India, whose ecclesiology is still under the influence of western theology.

The Christ Groups had no preconceived ideas. The members of Christ Groups themselves defined their own identity as Christians and Churches. They saw themselves as a household. Their understanding of church, namely their ecclesiology, arose out of their experience of Christ and their own background. Their Lingayat background or its influence meant they were already well prepared with an anti-Brahminical understanding of religion. This meant they already had an understanding of priesthood and religion "from below". They drew on their own traditions that were compatible with Christian church order. For Lingayats, faith is holistic and affects the whole of life. So Christ Groups easily related to a holistic understanding of the Christian faith.

The western mission wanted to dissolve Christ Groups rather than continue them. The mainline churches did not embrace them, because they did not look like them. In Samuel's words 'they were not the "products" of the west, they were not built on resources tied to western mission enterprise because they cannot be controlled or limited by the power from above'.[51] Samuel cautioned 'that western mission is increasingly becoming hegemonic in this post colonial period and now sees itself as investment driven and shaped by globalisation, which seeks power and control over its clients'.[52] Christ Groups have passed the test of time over these decades. Without recognition, they have continued due to their past religious experience and the new message they received. Without divorcing themselves from their

---

[47] D'Epinay, L. Christian, 1969, 'Haven of the Masses', in Sugden, 1991, *AD 2000 and Beyond, A Mission Agenda*, 64
[48] Gutierrez, Gustavo, 1991, in Sugden, *AD 2000 and Beyond*, 77
[49] Ana, Julio De Santa, 1978 (1977,WCC), *Good News to the Poor*
[50] Ibid.
[51] Ibid.
[52] Ibid.

culture, they have become the bearers of the good news. This movement may shed more light on the how the mission in rural India may emerge.

Christ Groups provided a new social dimension for the rural populace, bringing people of all classes and castes and genders on an equal platform to worship and have fellowship with each other, which gave the members self-worth and empowerment; though it did not eradicate the age-old Indian caste system. It provided glimpses of harmony and unity to the rural populace when they saw the incarnation of Christ, His atonement and love for humanity, which transcended all man-made barriers and clash of cultures. Members' past religious experience and the influence of Bhakti, Lingayatism and Nudi which affected peoples' religious experience gave them the ability to continue in Christian faith and withstand any hostile context, or indifferent attitudes of its originators and leaders. This was the Christ Groups' unique contribution to the Indian rural populace, when India's social fabric was under threat from anti-social elements, which were causing divisions and disharmony among all classes and castes of Indian society, while churches were looking more to the west for their continuity and growth.

Thus, Christ Groups are a 'New Vision of Rural India' and they fulfil the long desire and aspirations of Indian missions in providing one more indigenous, yet Scripture-based, non-syncretistic and non-accommodationist, but an appropriationist Church Planting Tradition for rural India.

Critique of Christ Groups

The study may be romantic about the success of Christ Groups. Christ Groups may have to face up to sectarian teachers who will confuse and mislead them. Christ Groups are rather secluded and need to relate to other Christian groups to know them better and also other Christian traditional churches to relate to them to protect them from divisive forces.

In Matthew chapter 13 Christ uses the illustration of a mustard seed which grows into a tree and becomes the nesting place for birds of the air. In this passage Christ taught his disciples to be careful about the teachings of various sectarian groups who would come and confuse the vulnerable followers of Christ. The Christ Groups are no exception in having to face up to such divisive forces.

Christ Groups members who hitherto have been taught by the non-trained simple faith evangelists appear to be vulnerable and easily misled by other Christian groups with a more cultic or sectarian emphasis. This is not new among new Christian communities. Paul while writing to the Hebrews advises believers to move from drinking milk to eating solid food. (Heb 5:11-14). This raises the question of how they will moveointo the next stages of appropriation of the full summary of Christian teachings while retaining their own cultural identity. This will be particularly important as the faith is passed on to the next generation.

For this reason, traditional churches to protect their fold remained traditional to guard their members from such sectarian emphases. Christ Groups should develop to know what other churches are so that they retain and develop their Christian identity when they come in contact with many more sectarian groups. This would be another topic for future research.

Christ Groups and Change: Now Christ Groups have entered into the next generation where the whole leadership has to face change. Rural culture in India continuously faces increasing modernization. Will the rural people be able to resist modernity? Will rural culture be able to engage successfully with the modernity which others will bring to their rural life? A next generation of young people in villages faces technological advancement. Will they be able to relate the Christian faith of their parents to it? Will they be attracted by the modernity of modern India while retaining the faith of their parents?

It can at least be said for WLC that it attempted to harness the forces of modernity in technology and communication for the cause of Christ, in the belief that these forces could be the servants of Christian faith. Time has shown that those forces can become masters too. Nevertheless, WLC people gave their allegiance to the cause of Christ.

Contribution of Christ Groups to the Ongoing Discussion on Missological Approaches, especially in Relation to David Bosch's 'Transforming Mission', David Smith's 'Mission after Christendom' and Samuel and Sugden's 'Mission as Transformation'

Bosch provides a comprehensive account of current Mission Theologies and Practice in Transforming Mission but there is a gap in his work as Sugden points out that Bosch overlooks 'the epistemological priority of the poor, the categories of covenant and family, the integration of evangelism and social action, the understanding of power (and) the role of Pentecostalism'[53] which are marks of the growing churches in the Two-Thirds world. Christ Groups fill part of that gap by showing the way in which rural communities in the so-called Two-Third World have responded to the gospel.

In order to locate the contribution of Christ Group, I refer to three works: *Transforming Mission, Mission as Transformation* and *Mission After Christendom*. David Bosch, in effect, outlines the mission of mainstream churches. Samuel and Sugden fill more of the gap that Bosch leaves and

---

[53] Sugden, Christopher, 1996, 'Placing Critical Issues in Relief: A Response to David Bosch' in Willem Saayman and Klippies Kritzinger (eds.) *Mission in Bold Humility: David Bosch's Work Considered*, 150

identify the development of the wholistic mission coming from the Two-Thirds World. David Smith describes the changed contexts of mission from the point of western evangelical churches, especially of Northern European churches.

Christ Groups' approach is focusses on the experience of church planting. *Mission as Transformation* focussed particularly on the experience of development work beginning with issues of poverty. Christ Groups focus on and begin with evangelism. The study provides further material to fill the gap identified in David Bosch's work. Christ Groups are also in contrast to the conversion approach of WLC that focused on the conversion of the individual and neglected the community and the implications for the culture.

Bosch suggests that churches to have 'change within' seeing changes in the context. Bosch speaks critically of traditional approaches that sought to justify certain preconceived understandings of mission by proof texts in the Scripture. He rather stressed a rediscovery of the intrinsically missionary nature of the church, based on the witness of the Bible. He further adds that the Bible functions as a foundational source and standard by which the church understands its identity in Christ, as well as a source of paradigms and models for current missionary engagement with the world.[54]

In the changed mission contexts of the world, David Smith stresses that churches seeing the changes in the mission contexts of world today should 'change all'. He explains that while mission is a biblical universal, the modern missionary movement was a specific, culturally conditioned initiative which, while amazingly successful in its time, is likely to become increasingly dysfunctional if the attempt is made to preserve it in the new context... and the modern missionary movement has almost reached the end of its life.[55]

In Walls' words, 'the missionary movement is now in its old age. It is not a useless and decrepit old age. There situations where it provides the most effective, perhaps the only foreseeable means of making any witness to Christ or any proclamation about him... But the conditions that produced the movement have changed, and they have been changed out of all recognition by the agency of the missionary movement itself'.[56]

Bosch failed to give adequate attention to the emerging theologians and perspectives of the church in the Two-Thirds World.[57] Smith recognizes this but asks western evangelical churches to play some kind of a role as

---

[54] Livingston, J. Kevin, 1999, David Jacobus Bosch 1929 to 1992, *International Bulletin of Missionary Research*, January, No 1, 26-32

[55] Smith, David, 2003 (2007), *Mission After Christendom*, 117

[56] Walls, Andrew, 1996, *The Missionary Movement in Christian History*, 261

[57] Sugden, Christopher, and Frans Verstraelen, 1996, *Mission in Bold Humility* and the foreword to Norman Thomas, *Classic Texts in Mission and World Christianity*, 1995: *A Reader's Companion to David Bosch's Transforming Mission*

referees because of their past theological heritage to correct any imbalance in emerging theologies of the Two-Third World.

For Bosch and Smith, the church and its expansion is central to their thinking. Both are genuinely concerned about church's development and effective witness. As Frans Verstraelen noted, Bosch had difficulty in giving 'context' a central place in his theologising because he remained in the category of an 'idealist' theologian who theologizes from above rather than from below.[58]

In contrast, the Christ Group movement is a 'peoples movement' where people owned it and are central to its thinking. In Jesus' words they may be seen as a 'little flock' (Lk 12.32) or 'flock' (Jn 10:16). Because of the involvement of the people in the movement, a theology from below emerged, which gave people space and time to mature and bear witness for Him without threatening any communities and cultures. Christ Groups take a similar approach as *Mission as Transformation* but beginning from evangelism rather than development. This is an example of the complete change in approach that David Smith argues for away from the initiative of the western churches: it focuses on the community response and changing the culture in contrast to WLC's focus on individual conversion as the sole outcome.

---

[58] Verstraelen, Frans, 1996, 'Africa in David Bosch's Missiology', 14, op.cit., in Willem Saayman and Klippies Kritzinger (eds) *Mission in Bold Humility*

Appendix 1
Chapter Notes

Chapter1: The relational context sometimes called the cyclical worldview, finds its roots in tribal cultures. It is intuitive, non-time oriented and fluid. The balance and harmony in relationships between multiple variables including spiritual forces make up the core of the thought system. Every event is in relation to all other events regardless of time, space or physical existence.

Chapter 2: Evangelism is the proclamation of the good news to non-believers, calling for repentance and salvation and inviting them to become the members of the church and preparing them for the service of God. However, Mission includes evangelism as one of its responsibilities. Mission primarily refers to *'missio Dei'* (God's mission), that is, God's self-revelationas the One who loves the world, God's involvement in and with the world, and in which the church is privileged to participate (Bosch:1991 (2005):10,11).

Print, radio and television are grouped under 'mass-media'. Print or literature can be used for personal or mass evangelism (distribution). The main difference between big crusades and mass distribution is that in the former one reaches thousands at a time but in the latter hundreds or thousands of distributors reach the thousands. www.pgmindia.org

Chapter.3: One of the Enlightenment precepts was that everyone was an autonomus individual. Its effect on Christianity was the rampant individualism in which each individual not only had the right but also the ability to know God's revealed will. This led to a belief that individuals were liberated and independent, and they could make their own decisions about what they believed (Bosch:1991:273).

'World Evangelism' assumed that the current generation is evangelized. This is now questioned. Hesselgrave (2007:121-149) while writing on 'Edinburgh 1910' called to 'Correct the Ediburagh Error'which suggested that approach to world mission was narrower and the whole conference was represented by some selected band of Protestant evangelicals. But the 'Edinburagh 2010' pledge to do away with this tradition and plans to bring the whole range of Christian traditions and confessions. However, it is not certain whether it will even bring all sectarian, cultic, exclusive and fundamentalist Christian groups too.

There are conflicting figures mentioned about the deal. The total price for the mill was for 4.1 million US dollars. The first payment of $500,000 was made in November 1977. Another 1 million was raised and paid in 1978. McAlister, Jack, 'God impressed me with this fact', 'It is my paper mill', *Everybody*, 1978, Feb., Vol. 4, No. 2, .3, *Everybody*, Jan., Vol. 1, No. 1, 8.

Chapter 4: India Missions Association. 1997, Languages of India, Chennai. According to SIL's Ethnologue web site http://www.ethnologue. com/show_country.asp?name=India there are about 850 languages in daily use in India. *The World Christian Encyclopedia* (2nd ed., 2001; Vol.1, 359) cites 1650 mother tongues in addition to the 18 official languages recognised in the Constitution

Singh, K.S., 2000, Cited in a Research Workshop on February 3, 2000. Dr. Singh's categories are based on people's perceptions and self-perceptions, identifying 76 cultural traits, and including dimensions of biology/morphology, language and culture. The commonly cited number from Dr. Singh's 1991 study is 4,635 people groups but in the last decade he has identified several dozen more

Sunder Raj, Ebenezer, 2001, *National Debate on Conversion*, Chennai, Bharat Jyoti, Chennai, India.

World Christian Encyclopedia, 2001. The percentages given in this section relating to castes and Christians have been deduced from the 2001 edition of *Operation World*, edited by Patrick Johnstone and Jason Mandryk. It looks "deduced" because on page 309 they list percentages by caste, but these appear to be percentages of the Hindu population (not the total population), which they identify on page 310 as 79.83% of the total population. On page 315, the number of Brahmins is given as 40 million (i.e. 4% of the total population). Somewhat different percentages have been cited by Dr. Raju Abraham, and by S.D. Ponraj and R. Bruce Carlton in *Strategic Coordination in Mission* (Chennai: Mission Educational Books, 2001). In *The National Debate on Conversion* (Chennai: Bharat Jyothi, 2001:150), Ebenezer Sunder Raj warns that, 'Our (Indian) Census figures on religions are very unreliable data and the cause for great communal tensions. They cannot be made the authentic base for any legal or legislative purpose.'

Vasanthraj, S. Albert, 1999, *Unreached Mega Peoples of India*, 6, Chennai, India Missions Association. India (Albert Vasanthraj, estimates in Unreached Mega Peoples of India, Chennai, India Missions Association, that there are 45 million Christians in India, in addition to 10 million crypto-Christians or secret believers. *World Christian Encyclopedia* (2nd ed., 2001; Vol.1, 360) estimates 40.8 million Christian adherents and 21.5 million crypto-Christians).

Chapter 5: 'The Bible Study Groups', 'Koinonia' and 'Christ Groups' are synonyms names used for the newly formed believers groups but these names were used in the different stages or periods of the ministry. The name 'Christ Group' was the final one that WLC/IEHC started using from 1972. The Christ Groups stayed part of IEHC but under pressure from

WLC, IEHC distanced and showed indifferent attitude towards them. Only WLC disowned them but not IEHC.

The word 'Growth' here means what was it that helped Christ Groups to continue in spite of hurdles it faced. It does not explicitly deal with their physical or spiritual growth but those elements affected or contributed towards their continuity.

Farquhar, J. N., 1913, *The Crown of Hinduism*. The key word in Farquhar's missionary theology was fulfilment. He... popularized the idea that Christ came to fulfil and bring to completion not only the law and the prophets (Mt 5:17) but all the world's higher religions. It is in this sense that Christ is the crown of Hinduism. Accessed on 15-06-09 www.diglib.bu.edu. Hugh McLeod echoes the same about Farquhar that some 'sought to be more inclusive of other religious traditions and interpret that the Christian message as fulfilling other religions', *Christianity, World Christianities*, c.1914-c.2000, 2006, 513.

Chapter 6A: After going through the open-ended interviews. I made missionaries cum pastors go over them again with the respondents for better clarification and then the questionnaires were filled in. The questionnaire was translated into the local language, Kannada, so that it was better understood by people and pastors, since English was not their first language. To get needed data in an oral culture like this, a quantitative survey may not alone be sufficient. It would be time consuming to get data from four different Christ Groups, which were situated in different parts of Karnataka State from the far North to the South and East to West, and it needed more resources to meet the cost. Data were collected in the centrally located parts of these groups and by key informants. To obtain data through postal questionnaires would have taken more time and the validity of information may have been vague. The postal services in these areas are not reliable. To collect the data took 3-4 days in each of these four CG centres, including the journey time.

Chapter 7: This research is based on four Christ Groups: Bagepalli, Hosadurga, Pavagada and Bijapur. The survey data includes a questionnaire and interviews with the members and evangelists-cum-pastors. Information was also gathered from the published materials of IEHC, such as reports and magazines, in order to see whether the accounts, either in the mission fields or testimonies of individuals with whom interviews were conducted, tally or any important issues are missed out.

Figure 7A.3 Age Distribution of Members of
Four Christ Groups Survey in Karnataka

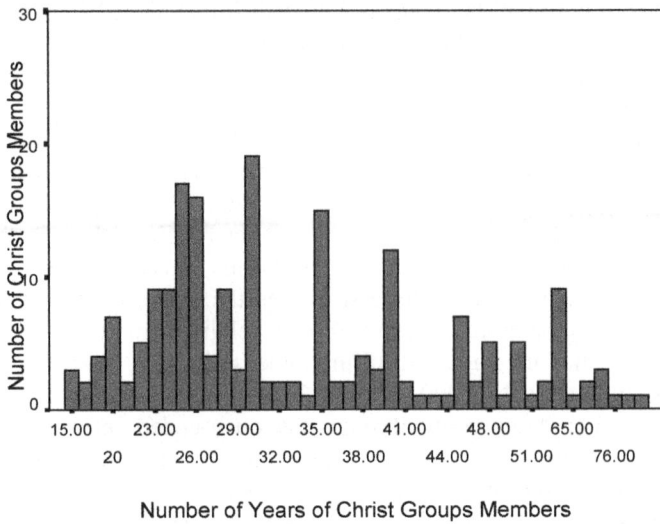

Number of Years of Christ Groups Members

Table 7B.5 Distribution of Members of Four Christ Groups 'Opinion about 'Christian Wedding' to become a Christian; CG Survey in Karnataka State

Representation of Members of Four Christ Groups		Numbers of Members Represent Four Christ Groups	Percentage of Representation of Members
Agree	.00	3	1.5
Strongly Agree	1.00	11	5.5
Disagree	2.00	13	6.5
Strongly Disagree	3.00	144	72.0
Neutral	4.00	29	14.5
Total		200	100.0

Chapter 8: www.ad2000.org accessed on 06-06-09, Samuel, Vinay, and Chris Sugden (eds.), 1991, *AD2000 & Beyond: A Mission Agenda.*, The Movement sought to encourage cooperation in establishing a church within every unreached people group and making the gospel available to every person by the year 2000. However, the movement was not successful in the end.

Stricland, Don, 'Charles Finney's assault upon Biblical Preaching'. *The Founders Journal*, main page, contents 9, accessed on 7th Sep 2006. Stricland argues that Finney's appeals for 'souls conversions' during his mass evangelistic camps were engineered to make people to become emotional and commit their lives to Christ. According to Stricland, "Finney changed evangelicalism's understanding of revival. The Edwardian idea that revival is "prayed down" was replaced by Finney's conviction that it is "worked up" (along the lines of mass evangelism). The former views God as the agent in salvation and the latter sees man as the instrument of his own spiritual birth.

William McLoughlin summarized Finney's major contribution to revivalism: Both he [Finney] and his followers believed it to be the legitimate function of a revivalist to utilise the laws of mind in order to engineer individuals and crowds into making a choice, which was ostensible, based upon free will.

Both Stricland and McLoughlin fail to mention the role of the Holy Spirit in the act (drama) of conversion.

This statement was confirmed by a staff member of OM in Lucknow (28th February 2009 in New Delhi) that OM has separately registered its wing to look after the church ministry. The days may not be far for OM to have its churches governed by a denominational body of its own.

Appendix 2
Conclusions of Chapters 2 – 7

Chapter 2

It was thought by the historians and social scientists that evangelicalism would not survive the onslaught of modernity that produced secularism. Modernization was expected to see religion decline to the point of non-relevance in the contemporary context. Hammond predicted, 'the whole conservative religious scene…was out of step with the America I knew. Therefore it could be dismissed'.[1]

That may be true in most parts of the West. However, it is becoming apparent that religions are competing well in this pluralistic society. The American evangelicalism's and mass-evangelistic organization's adaptation to the modern culture or use of the modern culture to spread the good news has shown an alternative understanding of religion's role in modern society. Marty suggests that 'there has been a symbiosis between unfolding modernity and developing Evangelicalism'. He adds further that 'Evangelicalism is the characteristic Protestant way of relating to modernity', and 'Evangelicals have adapted well to the characteristic features of the modern world'.[2]

In conclusion, in modern times, mass-evangelistic organisations in USA, through their enthusiasm for the culture of reading, the culture of performance, and the culture of mass media, have chosen to operate within the market place of a commodified commercial culture.

Chapter 3

WLC as a product of American culture of its time took up a huge world programme, which is sympathetic to American evangelicalism, to evangelize the world by placing a printed gospel booklet systematically in to every home. Although the strategy was 'every home', WLC used the western individualistic approach, which was quite contrary to the context of

---

[1] Ibid. 281

[2] Marty, Martin E., 1981, 'The Revival of Evangelicalism and Southern Religion', in *Varieties of Southern Evangelicalism*, ed. David E. Harrel, Jr,, 9

the countries, such as India, where relational contexts are paramount. WLC was driven with market values. It made economically viable plans in order to reach every home on the globe. McAlister used the effective new media of his time, such as radio, literature and television. Lee based his methods on science, like cells, and business, such as a paper mill.

To some extent , WLC's strategy of reaching every home on the globe is more of a vision than an accomplished goal. There are a large numbers of countries, like China and Islamic countries, that cannot be reached. Even in India, in spite of two nationwide house-to-house coverages, only every accessible home was reached. WLC's strategy was mass-evangelism through printed literature. That is one message for all. WLC thought printing gospel tracts in millions in a particular language would cut the cost considerably.However, the statistical data from India shows that only 7 to 10 percent of people made an enquiry for further courses and one percent of these enquirers were able to complete such a course. WLC was not keen to know about or analyse this huge number of non-responses.

WLC believed in the power of the printed page. It called this printed page its 'Paper Missionary'. This attempt aimed to replace foreign missionaries so that the cost to support such missionaries would be reduced. However, personal evangelism to the families is thought to be the best way in winning people. The 'Final Thrust-5000' of EHC in India proved that under its programme through personal evangelism 40 to 60 percent of people responded and most of them made a definite commitment to the Lord. The power in the printed word can be effectively achieved when personal evangelism and other forms of evangelism are involved in reaching homes or people.

WLC would have capitalized on its success in forming Christ Groups, if McAlister or Lee had continued in WLC. The change of leadership and policy made WLC to retreat to its 'every home' strategy or to move away from that to a 'catalyst' role. It became only sympathetic to Christ Groups work rather than to own the vision involved. WLC, instead of widening its vision to analyse what strategy was best suited for India, retreated to its western individualistic approach.

Chapter 4

WLC were successful in bringing pressure on Indian leaders and making them listen to their directives rather than allowing them to run the ministry according to their own convictions, to suit their (Indian) contexts, culture and people. However, all evangelistic methods have been pushed to the periphery, including WLC's main aim of 'systematic tract distribution'. Social concerns like adult literacy and vocational training have come to the front. What does the future hold for IEHC ministry in India? Will WLC continue funding their work in India? Will they desert their 'Jewel in the

Crown' in search of a 'Diamond'? Will IEHC on its own survive in India
and attempt to do what its relational context demands from it? Will it again
try to complete, or will it abandon its Third coverage or the Final Thrust-
5000 to gather the 'Harvest'? These look to be distant realities but other
targets could be achieved, if the leaders are alert to the tasks required, while
the harvest is nurtured to eventually complete the final task.

The data presented in this section shows that the members of the Christ
Groups had no idea about what the 'individualistic approach' meant. Their
response to the Good News comes out of the context they live in, that is, a
relational one, not only among blood relations but also with the other
families in their own community and in other communities in the village.
The social fabric of the rural community appears delicately and closely
knitted between one family and an other and one member and a other. In
such contexts, the Good News, instead of causing disharmony, alienation
and division may work towards building a better community having the
values of the Kingdom of God. In this context 'Family Evangelism' seemed
an appropriate approach to reach the rural community in building God's
Kingdom.

Chapter 5

IEHC made a big attempt to evangelize every home. IEHC broke new
ground. They made the gospel available to every accessible home and
person. IEHC brought fresh-air for people to breathe and to find meaning
and self-esteem in their lives. However, it also created a big vacuum in
doing so. The attempt brought good success but also brought challenges.
The afore-said factors ought to have forced WLC and EHC in India to shift
their emphasis from mass evangelism to Christ Groups. Christ Groups were
formed in India's relational context in reaction to mass-evangelistic,
individualistic methods of WLC. People not only read for themselves but
for their friends and family members,[3] and that became a starting point for
the formation of Christ Groups. As Paul said, 'the community shared its
experience quietly with their friends and relatives,'[4] According to
Newbigin, 'the Gospel spreading from village to village without any kind
of organization and finance'.[5]

The field survey shows that people were led to Christ and Christ Groups
because a friend or family member had shared the gospel with them. The
place of literature in evangelism seemed to be minimal. As IEHC puts it 'a
Christ Group has not come into existence just by obtaining Gospel message

---

[3] Sugden, Christopher, 1999, personal interview, Oxford, UK
[4] Ibid. 3
[5] Ibid. 4

on a printed page'.[6] Through the constant endeavour of the evangelists and
their contacts 'a Christ Group is formed'.[7] As Prasad said, the formation of
Christ Groups was not their original plan.[8] IEHC leaders were ready to
meet 'the newly arisen demands' in their evangelistic effort.[9] After Prasad's
death, the subsequent leaders were not visionaries like him nor were they
ready to convince their WLC's officials about the context and culture of
India. However, they weakly surrendered themselves to do what the WLC
leaders wanted them to do rather than committing themselves into the
hands of God to do what He wanted to do through them.

In spite of all sorts of indifferent attitudes from WLC's and IEHC's
leaders, it is interesting to see that after 30 years of Christ Groups,
beginning in 1968 Christ Groups have continued to survive the very severe
tests of the times. Even though Christ Groups never understood the
attitudes and behaviour of the WLC's and IEHC's, their enthusiasm was
never quenched nor were they disturbed by any financial crisis.

Some may question whether Christ Groups will continue in the Christian
faith, without assimilating into Hinduism, if, as the bearers of the Christian
message, they build God's Kingdom without inheriting the traits of the
entrepreneurial instincts of the WLC ministry. The question of whether
Christ Groups will assimilate into Hinduism and take up another form, may
not arise here as they have passed the test of time. They are growing
stronger in faith and some have become big churches and denominations.
As Christ said, 'upon this rock I will build my church; and the gates of hell
shall not prevail against it' (Mt 16:18).

Christ Groups members found new meaning for their past religious
experiences of pietistic movements. Christ Groups provided the social
equality between men and women and also removed the indifference of
caste system. It empowered men and women to become the leaders of their
groups. Christ Groups' ability to survive in a hostile context lies in their
past religious experience and the influence of Bhakti, Lingayatism and
Nudi movements that had given them the self-surviving, self-continuing
and self-growing capabilities against the Brahaminical hierarchical order. It
became once again their shield and strength when they took upon
themselves a new identity in Christ. Christ Groups were not deterred by the
hostile context they lived in, nor discouraged by the indifferent attitudes of
their WLC originators and IEHC leadership but continued to grow and
expand.

---

[6] Ibid. 17
[7] Ibid.
[8] Ibid. 24
[9] Ibid. 24

Chapter 6

The preference for combined methods as discussed in this chapter was based upon the following factors. To explain the structured questionnaire to an average rural people it was difficult for them to follow the logic of the questions in the survey. Due to this, a personal interview of each participant was conducted with open-ended questions to gather the data. After this stage, the evangelists cum pastors helped the participants provide the needed information to fill in the questionnaire. This was time consuming and expensive. This was the first time that social research has been applied to Christ Groups. It made the quantitative method a necessary approach because it provides triangulation and linkages with the qualitative data. To summarize, the combined methodology better served the objectives of this study and seemed more appropriate for contexts where there is a lack of social science research experience applied to the subject under investigation.

Chapter 7

The data presented here suggests the sort of changes the members of Christ Groups want when they become Christians rather than what changes evangelists or Christ Groups wanted to see in the lives of their members. It was significant to note that the changes came from the perceptions of the members of Christ Groups on Christianity rather than views imposed from the outside. The traditional Churches gave 'no choice to converts but to change their culture'.[10] Christ Groups widened the horizon and deepened the meaning of Christianity that it may grow in its soil and spread from there.

To change the concept of God looked possible but the Christian mission needs to provide space and time so that change may take place at its own pace rather than looking for 'Pure Christians'. The members saw the institutions of the church as something 'Sacred'; the past was replaced but found deeper meaning to them rather than just showing pious reverence for them. The observances of festivals were a sign of renewing social bonds rather than religious observances. The festivals were with the newfound truths, and thus transformed the meaning of them to flow with the stream with a distinct meaning to it. For example, Muniswamy of Bagepalli Christ Group, before he became a Christian used to make pilgrimages to the Himalayas to do *tapasya* (meditation). In a similar way, when he became a Christian he fasted and prayed on a mountain top for forty days and nights.

---

[10] Ibid. 12

Chapter 7

From the beginning , it was assumed that the 'Relational' factor might be the most important one. However, there were several other factors that helped members in the groups to play their roles, which may have been beneficial to them and to the larger community. Christian mission, while working in the rural parts of India, particularly in Karnataka State, may work better to some extent to meet the expectations of the rural community and build them to become members of His Kingdom. While nurturing members to maturity and make them worthy of God's Kingdom, it is also important for them to know their responsibilities towards the community at large and how to participate in nation-building and thus become better citizens of India.

As Christ trusted in His disciples that they will take His message across the nations and make people become His disciples, in a similar way 'the hearer of the good news has become the bearer of it'. There is a tremendous power in the gospel. Christ Groups' members, after tasting the gospel message, did not keep that for themselves but willingly and lovingly shared the good news with their friends, relatives and neighbours. Members did not realize either what their originator WLC, or their Indian parents (IEHC), thought about them. However, for members, finding Jesus was a wonderful experience that they were determined to share with others in the community and decided to carry out the task they were entrusted with.

Appendix 3
Varna Model or Indian Caste Ladder

VARNA MODEL (Sanskritic) – (from Campbell 1978)

Origin	Varna's	Binary Divisions			Hierarchy

Origin	Varna's				Hierarchy
Mouth	**BRAHMANS** Priests Scholars	R e l i g i o u s	T w i c e B o r n	I n s i d e S o c i e t y	▼ PURE
Arms	**KSATRIYA** Ruler Warrior	S e c u l a r			
Thighs	**VAISAYA** Merchants Traders				
Feet	**SUDRAS** Farmers Artisans Labourers		O r d i n a r y		
	UNTOUCHABLES			O u t s i d e Society	▼ IMPURE

Appendix 4
Fatalism

Is the degree to which an individual recognizes a lack of ability to control his future? Fatalistic attitudes are widely reported as characteristic of peasant peoples (Banfield 1958, Levi 1947, Bista 1991). Some believe that peasants' fatalism stems from their inability to transform class relationships that would change their lives, and is emphasized in passive resignation, and destructive internal conflict (Keesing 1981). Lewis (1960) feels that peasants' fatalism stems from authoritarian family structures, which tends to produce passive and dependent children.

In peasant societies, there is a very low degree of mastery over nature and social conditions. Drought or flood are visitations from gods or evil spirits, whom man can propitiate but not control. Feudal forms of land tenure and non-productive technologies may condemn a farmer to a bare subsistence living. Medical and social services are lacking, and people die young. Under such circumstances, it is not surprising that people have few illusions about the possibility of improving their lot. A fatalistic outlook, the assumption that whatever happens is the will of God or Allah, is the best adjustment the individual can make to an apparently hopeless situation (Foster 1973).

This view is supported by many: Fals Borda (1955) in Brazil and Bista (1991) in Nepal. Bista tells us that many Nepalese, especially high caste Hindus (the elite power holders) have been brought up according to a belief system them posits that one's circumstances have been determined by a supreme deity; that their lives have been determined. This is called *karma*, and is thought to be predestined and as something that cannot be altered in any way. Fatalism, in this context, finds expression in a lack of purposeful problem-solving and goal-achieving behaviour, in education that just becomes ritualistic behaviour, in a lack of internalized responsibility towards society at large; in difficulty with the attribution of success or failure for individual action, in keeping to contractual relations, in its affect on competitive behaviour and profit-motive, in planning for the future and 'time management'.

By contrast, low caste people, when opportunities arise, have found that hard work leads to economic success and, as a result, they are improving their economic status. Bista argues that fatalism has had a devastating effect on the work ethic and achievement motivation, and through these on the Nepali response to development. Followers of primal belief are generally not fatalistic but are indirectly affected if the elites that oppress them are fatalistic.

Appendix 5
A Report on Christ Groups in India
– Option for Adoption

At the request of Dr, Dale Kietzman and the World Literature Crusade Executive Committee, a quick but intense study has been done 'on the alternatives available to us for the adoption of the Christ Groups by established churches or missions within India'.The study has been made necessary as I see it by 1) The mandate of World Literature Crusade 'that Every Home Crusade exists to serve, motivate, and mobilize the Church to participate actively in the systematic personal presentation of a printed or repeatable message of the Gospel of Jesus Christ to every home in all the world, helping new believers to responsible members of the Body of Christ'. 2) That WLC wishes to have its Every Home Crusade vision implanted an operative in every nation by 1996... 4) That India Every Home Crusade appears now to be primarily 'helping new believers to become responsible members of the Body of Christ'. 5) That limited income demands that WLC make every effort to use its funds wisely as directed by its mission statement, and expected it to do by its supporting constituency....7) What appears to be a quiet confusion in how WLC understands its task at the present moment, given its present resources, and how IEHC sees the work it is to do now, i.e., in terms of whether the weight of things is to be on initial evangelism or follow up.

Excerpts from Charles A Wickman's report on Christ Groups in India – Option for Adoption.

Appendix 6
Resolution, Board of Directors, February 27, 1985, Dallas, Texas, World Literature Crusade

Whereas, the Board discussed the current cross road transition and reorganisation taking place under God's direction in this His ministry and felt moved of the Holy Spirit to make an informal statement of our love, worship and praise of our Heavenly Father and His only begotten son, and our Lord and Savoir Jesus Christ; and

Whereas, seeking to be in the centre of Almighty God's perfect will by obeying Him and taking a stand before the world on issues that are vital toward that end, the board spoke with one mind and heart; and

Therefore, after deliberation, prayer, worship and praise, on a motion duly made by John Aycock, and seconded by Wayne Olson, the following resolution was unanimously adopted:

Resolved, in the precious name of Jesus Christ we humbly repent of our sins, and to His glory and in His Holy name we publicly declare and confess that Jesus Christ is Lord of our lives and Leader of World Literature Crusade throughout the world, and we proclaim to the world that this Ministry is part of His Church; and

Resolved further, that 'integrity' shall be the watch word and motto of World Literature Crusade and Every Home Crusade throughout the world, as this Ministry is here to serve god and for no other purpose, as God reminds us in (Proverbs 12:22) 'The Lord detests lying lips, but He delights in men who are truthful'; and

Resolved further, that any giving of false information or half-truth to this Board, the Ministry Staff, Donors and Public will not be tolerated; and

Resolved further, that we reject worldly wisdom which places great value on pleasing men, we accept Heavenly wisdom which says nothing is more important than pleasing Jesus Christ, our Lord and Saviour; and

Resolved further, that we reject worldly wisdom that would tell us to raise more funds for God's work by manipulation of donors, we accept Heavenly Wisdom which says, Have faith in God and follow Jesus with gladness and joy always being careful to give him all the glory as we obey Him; and...

Resolved Further, that all Ministry communication and everything this Ministry does must pass the highest in standards of truth, as we are reminded that Acts Chapter V, Ananias lied and instantly died; (His wife) Sapphira lied and instantly died; (If World Literature Crusade permits lies it will surely die.)

Resolved further, we declare to all that God is in total control of this Ministry. The Lord God omnipotent reigns, let us rejoice and be glad and give him the glory! Amen!

Appendix 7
IEHC Boards Report / Resolution on Koinonia (an earlier name for the Christ Groups) Green Park, New Delhi, 9, May 15 1972

Koinonia

We had the joy of starting several Koinonia groups during 1970-71 but this has been temporarily suspended under the instructions of our Overseas Director

Bibliography

Primary Sources

Interviews

A Staff of OM, 2009, Personal interview in February 28, at YMCA, New Delhi, India

Augustine, John, 1998, Personal Interview, UTC, Bangalore, India

Bowman, Jim, 2000, Personal Interview, Bangalore, India (a former staff of Interdev and founder of Scripture in Use, USA

Christopher, David, 2002, Personal Interview, Bangalore, India

Das, Madhusudan, 2006, Personal interview, Elim Retreat Centre, Whitefield, Bangalore, India

D'Souza, George Steven, 2007, Personal Interview, Pastor, Calvary Sharon Church, Hosadurga, India

Early, Gene, 1999, Personal Interview, Oxford, UK

Eastman, Dick, 1999, Personal interview, 12th March, Colorado Springs, USA

Guruprasad, G., 1998, Personal Interview, March, Bangalore, India

Jairaj, P., 1998, Personal Interview, February, Pastor of Hosadurga Christ Groups Church, Hosadurga, India

Jairajan, P., 1998, Personal Interview at Bangalore, March, Pastor of Hosadurga Christ Groups Church, India

Jayananda, R., 1998, Personal Interview, February, Pastor of Pavagada Christ Groups, Pavagada, India

Jayananda, R., 1998, Personal Interview at Bangalore, March, Pastor of Pavagada Christ Groups, India

Jayaprabhu, B, 1999, Personal Interview, February (a former field staff of IEHC, Karnataka, a lead worker of Christ Groups work in Hosadurga). Yellapur, India

Leach, Eric, 1998, Personal interview, 12th November, London, UK

Maxton, M. M., 1998, Personal Interview, IEHC, Lucknow, India

McAlister, Jack, 1999, Personal interview at his residence, 22nd March, founder and former President of WLC, Los Angeles, USA

McAlister, Hazel, 1999, Personal Interview, 22nd of March, Los Angeles, USA

Muniswamy, 2003, Personal Interview (Pastor of independent churches, Chelur and Tippasandra, Bagepalli taluk) Bangalore, India

Peter, Manik, 1998, Personal interview at his residence in Bijapur, February and March, a staff of IEHC, Karnataka, Bijapur, India

Prasad Rao, 1998, Personal Interview, Pastor of an independent church, Kalghatagi, India

Prathapkumar, B.A., 1998, Personal interview, Secunderabad, India

Pushpamma, R., 1998, Personal Interview, Hosadurga, India

Samuel, C. Samuel, 1998, Personal Interview, Bangalore, India

Samuel, Vinay, 1998, 2000, 2002, 2003, 2004, Personal Interview, Oxford, UK

Shettian, D.P., 2001, Personal Interview, a former Bishop of Karnataka Southern Diocese, Mangalore, Karnataka, India

Soans, Murphy, 2004, Personal interview, an ordained clergy of CSI Church, Bijapur, India

Solomon, B.G., 2000, Personal interview, Bangalore, India

Sudershan, Albert, 2003, Personal Interview (A Present Manager of IEHC, Karnataka), Bangalore, India

Sugden, Christopher, 1999, 2002, 2003, 2004, 2009, Personal Interviews, Oxford, UK

Thomas, P., 1998, Personal Interview, a field coordinator for Marthoma Evangelical Church, Devanhalli, Bangalore, India

Vasudev Rao, 1998, Personal Interview, A Field and Follow up Coordinator of IEHC, Bangalore, India

Venkatswamy, C., 2003, Personal Interview (Pastor, Christ Groups Church, Oodavarpalli, Bagepalli taluk), Bangalore, India

Vinaykumar, Stanley, 1998, Personal Interview, a pastor of an independent church, Bangalore, India

Willmer, Haddon, 2000, Personal Interview, Oxford, UK

Wilson, Wes, 1999, Personal Interview, February, Colorado Springs, USA

Correspondence

Creighton, Fred, 1998, Letter (faxed), Hamilton, New Zealand

Creighton, Fred, 1994, Letter to Dick Eastman on 21st October, Hamilton, New Zealand

Creighton, Fred, 1994, (2) Letters to Dick Eastman on the 4th of November, Hamilton, New Zealand

Creighton, Fred, 1994, Letter to Dick Eastman on 20th December, Hamilton, New Zealand

Creighton, Fred, 1994, Report on Indian Leadership to Dick Eastman, Hamilton, New Zealand

George, C., 1978, Letter to all IEHC directors, New Delhi, India

Goodwin, Paul N., 1985, Letter to U S Board of Directors WLC/EHC Executives World Wide, February 14th

Goodwin, Paul N., 1985, Letter to WLC/Executive Staff on the April 29th, Studio City, California, USA

Guruprasad. G., 1964, Invitation Letter, 5th December, India Every Home Crusade, Bangalore, India

Kietzman, Dale, 1985, Letter to National Directors & Executive Directors, November 4, Studio City, California, USA

Kietzman, Dale, 1986, Letter to BAG Prasad on 18th April, Studio City, California, USA

Lee, Yohann, 1977, Letter to all the Regional Directors on 21st of September, Studio City, California, USA

Lee,Yohann, 1977, Circular Letter to C George, J J Oliver, Robert Louis, BAG Prasad, M M Maxton, Peter Bose, James Ebenezer, D C Kaushal, E D Ashwal and S C Samuel, on 18th of October, Studio City, California, USA

Lee, Yohann, 1977, Letter to All Every Home Crusade Directors on 20th of September, Studio City, California, USA

Lee, Yohann, 1980, Letter, WLC, Studio City, California, USA

Louis, Robert, 1970, Letter addressed to G Guruprasad, Raichur, India

McAlister, Jack, 1970, Letter to Josias S Riberio of Sao Paulo, Brazil, September 4, WLC, USA

Oliver, J. J., 1994,   Letter, 22nd of November, to Dick Eastman, a former director and one of the founding members of IEHC, Mhow, India

Prabhakar, B.A., 1969, Letter to all IEHC Directors on 20th October, Bangalore, India

Prasad, B.A.G., 1985,   Letter to all the Directors in South Asia on 13th May, National Director and a founding members of IEHC, Central Office, Secunderabad, India

Prasad, B.A.G., 1985,   Letter to Paul Goodwin and All IEHC Directors on 13th May, Secunderabad, India

Prasad, B.A.G., 1985, Letter to Paul Goodwin on 11th May, Secunderabad, India

Prasad, B.A.G., 1986, Letter to C George, a copy to Dale Kietzman on 20th March, Secunderabad, India

Prasad, B.A.G., 1986, Letter to Dale Kietzman on 1st May, Secunderabad, India

Prasad, B.A.G., 1986, Letter to Dale Kietzman on 2nd May, Secunderabad, India

Prasad, B.A.G., 1986, Letter to Dale Kietzman on 3rd May, Secunderabad, India

Prasad, B.A.G., 1986, Letter to Martin Wilson on 20th June, Secunderabad, India

Prasad, B.A.G., 1986,   Letter to Dale Kietzman on 22nd December, Secunderabad, India

Prasad, B.A.G., 1986,   Letter to Dale Kietzman on 22nd December, Secunderabad, India

Prasad, B.A.G., 1987, Letter to Dale Kietzman, Hyderabad, India

Prasad, B.A.G., 1988,   Letter to Faustino Ruivivar on 8th March, Secunderabad, India

World Literature Crusade

Everybody, 1968
Everybody, 1976, Vol 2, No 2, February
Everybody, 1976, Vol 2, No 5, May
Everybody, 1976, Vol 2, No 8, August
Everybody, 1977, Vol 3, No 1, January
Everybody, 1977, Vol 3, No 5, May
Everybody, 1977, Vol 3, No 6, June
Everybody, 1977, Vol 3, No 7, July
Everybody, 1977, Vol 3, No 8, August
Everybody, 1977, Vol 3, No 9, September
Everybody, 1978, Vol 4, No 1, January
Everybody, 1978, Vol 4, No 3, March
Everybody, 1978, Vol 4, No 5, May
Everybody, 1978, Vol 4, No 7, July
Everybody, 1978, Vol 4, No 11, November
Everybody, Spring 1980
Everybody, 1980, Third Quarter
Everybody, 1980, Fourth Quarter

Editorial, 1970, *Everybody*
Editorial, 1972, *Everybody*
Editorial, 1976, *Everybody*, July
Editorial, 1976, *Everybody*, March
Editorial, 1976, *Everybody*, September
Editorial, 1977, *Everybody*, January
Editorial, 1980, *Everybody*, January
Editorial, 1980, *Everybody*, June

Read and Pray, 1960 Editorial

Eastman, Dick, 1977, *Everybody*, '33 centuries of prayer', September
Lee, Yohann, 1976, *Everybody*
Lee, Yohann, 1976, *Everybody*, January
Lee, Yohann, 1976, *Everybody*, March
Lee, Yohann, 1976, *Everybody*, April
Lee, Yohann, 1976, *Everybody*, September
Lee, Yohann, 1977, *Everybody*, 'Why the Amazing Harvest?' March
Lee, Yohann, 1978, 'Dog Soup', *Everybody*, February
Lee, Yohann, 1978, *Everybody*
Lee, Yohann, 1980, *Everybody*, 'World Progress Report', June
Lee, Yohann, 1980, *Everybody*
Lee, Yohann, 1983, *Everybody*, Vo.1 1, No. 2, 37 years of the Vision, February
Lee, Yohann, 1984, *Everybody*

McAlister, Jack, 1970, *Everybody*
McAlister, Jack, 1972, *Everybody*
McAlister, Jack, 1972, *Everybody*
McAlister, Jack, 1976, *Everybody*, January
McAlister, Jack, 1976, *Everybody,* March
McAlister, Jack,1976, *Everybody*, 'Come meet us... here's what we are', July
    McAlister, Jack, 1976, *Everybody*, September
McAlister, Jack, 1976, *Everybody*
McAlister, Jack, 1978, *Everybody*, 'Attitude toward other Christian organisations', June
    McAlister, Jack, 1978, *Everybody*, February
McAlister, Ruth, W. E. 1977, My First Born, *Everybody*, April
McGavran, Donald A., 1976, 'Testing Your Investment in India', *Everybody*, February,

Oliveira, de, A B., 1978, *Everybody*, 'Here & There', June
Patterson, David, 1978, *Everybody*, 'Here & There', February
Patterson, David, 1978, *Everybody*, 'Here & There', June
Patterson, David, 1980, *Everybody*, 'WLC-a charter member.' June
Peters, George, 1976, *Everybody*, Lausanne Congress on World Evangelisation

A Report, 1976, *Everybody*, 'They send missionaries by the millions', no1
A Report, 1978, *Everybody*, January
A Report, 1994, *Everybody*

Read and Pray, 1960 Editorial

A Booklet, 1970, "Individual", A WLC's booklet on winning Individuals, WLC, Studio
    City, California, USA
Goodwin, Paul N., 1984, A Report, WLC, USA, WLC, Studio City, California, USA
Goodwin, Paul N., 1985, A Report of US Board of Directors WLC/EHC Executives,
    10th March, Studio City, California, USA
Goodwin, Paul N., 1985, A Report, Studio City, California, USA
Goodwin, Paul N., 1985, A Report, Studio City, California, USA
Hinman, Nelson, E., 1962, Japan's Golden Harvest, Jack McAlister (ed), Part II, Let's
    Finish The Work! A "One Evening" World Tour, WLC, Studio City, California,
    USA
Kietzman, Dale, 1985, A Report

Kietzman, Dale, 1986, A Report, International Policy Guidelines, Studio City, California, USA

Kietzman, Dale, 1986, A Report, WLC, Studio City, California, USA

Kietzman, Dale, 1987, Memorandum to Wickman, dt April 10, Re: Strategies of ministry, the same was sent to all the leaders, WLC, Studio City, California, USA

Lee, Yohann, 1962, *Dawn of New Era*, A 'One Evening World Missionary Tour', Studio City, California, USA

Lee, Yohann, 1962, *Japan's Golden Harvest, Part II*, Jack McAlister (ed), EHC Action in Asia, A Hungry, Angry Giant Without Christ, A 'One Evening' World Tour,

Lee, Yohann, 1964, *India Giant of Asia*, A One Evening World Missionary Tour... no 14, World Literature Crusade, California, USA

Lee, Yohann, & Jack, McAlister, 1965, *'I Survived a Communist Slaughter'*, One Evening World Missionary Tour...no 9, World Literature Crusade, California, USA

Lee, Yohann, & Jack, McAlister, 1966, *The Other Half*, One Evening World Missionary Tour no. 12, World Literature Crusade, California, USA

Lee, Yohann, 1966, *Are You Happy?*, a tract of WLC though printed in India but written in USA and used in all the offices of IEHC for distribution, Bangalore, India

Lee, Yohann, 1968, *Fruit that shall Remain*, One Evening World Missionary Tour no 16, World Literature Crusade, California, USA

Lee, Yohann, 1971, *The 25th Hour in Southeast Asia*, One Evening World Missionary Tour no 18, World Literature Crusade, California, USA

Lee, Yohann, 1971, *Christ Wept,* One Evening World Mission Tour Series...no 19, World Literature Crusade, California, USA

Lee, Yohann, 1972, *On the Road to Damascus Today*, One Evening World Missionary Tour no 20, World Literature Crusade, California, USA

Lee, Yohann, 1974, *Operation Last Home*, A One Evening World Missionary Tour no 21, World Literature Crusade, California, USA

Lee, Yohann, 1975, *The Story Behind Television*, WLC, Studio City, California, USA

Lee, Yohann, 1976, 'Christ Groups', *Everybody*, WLC, Studio City, California, USA

Lee, Yohann, 1976, *Christ Group Manual*, WLC, Studio City, California, USA

Lee, Yohann, 1976, *Production Manual*, Fall, World Literature Crusade, USA

Lee, Yohann, 1976, *Operational Manual*, Early Winter, World Literature Crusade, California, USA

Lee, Yohann, 1980 (1965), *'I Survived a Communist Slaughter'* (a revised edition), WLC, Studio City, California, USA

Lee, Yohann, 1982, Annual Report, World Literature Crusade, California, USA

Lee, Yohann, 1999, A Christ Groups Questionnaire, Los Angeles, USA

McAlister, Jack, 1959, *Prayer Mobilisation Manual*, September, World Literature Crusade, California, USA

McAlister, Jack, 1960, *Alaska Assignment Accomplished*, A One Evening World Missionary Tour, World Literature Crusade, California, USA

McAlister, Jack, 1963, *The Song of the Soul Set Free*, 'Preface...Tried by Fire', WLC, Studio City, California, USA

McAlister, Jack, 1963, *Daily Diamonds*, WLC, Studio City, California, USA

McAlister, Jack, (ed), 1964, *Men or War and Peace*, One Evening World Missionary Tour no 8, World Literature Crusade, California, USA

McAlister, Jack, 1966, *One Million Every Day*, Preface, A One Evening World Mission Tour, No 13, WLC, Studio City, California, USA

McAlister, Jack, 1974, *Operation Last Home*, A 'One Evening' World Missionary Tour no 21, WLC, Studio City, California, USA

McAlister, Jack, 1975, *The Story Behind the Television*, back cover, WLC, Studio City, California, USA

McAlister, Jack, & Yohann Lee, 1975, *2 Giants*, 'One Evening' World Mission Tour Series...no 24, WLC, Studio City, California, USA

Smith, Paul B., 1962, Foreword, *Dawn of New Era*, Johnny Lee, WLC, A 'One Evening' World Missionary Tour, Studio City, California, USA

Wickman, Charles, 1984, A Resolution of the WLC's Board, Colorado Springs, USA

Wickman, Charles, 1986, A Report on, Christ Groups in India Options for Adoption EHC-I, Colorado Springs, USA

Every Home Crusade

A Report, 'Country-by-Country Summary of EHCs', 'Canada', A Statistical Details File of EHC-I, Colorado Springs, USA

Eastman, Dick, 1992, A Report, Points for Praise, Summer, From the President's Pen, EHC-I, Colorado Springs, USA

Leach, Eric, History of Australia and New Zealand, Every Home For Christ, Australia

Statistical Data, 1995, A Status Report of Every Home Christ International, Colorado Springs, USA

Statistical Data, 1998, A Status Report of Every Home Christ International, Colorado Springs, USA

Statistical Data, 1999, Worldwide Progress Report, Every Home Christ International, Colorado Springs, USA

India Every Home Crusade

A Report on Kasargod Seekers Conference, 1974

A Report on India, 1990,

A Report, 1968, a publication of IEHC Karnataka, where 167 baptisms took place in a day by the Rev. William Shatanada of Chintamani church, Karnataka, India

A Report, 1972, January 1970 to April 1972

A Report, 1974, India Every Home Crusade, Bangalore, India

A Report, 1980, A Report on Karnataka

A Report, 1980, A Statistical Details of IEHC

A Report, 1982, a Report on Karnataka

A Report, 1985, A Report, 1995, A Statistical Details on Karnataka

A Report, 1995, A Statistical Details on Karnataka

Ashwal, E. D., 1984, Project Himalaya, One Evening Series...no 2, India Every Home Crusade, Secunderabad, India

Ashwal, E. D., 1987, Grace Before Gallows, 1987, One Evening Series...no 3, India Every Home Crusade, Secunderabad, India

Ashwal, E. D., Jesus in Jungle, 1987, One Evening Series...no 4, India Every Home Crusade, Secunderabad, India

Ashwal, E.D., 1989, It Can Be Done! Christ Groups, IEHC, Secunderabad, India

Ashwal E.D., Desert Blooms, 1993, India Every Home Crusade, Secunderabad, India

Ashwal E. D., Karnataka Crusade, 1994, India Every Home Crusade, Bangalore, India

Ask Us, 1981, India Every Home Crusade, Bangalore, India

A Statement of Faith, 1966, India Every Home Crusade, Bangalore, India

Brayard (Brian), Taylor, 1989, op.cit., Ashwal, E.D, *It Can Be Done!* IEHC, Secunderabad, India

Christ Groups, 1984, Vol. 3, No. 3, July, India Every Home Crusade, New Delhi, India

George, C., 1978, A Report of Christ Groups, presented in the Asian Directors Conference, 7-14 January in Bangkok, Thailand

George, C., 1983, Christ Groups, IEHC, August, New Delhi, India

George, C., 1985, Christ Groups, IEHC, January, New Delhi, India

Guruprasad, G., 1969, Do you know this? India Every Home Crusade, Bangalore, India

Harvest in India, 1996, Central Office, India Every Home Crusade, Secunderabad, India

IEHC, 1994, India at a Glance. Bangalore, India

India Mission Association, 2000, Editorial, Chennai, India

Louis, Robert, 1974, A Report On Karnataka IEHC, Bangalore, India

Louis, Robert, 1976, A Report on Karnataka, Bangalore, India

Louis, Robert, 1976, A Report on Karnataka, December, IEHC Bangalore, India

Louis, Robert, 1978, A Report on Karnataka IEHC, presented in a meeting arranged by the Bible Society of India Auxiliary, Bangalore, India

Munnade (Forward), 1970, News Letter-5, India Every Home Crusade, Bangalore, India

News Letter-7, 1970, Forward, India Every Home Crusade, Bangalore, India

News Letter, 1975, 30th January, India Every Home Crusade, Bangalore, India

Oliver, J. J., 1994, An Address in IEHC directors meeting at Hyderabad, India

Onward, 1969, News Letter-5, India Every Home Crusade, Bangalore, India

Pitts, Glen, 1988, an address in an IEHC Directors Conference in Bangalore, India. (Glen Pits was the Vice President of WLC, USA)

Prabhakar, B.A., 1970, A Circular dated 21st August, to various evangelical mission heads, Bangalore, India

Prabhakar, B.A., 1970, A Boards Resolution, IEHC, The Central Office, Bangalore, India

Prarthisu, 1966 Editorial

Prarthisu, 1969

Prasad, B.A.G., 1991, Prayer Bulletin, IEHC, December, Secunderabad, India

Prasad, B.A.G., 1992, Final Thrust 5000, a manual and publication of IEHC, Secunderabad, India

Prasad, B.A.G., 1993, Prayer Bulletin, 300,000 Christ Groups by the end of 2000 AD, IEHC, Secunderabad, India

Prasad, B.A.G., 1994, An Address in IEHC Directors conference, Hyderabad, India

Prasad, B.A.G., 1999, Prayer Bulletin, November (a posthumously published material of Prasad), an IEHC Publication, Secunderabad, India

Statistical Data, 1994, A Report on Karnataka IEHC, Bangalore, India

Statistical Data, 1996, A Status Report of Karnataka IEHC, Bangalore, India

Statistical Data, 1998, A Status Report on Karnataka IEHC, Bangalore, India

Statistical Report, 1998, A Statistical Report of IEHC Karnataka, Bangalore, India

Taylor, Bayard (Brian), 1986, Every Home Crusade Christ Groups Village Survey, Karnataka, South India, World Christian Magazine, USA

What is Every Home Crusade? 1983 & 1985, India Every Home Crusade, Secunderabad, India

Secondary Sources

Accorda, Corrie, 1993, Tradition, Modernity and Christian Mission in Asia, *Transformation*, October

Aikman, David, 1998, *Great Souls*: Six who changed the century, Waco, Texas: Word

Ainlay S. C., and J.D. Hunter (eds.), *Making Sense of Modern Times: Peter L. Berger and the vision of interpretative sociology, London: Routledge*

Ana, Santa, Julio de, 1977 (1978), *Good News to the Poor*, Geneva: WCC

Anderson, Leith, 1998, *Dying for Change*, Bethany House, Minnesota

Anderson, Rufus, 1967, *To Advance the Gospel*, in Selections from the Writings of Rufus Anderson, ed. R. Pierce Beaver, Grand Rapids, Michigan: Wm. B. Eerdmans

Armstrong, B. *The Electric Church.*

Baker, Edwin, & Alan Greenbank, 1995, *A Handbook on Open-Air Evangelism*: the Open-Air Mission, London

Barna, G., 1990, The Church of the '90s: Meeting the Needs of a Changing CultureBass, Bernard M., 1985, *Leadership and Performance beyond Expectations*, New York: Free Press

Berger, P.L., 1969, *The Sacred Canopy*, Anchor, New York: Doubleday

Berger, P.L. and D Nash., 'Church commitment in An American Suburb: An Analysis of the Decision to Join,' Archives of the Sociology of Religion,

Billington, Harper, Susan., 2000, *In the Shadow of Mahatma*, Grand Rapids, Michigan: William, B. Eerdmans

Blodget, Harold W, 1953, *The Best of Whitman*, New York: Ronald Press

Bosch, David J., 2006 (1991), *Transforming Mission* (Indian Edition), Bangalore: Centre For Contemporary Christianity

Bouma, G.D., & Atkinson, G.B. 1995, *A Handbook of Social Science Research*, Oxford: Oxford University Press

Bowman, Jim, 2002, Discipleship through Story Telling: A manual, Arizona

Bromley, D. G., and A Shupe, *Rebottling the Elixir: The Gospel of Prosperity in America's Religio-economic Corporations*, in T Robbins and D Anthony, *In Gods We Trust: New Patterns of Religious Pluralism in America*, 1981, New Brunswick, New Jersey: Transaction

Brouwer, Steve, Paul Gifford, Susan D. Rose, 1996, *Exporting the American Gospel: Global Christian Fundamentalism*, London: Routledge

Bryman, A C., 1999, *Quantitative Data Analysis*, London: Routledge

Carpenter, Joel A., and Wilbert R Shenk, 1990, *Earthen Vessels*: American Evangelicals and Foreign Missions, 1880-1980, Grand Rapids, Michigan: William B. Eerdmans

Carpenter, Joel A., 1997, *Revive Us Again*: The reawakening of American Fundamentalism, New York: Oxford University Press

Carvalho, S., & H. White, 1997, *Combining the Quantitative and Qualitative Approaches to Poverty Measurement and Analysis*: The Practice and The Potential (World Bank Technical Paper no 366). Washington D. C.

Cho, Paul Yongi, 1981, *Successful Home Cells Groups*, Seoul: Church Growth International

Colquhoun, Frank, 1948, *Give Ye Them To Read*, Bible Churchmen's Missionary Society

Cootie, Robert, 1991, *Evangelical Mission Quarterly*, 'The number game in world evangelisation', April

Corner, J., 1991, *In search of more complex answers to research questions: qualitative versus quantitative research methods: is there a way forward?* Journal of Advanced Nursing

Cowman, Charles E. [Lettice] Mrs. 1939, Charles E. Cowman: *Missionary Warrior*, Greenwood, Indiana: OMF

D'Souza, Joseph, 2000, 'The Indian Church and Missions face the Saffronization Challenge', *Global Missiology for the 21st Century*, ed. William D. Taylor, Grand Rapids, Michigan: Baker Academic

D'Epinay, L. Christian, 1969, *Haven of the Masses*: A study of the Pentecostal Movement in Chile, London: Lutterworth Press

Derne, Steve, 1995, *Culture in Action: Family Life, Emotion and Male Dominance in Banaras India*, Albany: State University of New York Press

Desai, Neera, and Maithreyi, Krishna Raj, 1987, *Women and Society in India*, Ajantha

Durkheim, Emil, 1912 (1915), *The Elementary Forms of the Religion Life*, Translated by Joseph Ward Swain, London: George Allen & Unwin (Les formes elemetaires de la vie religieuse: Le systeme totemique en Australie)

Eastman, Dick, 1971, *No Easy Road*, Baker House Company, Grand Rapids, Michigan

Eastman, Dick, 1997, *Beyond Imagination*, A simple plan to save the World, Chosen Books, Grand Rapids

Encyclopaedia of Religion, 1987,' Hinduism', Eliade, Mircea and Adam, Charles (eds.), MacMillan, New York

Escobar, Samuel, 1991, A Movement Divided, *Transformation*, October

Fairely, E., 1997

Fernandes, Walter, 1981, *Caste Conversion Movements in India*, New Delhi: Indian Social Institutei

Findlay, James F., 1969, *Dwight L Moody: American Evangelist*, Chicago: University of Chicago Press

Firth, C.B., 1961, *An Introduction to Indian Church History*, London: SPCK

Frykenberg, Eric, Robert, & Alaine M. Low, 2003, *Christians and Missionaries in India:*

Cross-Cultural Communication since 1500, with special reference to caste, conversion, and colonialism, Grand Rapids, Michigan: William, B. Eerdmans

Gitari, David M. and G.P. Benson (eds) 1986, *Witnessing to The Living God in Contemporary Africa*, UZIMA, PRBS, Nairobi

Gnanadasan, 1989, *A. Mission Mandate*, L.D.Pate (ed.), From Every People: A Handbook of Two-Thirds World Missions, Monrovia, California: MARC

Green, Bryan, 1951, *The Practice of Evangelism*: Missions and Mass-Evangelism, London: Hodder and Stoughton

Guba, E. G., and Lincoln, Y.S, 1989, *Fourth Generation Evaluation*, Newbury Park, California: Sage

Hammond, Phillip E., 1983, In Search of a Protestant Twentieth Century: American Religion and Power since 1900, *Review of Religious Research* 24, March

Haralambos, Michael, R.M Heald, and Martin Holborn, 1995, *Sociology: Themes and Perspectives*, Collins Educational

Hargreaves, A.C.M., 1979, ed., *Report of the Conference of British Missionary Societies*, by Leslie, Newbigin, JE, 1958, 9 Meeting

Hargreaves, Cecil, *Asian Christian Thinking: Studies in a Metaphor and its Message, Evangelism,2nd ed., New Delhi: ISPCK, 1979*

Hatch, Nathan O., 1989, *The Democratization of American Christianity*, Yale

Hedlund, Roger E., 2004, *Christianity is Indian: The Emergence of an Indigenous Community*, New Delhi: ISPCK

Hewitt, Brian, 1995, *Doing a New Thing*, London: Hodder and Stoughton

Hiebert Paul, Missiological Issues in the Encounter with Emerging Hinduism, *Missiology*, Vo.l 28i, no. 1, January 2000Hobson, Sara, 1978, *Family Hub*: A Story of India, London: John Murray

Hogg, A.G., 1947, *The Christian Message To The Hindu*, London: SCM Press

Hooker, Roger, 1979, *Voices of Varanasi*, London: CMS

Holman H.R., Qualitative inquiry in medical research Journal of Clinical Epidemiology, 1993:46(1):29-36,

Houghton, Graham, 1983, *The Impoverishment of Dependency*, Madras: Christian Literature Centre

Hunshall, S.M., 1947, *The Lingayat Movement, A Social Revolution: The Ethics of Lingayatism (Bhaktisthal)*, Dharwar: Karnataka Sahitya Mandir

Hunter, Alan, and Kim-Kwong Chan, 1993, *Protestantism in Contemporary China*, Cambridge: Cambridge University Presse

Illich, Ivan 1974 *Mission and Midwifery: Essays on Missionary Formation, Gwalo: Mambo Press,*

India Missions Association, 1997, *Peoples of India*, Chennai

India Missions Association, 1997, *Languages of India*, Chennai

Jayakumar, Samuel, 1999, *Dalit Consciousness and Christian Conversion*, Oxford: Regnum International

Jenkins, Philip, 2006, *The New Faces of Christianity*, New York: Oxford University Press

Jayaprakash, L.J., *Evaluation of Indigenous Missions in India*, CGRC, Madras

Johnson, Paul, 1991, *The Birth of the Modern*, New York: Harper Collins,

Johnstone, Patrick, and Jason, Mandryk, (eds) 2001, *Operation World*, Waynesbor:, Paternoster

Johnstone, Patrick, 1993, *Operation World*, OM Publishing

Johnstone, Patrick, 1998, *The Church is bigger than you think*, Christian Focus

Jongeneel, Jan, A.B., (1995) 2006 (Indian Edition), Conclusion and Perspective, *Missiological Encyclopedia*, Part II, Bangalore: Centre For Contemporary Christianity

Kannada Vishwa Kosh, (Kannada Encyclopaedia) 1990, Karnataka Sahitya Academy, Bangalore

Karnataka Encyclopaedia, 1978, Bangalore: Kannada Sahitya Prakashan

Kreider, Alan, 1995, *Worship and Evangelism in Pre-Christendom*, Cambridge: Grove Books

Lears, Jackson T J., 1981, *No Place of Grace*, New York: Pantheon Books

Livingston, J. Kevin, 1999, David Jacobus Bosch 1929 to 1992, *International Bulletin of Missionary Research*

Macchia, F.D., 1999, *The Struggle for Global Witness: Shifting Paradigms in Pentecostal Theology, in The Globalisation of Pentecostalism* (8-29), Oxford: Regnum Books

Marsden, George M., *Fundamentalism and American Culture*, 1980, New York: Oxford University Press

Marty, Martin E., 1981, *The Revival of Evangelicalism and Southern Religion*, in Varieties of Southern Evangelicalism, ed. David E. Harrel, Jr, Macon, Georgia: Mercer University Press

Maynard, James G., 1945, *Evangelize*, Essex: Evangelical Publishing House

McGavran, Donald A., 1971, in *Concise Dictionary of the Christian World Mission*, (ed) S.Neill et al., London: Lutterworth Press

McGavran, Donald Anderson., 1988 (1970, 1980), *Understanding Church Growth*, Grand Rapids, Michigan: Wm. B. Eerdmans

McLoughlin, William G., 1959, *Modern Revivalism, Charles Grandison Finney to Billy Graham*, New York: Ronald Press

McLuhan, Marshall, 1964, *Understanding Media*, New York: McGraw-Hill

Moslem World, 1937, January, Vol. XXVII

Nadimutt, S.C., 1941, A Hand Book of Virasaivism, Dharwar: Literary Committee, Lingayat Educational Association

Neighbour, Ralph W., 1990, *Where Do We Go From Here?* A Guide Book for the Cell Group Church, Houston: Touch

Neill, Stephen, et al. (eds.), 1971, *Concise Dictionary of the Christian Mission*, London: Lutterworth Press

Neill, S. 1964, *A History of Christian Mission*, Harmondsworth: Penguin Books

New Dictionary of Theology, 1988, Ferguson & Sinclair (eds), IVP

Patton, Cornelius H., 1924, *The Business of Mission*, New York: Macmillan

Pickett, J. W., 1933, *'Christian Mass Movements in India'*, New York: Abingdon Press

Pityana. N., 1973, 'What is Black Consciousness', in B. Moore (ed), *Black Theology, The South African Voice*, London: C. Hurst

Pollock, John, 1966, *Billy Graham*, London: Hodder & Stoughton

Postman, Neill, 1985, *Amusing Ourselves to Death*: Public Discourse in the Age of Show Business, 1985, New York: Viking

Rajendran, K., 2000, The Impact of Christianity in India, Global Missiology for the 21ˢᵗ Century, ed., William D Taylor, Grand Rapids, Michigan: Baker Academic

Rajshekar Shetty, V.T., 1983 (1977), Apartheid in India, Bangalore: Dalit Sahitya Academy

Ramalinga, 1987, 'Nitivantan Bhikar Kole' (Murder of an Innocent), Mysore

Richard, H.L., 1998, *Following Jesus in Hindu Context*: The Intriguing Implications of N.V. Tilak's Life and Thought, New York: William Carey Library

Ritson, John H., 1910, *Christian Literature in the Mission Field*, Papers presented in Continuation Committee of the World Missionary Conference, Edinburgh

Rossman, G.B., & Wilson, B.L, 1984, Number and Words, Combining Quantitative and Qualitative Methods in a single large-scale evaluation study, *Evolution Review*, 627-643, 9(5)

Rudolph, Lloyd I. & Susanne Hoeber Rudolph, 1984, *The Modernity of Tradition: Political Development in India*, Chicago: University of Chicago Press

Saayman, Willem and Klippies Kritzinger (eds.) *Mission in Bold Humility*: David Bosch's work considered, Orbis Books, Maryknoll, New York

Sampson, P., Vinay Samuel, Chris Sugden (eds.) 1998, *Faith and Modernity*, Oxford: Regnum Books International

Samuel, Vinay Kumar, and Chris Sugden, 1987, *The Church in Response to Human Need*, Grand Rapids, Michigan: William B. Eerdmans

Samuel, Vinay Kumar, and Chris Sugden (eds), *AD2000 & Beyond: A Mission Agenda*, 1991, Oxford: Regnum Books

Sanneh, Lamin, 1989 (2002), *Translating The Message*, New York: Orbis Books

Sargent, N.C., 1969, The History of the Christian Church in Mysore State, *The Karnataka Christian Council, A Souvenir of its Silver Jubilee, 1944-1969*, and the Pastors' Conference (This was earlier published in the Bulletin of Church History Association of India, May 1962), Bangalore

Seel, J. Modernity and Evangelicals: American Evangelicalism as a Case Study in *Faith and Modernity*, Phillip Sampson, Vinay Samuel, Chris Sugden (eds.), Regnum Books International, Oxford, 287-313

Shaffir, W.B., and Stebbins RA, eds., 1991, *Experiencing fieldwork: an insider's view of qualitative research*, Newbury Park, California: Sage

Smith, David, 1996, A Report: William Carey and Religion in Europe and Asia: An Enquiry into the Founding and Early Influence of the Baptist Missionary Society, Oxford

Smith, David, 2003 (2007), *Mission After Christendom*, London: Darton, Longman and Todd

Stanley, Brian, 1990, *The Bible and The Flag*, Leicester: Apollos

Statements from the WCC Executive Committee Meeting, 1968 (February, 1968), *The Ecumenical Review*, vol. 20, no. 2, April

Steiner, A. George, 1979, Government's Role in Economic Life, 1953, *Capitalism and Progress*, New York: McGraw-Hill

Stott, John, 1975, *Christian mission in the modern world*, Falcon Books, London

Stout, Harry S., 1991, *The Divine Dramatist George Whitefield and the Rise of Modern Evangelicalism*, Grand Rapids, Michigan: William B. Eerdmans

Sugden, Christopher, 1991, What is Good about the Good News, in *AD 2000 and Beyond, A Mission Agenda*, Oxford: Regnum Books

Sugden, Christopher, 1996, Placing Critical Issues in Relief: A Response to David Bosch' in Willem Saayman and Klippies Kritzinger (eds.) *Mission in Bold Humility*: David Bosch's work considered, Maryknoll, New York: Orbis Books

Sugden, Christopher, 1997, *Seeking the Asian Face of Jesus*, Oxford: Regnum Books International

Sunder Raj, Ebenezer, 2001, *National Debate on Conversion*, Chennai: Bharat Jyothi

Sunder Raj, Ebenezer, 1998, *The Confusion Called Conversion*, Chennai: Bharat Jyothi Publication

Thomson, Luckman, 1991, *Printing and Publishing Activities of the American Tract Society from 1825 to 1850*, Papers of the American Bibliographical Society of America

Uchimura, Kanzo, 1926, *Can Americans Teach Japanese in Religion?* Japan Christian Intelligencer 1

Verstraelen, Frans, 1996, Africa in David Bosch's Missiology, in Willem Saayman and Kilppies Kritzinger (eds), *Mission in Bold Humility*, Maryknoll, New York: Orbis Books

Veerhoef, M.J., Casebeer, A.L, & Hilsden, R.J, 2002, Assessing Efficacy of Complimentary Medicine, Adding Qualitative Research Methods to the 'Gold Standards', Journal of Alternative and Complementary Medicine, 2002, Vol.8(3), pp.275-281

Verwer, George, 1963, *Literature Evangelism*: A Manual, Chicago: Moody Bible Institute

Vine, W.E., 1944, *Expository Dictionary of New Testament Words*, Vol.2, E-Li, London: Oliphants

Walker, Andrew, 1998, *Restoring the Kingdom*, Surrey: Eagle, Inter Publishing Service

Walls, Andrew F., 1982, The Gospel as the Prisoner and Liberator of Culture, *Missionalia*, Vol. 10:3

Walls, Andrew F., 1990, The American Dimension in the Missionary Movement, in *Earthen Vessels*, Joel A. Carpenter and Wilbert R. Shenk (eds.), Grand Rapids, Michigan: William B. Eerdmans

Walls, Andrew F., 1996, *The Missionary Movement in Christian History*, Edinburgh: T&T Clark

Walls, Andrew F., 2002, 'Missologist of the Road', *The Cross-Cultural Process In Christian History*, Maryknoll, New York: Orbis Books

Weber, M., 1904, *The Protestant Ethic and the Spirit of Capitalism* (2nd ed.), London: Allen and Unwin

Webster, C. B., 1976, *The Christian Community and Change in Nineteenth Century North India*, New Delhi: Macmillan

Weller, S., 1998, Structured Interviewing and Questionnaire Construction in Bernard, H. Russell *Handbook of Methods in Culture Anthropology*, Walnut Creek, California: Alta Mira, 363-407

Winter, Ralph, 1975, *Let the Earth Hear His Voice*, ICOWE, Pasadena

Wolpert. Stanley A., 1993, *A New History of India*, New York: Oxford University Press, New York

World Christian Encyclopaedia, 2001 2nd ed., David B. Barrett (ed)., Oxford: Oxford University Press

Wurth, 1920, *The Journals of Basel Missionaries of South Maratha*,

Young, William G, 1999, *Handbook of Source Materials*, for students of Church History, Delhi: ISPCK

Yung, Hwa, 1997, *Mangoes and Bananas*: The Quest for an Authentic Asian Theology, Oxford: Regnum Books International

Theses and Unpublished

Barna, G., 1991, 'Marketing the Church' Seminar, Atlanta, Georgia, 29th January

D'Souza, Joseph, 2006, A Public Address on Times Now T.V news channel, New Delhi, India

D'Souza, Oliver, 2003, a public address, the All India Christian Council on "Atrocities against Christians in Karnataka", Bangalore, India

D'Souza, Oliver, 2003, Atrocities against Christians in the State of Karnataka, All India Christian Council, Bangalore, India

David, D. R., India Leadership Study, 2002, USA (unpublished)

Duke, H.M., 1989, Christianity in Karnataka, 'The Contribution of Karnataka Churches', M. A. Thesis, Fuller Theological Seminary, Pasadena, USA

Ford, Leighton, 1985, A Paper on Methods on Evangelism presented at the Manila Congress on Evangelism, Philippines

Geertz, Clifford, 1999, A Life of Learning, 'Thick Description', Lecture Charles Homer Haskins, USA

Hong, Young-Gi, 2000, Dynamism and Dilemma: The Nature of Charismatic Pastoral Leadership in the Korean Mega-Churches, Ph.D. Thesis, University of Wales, UK

Marshall, P.G. (1998), Modernization and Post-Modernization of Ecclesiology, M. Phil. Thesis, The Queen's University, Belfast, Northern Ireland

Samuel, Vinay, 2009, Mission and Power, A Seminar Paper, Oxford, UK

Shettian, D.P., 1990, a public address, Wesley Church, Mysore (a former Bishop of Karnataka Southern Diocese, Mangalore, during the dedication service of IEHC evangelists), Mysore, India

Singh, K.S., 2000, Cited in a Research Workshop on February 3,

Studdley, John, 1992, op. cit. Banfield 1958, Levi 1947, Bista 1991, 'Fatalism', M.A Thesis, Religious Belief and Development, -4, University of Reading, Reading, UK

Sunder Raj, Ebenezer, op.cit., David, D.R. 2001.India Leadership Study, USA

Vasanthraj, Albert S., 1999, op.cit in D. R. David, India Leadership Study, an (unpublished), USA

Walls, Andrew F., 1999, a lecture in a Seminar, 'The Impact of Non-Western World Christianity in the 20th Century', 15th of November, at the Oxford Centre for Mission Studies, Oxford, UK

Yung, Hwa, 2000, Kingdom Identity and Christian Mission, A Lecture at OCMS August 31 (originally the paper was presented in 5th David Adeney Memorial Centre, Discipleship Training Centre, Singapore)

Internet

Ann L Casebeer, and Marja J Verhoef, 200?, 'Title' Available at http://www.phc-aspc.gc.ca/publicat/cdic-mcc/18-3/c_e.html, Accessed 2006-11-07

Bush, Luis, 1996, A Brief Historical Overview of the AD2000 & Beyond Movement and Joshua Project 2000, Seoul, Korea Available at http://www.ad2000.org/ histover.htm Accessed on 06-06-09

Camilleri, Natalino, Introduction to Missiology, Blata 1-Bajda – Malta, Available at www.dictionary.reference.com Accessed on the 26 August 2008

Eckman, Ben, 2008, 'Title' in Elwell Evangelical Dictionary, A.F. Glasser, Available at http://mb-soft.com/believe/indexaz.html, Accessed 26 August 2008

GNU Free Documentation License, Accessed on 21:12, 6 November 2006,

Mahesh, B.G., 1996, Available at www.karnataka.com/images/karnataka.gif Accessed on 19-12-03 www.karnataka.com/images/bijapur.gif

Natalino, Camilleri, sdc, Blata l-Bajda – Malta, 2008, Introduction to Missiology, Available at www.dictionary.refrence.com, Accessed on the 26-08-08

National Informatics Centre, 1987, Department of Information and Technology Government of India, Ministry of Communication, Available at www.kar.nic.in (new site), www.nitpu3.kar.nic.in/samanyamahiti (old site) Accessed on 22-12-03

Noll, Mark A., 2005, an article accessed from the web, USA

Population Reference Bureau, 1997, Data by Geography>India>Summary, Avilable at www.prb.org/Datafinder/Geography/Summary.aspx?region=142region_type=2 (new site 2009): (old site, not available http://nyac.aed.org.factsheets/india 1.htm) Accessed on 24-08-2000

Ravillion, Martin, 2001, 'Shaohua Chen', a file, World Bank, Washington, USA, Available at www.worldbank.org Accessed on 15-03-2006

Registrar General & Census Commissioner, 1991, Government of India, Home Ministry Department, Available at www.censusindia-1991 Accessed on 07-11-2006

Science Encyclopedia, The History of Ideas, Available at www.science.jrank.org/ pages/9079/Education-in-Europe-From-Protestant-Reformation-Nineteenth-Century Accessed on 8 June 2009

Stricland, Don, 2006, 'Charles Finney's assault upon Biblical Preaching'. The Founders Journal, main page, contents 9, Accessed on 7th Sep 2006

Walls, Andrew F., 2009, The Great Commission, From 1910-2010, Available at www.towards2010.org.uk/downloads/t2010paper01walls.pdf, accessed on 20-05-09

Weinreich, Nedra Kline, 2006, Integrating Quantitative and qualitative Methods in Social Marketing Research. 1996-2003 Weinreich Communications / Available at webmaster@social-marketing.com Accessed on 07-11-2006

Index